# THE FAIR LADY COOKBOOK

Annette Kesler

**Hamlyn** London · New York · Sydney · Toronto
**Tafelberg** Cape Town

**Acknowledgements**

The author and publishers would like to thank all who contributed the fine accessories which were such an important feature in the colour pictures.

The dishes came from such famous china and pottery houses as Arabia of Finland, Johnson Brothers of England and Thomas of Germany. The stockists who kindly loaned them were La Maree and Etceteras, Sea Point, Cape Town, and Binnehuis of Cape Town.

The exquisite glassware was by Arabia, Dartington, and Piedel of Austria.

The cutlery by Georg Jenson of Denmark and Christofle of France was kindly supplied by Spilhaus of Cape Town.

Illustrations by Marilyn Day

Published by
The Hamlyn Publishing Group Limited, Astronaut House, Feltham, Middlesex, England in association with Tafelberg Publishers Limited, Cape Town

ISBN 0 600 36163 2
Printed by Cox and Wyman, Fakenham, England

The front cover shows chilled curry soup (see page 27), roast leg of lamb and a mixed salad.
The back cover shows cream of avocado soup (see page 23), duck and orange salad (see page 102), noodles with ham and cream cheese (see page 90) and Fair Lady pashka (see page 118).

# Contents

# Useful facts and figures

## Metric measures

In this book quantities have been given in both metric and Imperial measures. As a general guide 30 g. equals 1 oz., 1 kg. (1000 g.) equals 2.2 lb.; 1 litre (1000 ml.) equals 1.76 pints or about 1¾ pints. Each column of ingredients has been balanced individually in order to give a satisfactory result in both measures. Therefore you will find that, for example, 100 g., 110 g. and 125 g. will all have been converted to 4 oz. in the Imperial column and the other ingredients adjusted as necessary.

## Oven temperature chart

| | °F. | °C. | Gas Mark |
|---|---|---|---|
| Very cool | 225 | 110 | ¼ |
| | 250 | 130 | ½ |
| Cool | 275 | 140 | 1 |
| | 300 | 150 | 2 |
| Moderate | 325 | 170 | 3 |
| | 350 | 180 | 4 |
| Moderately hot | 375 | 190 | 5 |
| | 400 | 200 | 6 |
| Hot | 425 | 220 | 7 |
| | 450 | 230 | 8 |
| Very hot | 475 | 240 | 9 |

As different makes of cookers vary and if you are in any doubt about the setting it is recommended that you refer to the manufacturer's temperature chart.

All spoon measures are level unless indicated otherwise and plain flour is used in the recipes.

The preparation times have been given as a guide to help you plan ahead when entertaining. You may find that you are able to prepare some of the recipes more quickly and of course the more often you prepare a recipe, the quicker you will become.

## A guide for American users

| *Imperial* | *American* |
|---|---|
| 1 lb. butter or other fat | 2 cups |
| 1 lb. flour | 4 cups |
| 1 lb. granulated or castor sugar | 2 cups |
| 1 lb. icing or confectioners' sugar | 3½ cups |
| 1 lb. brown sugar | 2 cups (firmly packed) |
| 12 oz. golden syrup or treacle | 1 cup |

| *Imperial* | *American* |
|---|---|
| 8 oz. stoned dates | $1\frac{1}{4}$ cups |
| 1 lb. dried fruit | 3 cups |
| 4 oz. chopped nuts | 1 cup |
| 8 oz. glacé cherries | 1 cup |
| 4 oz. cocoa powder | 1 cup |
| 8 oz. mincemeat | 1 cup |
| 14 oz. rice | 2 cups |
| 1 lb. chopped or minced meat | 2 cups (firmly packed) |
| 1 lb. lentils or split peas | 2 cups |
| 2 oz. soft breadcrumbs | 1 cup |
| 1 oz. flour | $\frac{1}{4}$ cup |
| 1 oz. sugar | 2 tablespoons |
| 1 oz. butter | 2 tablespoons |
| 4 oz. grated cheese | 1 cup |
| 4 oz. button mushrooms | 1 cup |
| 8 oz. cottage cheese | 1 cup |

## Liquid measures

| | |
|---|---|
| $\frac{1}{4}$ pint liquid (water, milk, stock etc.) | $\frac{2}{3}$ cup |
| $\frac{1}{2}$ pint liquid | $1\frac{1}{4}$ cups |
| 1 pint liquid | $2\frac{1}{2}$ cups |
| 2 pints liquid | 5 cups |

The Imperial pint is 20 fluid ounces whereas the American pint is 16 fluid ounces.

The following list gives American equivalents or substitutes for some terms, equipment and ingredients used in the book.

| *Imperial* | *American* |
|---|---|
| Baked/unbaked pastry case | Baked/unbaked pie shell |
| Baking tin | Baking pan |
| Biscuit mixture | Cookie dough |
| Dough or mixture | Batter |
| Frying pan | Skillet |
| Minced | Ground |
| Mixer/liquidiser | Mixer/blender |
| Muslin | Cheesecloth |
| Pastry cutters | Cookie cutters |

| *Ingredients* | *Ingredients* |
|---|---|
| Aubergine | Eggplant |
| Bacon rashers | Bacon slices |
| Bicarbonate of soda | Baking soda |
| Biscuits | Cookies or crackers |
| Black olives | Ripe olives |
| Broad beans | Fava or lima beans |
| Chicory | Belgian endive |
| Chilli | Chili |
| Cocoa powder | Unsweetened cocoa |
| Cooking apple | Baking apple |
| Cornflour | Cornstarch |
| Courgettes | Small zucchini |
| Curly endive | Chicory |
| Desiccated coconut | Shredded coconut |
| Double cream | Whipping cream |
| Gherkins | Sweet dill pickle |
| Haricot beans | Navy beans |
| Icing | Frosting |
| Single cream | Coffee cream |
| Spring onion | Scallion |
| Sultanas | Seedless white raisins |
| Tomato purée | Tomato paste |
| Vanilla pod | Vanilla bean |

# foreword

Almost every woman's magazine must dream of publishing a cookbook. This isn't because a magazine's life is short and a hardcover book lasts longer, nor is it for the prestige, though both these factors apply.

Really, it's because *Fair Lady* believes that a magazine's approach to food is part of its philosophy, a clearly defined and recognisable attitude to life. To us, food has never been 'fodder', but rather one of the pleasures in life. Cooking is an art, an admirable skill, and most important of all, a means of giving and sharing pleasure. We don't see it as a chore and hope we've encouraged you to feel the same way. We'd like you to entertain with gay abandon rather than painstaking precision. Our readers should be able to have their cake and eat it too!

Annette Kesler is one of a small band of cookery writers who bring a truly creative passion to their work. She loves food and cooking and actively enjoys entertaining. Best of all is her ability to share her pleasure and this is why her recipes always sound so mouthwatering. We suspect that Annette's approach to food has been one of the strongest influences on *Fair Lady's* short but successful life, and we're glad to have a chance to salute one of our favourite specialists, Volker Miros, the photographer whose luscious pictures look good enough to eat. In fact, he's no mean cook himself and the enthusiasm and appreciation he puts into his photographs elevate them to artistry.

This book, like all *Fair Lady* projects, has been a group effort and we are all proud of it, but Features Editor Liz Burnet and Art Director Vera Utermöhlen in particular, have provided invaluable encouragement, advice and assistance. Lastly, this book would not be complete without acknowledgement to Kathy Jowell, whose inspiration and enthusiasm was the spark which started off the whole venture.

# Planning your menus

The nicest thing you can say to anyone is 'stay for dinner'. If all entertaining were conducted as spontaneously and informally as that it would be as easy as pie. A perfect hostess enjoys her own evenings as much if not more than her guests, and that enjoyment is relaxing and infectious and very good for the digestion. She need not be the best cook in the world to find entertaining a joy.

We can all share this pleasure because there is only one essential for fret-free hostessing – planning. It takes just the same amount of time to *plan* a dinner party for eight as it does for 30. Laying tables for larger numbers, cooking bigger quantities of food, sending more invitations all take longer. But it is less laborious when you're working to an efficient schedule, less terrifying when you know you're going to be ready on time and less tiring when the effort is spread over a longer period.

Entertaining does require effort and enthusiasm but fortunately it's no longer necessary to be extremely formal about food or flowers. The woman who prepares an unusual combination of dishes is admired for her originality. And I particularly like the movement away from stereotyped tableware. The new designs are not just a delight to the eye, they can be mixed and matched with older pieces to stunning effect.

The way you entertain says something about the kind of person you are. It is a revealing form of self-expression, so do make sure that you do justice to your own taste.

## Our master plan

### Guests

The people make the party but do suit your entertaining to your guests. For the younger crowd buffets, brunches, coffee parties and poolside suppers provide an informal, casual and relaxed atmosphere. For more conservative older guests, small dinner parties, later after-theatre suppers, or gracious tea or coffee parties with the children's pandemonium kept to a minimum are best. If it is an older family you want to invite, and lunches and dinners are beyond you, consider a really old-fashioned tea or coffee party with your own home-made specialities. From time to time think out a new idea to stun your friends, one that fits into your way of living.

Make lists of who you would like to have . . . to what. Many people loathe cocktail parties, however useful they are, or big parties of any description. Don't force these on them, it is often difficult to refuse an invitation. At biggish gatherings, however lovely it is to see old friends, include some fresh acquaintances – it adds to the interest.

When overseas guests arrive, serve them your own local foods, especially fresh fruit. Remember outdoor cooking will be a much-appreciated novelty.

People enjoy contact – the type of entertaining does not matter. How you do it is important.

A simple meal prepared with flair is a feast. Don't think you can't invite people unless you provide expensive food and drink. The quality of food and cooking, not the quantity of dishes, is what counts. Effortless entertaining on a lavish scale is impressive but so is warm, genuine unpretentious hospitality. Have friends in on a Sunday evening for soup, home-made bread and cheese. As long as the soup is good, the bread and cheese just right, you can be proud of your fare.

## Menus

When you have settled the occasion and the number of guests, go through your recipe file. Choose dishes your guests have not eaten with you before. Make sure the menu is appropriate.

This step should be one of the most time-consuming. Clever planning of courses is an art and many really good cooks can bungle like novices when it comes to balancing a menu.

Most people today are diet-conscious. Unless you know your guests want a favourite, fattening speciality of your very own, don't overfeed them with too many courses or rich dishes from start to finish. At a seated dinner particularly, they often cannot get away from their plates and become unhappy captive eaters. Three-course dinners with salad and cheese are more than enough. The day after the dinner has to be considered as well.

## To balance a menu: ten golden rules

1 Do not repeat ingredients, no matter how small the amount, in any course. If you have a fruity beginning, don't serve fruit in the salad or around the meat or as a sweet, unless it is part of a dessert, for example in an orange soufflé.

2 Balance dishes made with rich sauces. If your first course has one, omit it in the main dish. If you begin with a creamy soup, follow with a plain main course and end with a fruity sweet. You can serve a delicious rich confectionery after a simple main dish. If planning a pasta or heavily-starched dish, begin with a piquant salad and end with a light frothy sweet – never pastry or cake.

3 Colour counts in your menu. A classic example of a dull and unappetising menu, to be avoided at all times, is a cream soup, white fish, white potatoes, white meringues. Be particularly careful with vegetables. Cauliflower with a white sauce needs to be complemented with, for example, carrots, slightly crisp and glazed. Serve green beans with baby marrows in a smooth tomato sauce.

4 Always contrast flavour and texture. Bland-tasting dishes – creamy soups, fish, vegetables – should be varied with something crisp and spicy.

5 Keep the seasons in mind. Hot soup is *not* welcome on a boiling day. When there are last minute changes in the weather, be versatile. If the thermometer drops dramatically and you had planned a cold soup for a luncheon . . . heat it. Most cold soups adapt well.

6 Serve the best of whatever is in season: new peas and baby potatoes, young asparagus and beans.

7 Be adventurous, try new ideas. Serve grapefruit with slivers of ginger instead of mint. The unusual is always stimulating, for example, a fruit salad which is a blend of whole glazed fruit, fruit compote and fresh fruit. It's the little touches that add spice. Instead of serving duck with orange, try it with large red plums. Serve chicken with the fresh frozen peaches you prepared in summer with the pink bloom still on them.

8 Serve the right food at the right time. At a formal dinner party offer more formal dishes – they can still be simple. Keep the baby meatballs for that hearty buffet supper. If you are having a ladies' lunch, make the menu dainty and non-fattening.

9 Serve your food as beautifully as you can. Never overcrowd plates. When setting out, arrange for maximum colour effect. Only lightly garnish finished dishes – thin slices of lemon or orange, fresh watercress, parsley or celery, little clusters of olives. Don't have tortured vegetables and fruits to place around platters. Forget about those tricky vegetable cut-outs and radish

roses. When food is well prepared it has its own perfection and needs no camouflage.

10 Always end your evening with good coffee, freshly ground and brewed if possible. Serve with large jugs of hot frothy strained milk. If you use instant coffee, pour it from a glass jug. Offer both brown and white sugar. If it really is a late, late evening, hot soup with a basket of crunchy rolls is always enjoyable.

## Count-down

When your menu is decided, make a shopping list complete to the smallest detail in food and accessories, such as candles and napkins. Decide what wine you will serve with the food. For dinner parties of up to 30 people you will need about three days for preparation. For a smaller guest list, less time will be necessary, but the drill will be the same. Decide now on the look you want to create. This will be decided partly by the menu, partly by the setting and occasion. Are you going to use silver and good china, or pottery and country-type accessories?

**Day 1** Buy the wine. If you are having a large crowd arrange for the ice to be delivered on the day. Choose the linen and flowers you will use. Check that your cutlery is as shiny as you would want it to be. Shop completely. Bake or make any sauces you can now.

**Day 2** Do the bulk cooking. Buy flowers and stand them in water until needed.

**Day 3** Morning – arrange the table and flowers. Ensure all wooden surfaces are well protected. Afternoon – add the last minute touches. Make sure all containers are ready. Arrange the coffee tray.

If possible, leave the drink arrangements to your husband! He will need: glasses, jugs, dish cloths, dishes for lemon, openers, insulated containers for ice.

## Tableware

If you have one basic good set of china, it does not have to tie you down to the same monotonous table setting the year round. Use different tablecloths and flowers, all picking up a note from your china, for variety.

If your china is one colour, you have an even greater chance to experiment. Plain white is an excellent choice – there are many ways you can enhance it. For example, vary your tablecloths from florals, stripes, plain solid colours to dainty pastels and strong patterns.

Fashion in tableware has changed drastically, so do not indulge in too many expensive linens. One or two of these are sufficient. Curtaining makes excellent inexpensive tablecloths. If you sew, the scope is limitless. Just make sure the material is washable. Run up napkins to match. Paper napkins are fine if it is a buffet supper party but really not suitable for a small seated dinner, or in fact whenever there is a manageable number of people.

As you build up a selection of tableware, look around for toning soup plates, side plates, dinner plates, glasses and interesting containers. These do not have to match, they can contrast, for example, basic white plates can be teamed with patterned side plates; soup bowls or salad dishes in a deep colour picked out of the side plate, sets of glasses in matching shades.

If your china has flowers or stripes, choose a plain dark colour in soup bowls or sweet dishes; for example with rose pink, white and green patterned china, plain green or deep rose accessories would be good.

If you feel you do not have a flair for choosing the right accessories, look in shops, through books or magazines noted for their taste and keep designs simple. White candles go with most schemes and some are inexpensive enough to use lavishly in clusters. There is no better light for enhancing everything.

Be imaginative. To create a beautiful table setting does not mean that you have to rush out and buy new dishes, flower containers and platters. Take a fresh look at what you have. Think about new things to do with them. Most accessories can be multi-purpose, given a chance. The large brass tray in your hall can have a double use. Wonderful to display cold food, the inside covered with see-through adhesive film. Fill your large glass vase with layers of fruit instead of flowers. Serve salad in the heirloom china bowl.

## How to display and serve food at a big buffet supper

There are many ways to make life simpler for yourself and provide an informal relaxed evening for your guests.

If you are serving between 20 and 60 people, use large platters, big tureens and bowls. These are far better than small fiddly dishes; your table will look stunning . . . and you will have less washing up.

One question is always asked: should buffet food be ready on the table when the guests arrive? If you have a separate dining room or if it leads off your lounge and is not too near the action, smoke, heat, etc. . . . yes. But if being ready means your guests walking into a room and being confronted with a foil-covered table . . . no! Everything set out should be covered until the last moment. Keep hot dishes warm until needed. Cold foods can be arranged except for those in the refrigerator. Have heated warmers ready for the soup tureens and casseroles, large wooden boards with sharp knives for the meats, sauces ready to serve in pots. Breads look delicious in flat wicker baskets. Make sure there is a board provided for slicing them. Butter can be in pretty pots nearby. The buffet table should be bountiful and welcoming. Seated dinners can also be helped along by serving the meat beautifully sliced and arranged with rows of vegetables on the same dish. If necessary, prepare two of these platters.

## Shopping

If you are having a special cut of meat, discuss it with your butcher, whether in his retail shop or in the supermarket. If it is beef, make sure it has been well hung. Choose the fish yourself, making sure it is really fresh. Be very particular about vegetables and salad greens. When you get them home, place them immediately in the crisper. Even bread, rolls, pastry – if you are not going to bake your own or do not have the time – must be hunted around for. Find out in advance where the best specialised pastry shops and bakeries are. Usually they also sell home-made chocolates. Buy just a few to serve with coffee – the last touch of style in the perfectly planned meal. Now you can really relax and enjoy the company of your guests.

# Appetisers and soups

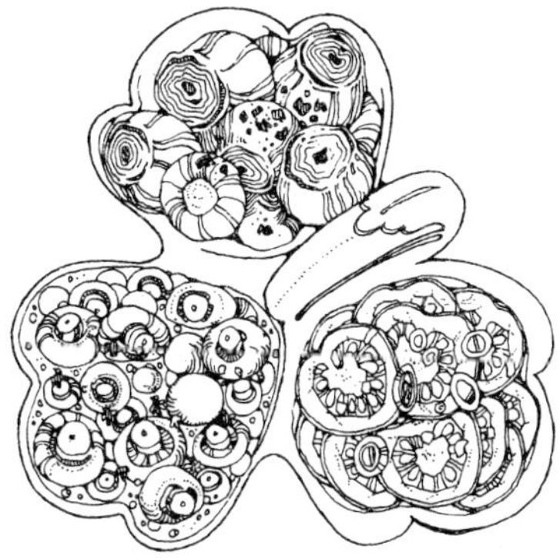

Every meal deserves a good start. However small, a first course always pleases. It should pique the appetite, anticipating the delights to follow. It need not be expensive, just well prepared and beautifully served. A few fresh ripe tomatoes on a leaf green plate with a little chopped basil and tangy dressing, or hollowed out and filled in a dozen ways. Good soups, thick and meaty or creamy. These can always be made well in advance and frozen. When vegetables are plentiful, liquidise them for a fresh treat. Have a supply of tiny crêpes in the freezer; these filled with savoury mixtures are a perfect beginning in cold weather. Eggs, one of the most versatile of starters, are wonderful for those last-minute occasions, baked in little pots or cloaked in home-made mayonnaise – herb, anchovy or seafood.

Good-looking dishes to have: large china or pottery soup tureen (a large vegetable dish can double for this); soup bowls with lids; small oval or round plates; small ovenproof pottery dishes for hot foods; a large round platter; small glass bowls for fruits. Available too are pottery vegetable shapes which are multi-purpose. White, leaf green, soft yellow and warm brown are good colours to serve starters on.

## Appetisers

### Stuffed cucumbers

Preparation time: 30 minutes, plus chilling time
Serves: 4

**2 large cucumbers**
**½ teaspoon salt**
**125 g./4 oz. cooked chicken, diced**
**1 hard-boiled egg**
**3 tablespoons chopped ham**
**¼ teaspoon freshly ground black pepper**
**2 tablespoons chopped pickled cucumber**
**2 teaspoons prepared mustard**
**6 tablespoons thick mayonnaise**
**4 tablespoons cream**
**2 tablespoons chopped chives**

Peel the cucumbers and cut off the tops. Remove centre pips and pulp, using a long, thin sharp knife or a potato peeler, working with a circular motion. Sprinkle ¼ teaspoon salt into each cucumber and allow to stand, covered, for 15 minutes. Drain, and pat dry with absorbent paper. Place the chicken in a bowl, finely chop the egg and add, together with ham, pepper, pickled cucumber, mustard and mayonnaise. Fill the cucumbers by standing them on end and spooning in the filling. Pack firmly until cucumbers are filled. Wrap in wax or greaseproof paper and chill for 2 hours, until the filling is firm. Slice on the cross into 1¼-cm. (½-inch) wedges. Arrange on a bed of crisp lettuce leaves. Pour a little cream over the wedges and sprinkle with chives.

# Artichokes with mustard sauce

Preparation time: 15 minutes
Cooking time: 35–40 minutes
Serves: 6

**6 large artichokes**
**1 tablespoon vinegar**
**3 litres/5 pints water**
**2 tablespoons salt**
**juice of 1 lemon**
**2 tablespoons prepared French mustard**
**3 tablespoons boiling water**
**125 ml./$\frac{1}{4}$ pint salad oil**
**$\frac{1}{2}$ teaspoon salt**
**pinch freshly ground black pepper**
**2 tablespoons finely chopped parsley**

Remove the stems of the artichokes then break off the small leaves at the base and trim to enable artichokes to stand upright. Slice 2 cm. (1 inch) off the centre core of the leaves. Using scissors, trim points of artichokes, and place in a basin of water with vinegar added. (This prevents discolouration.) Bring the water and salt to boiling point; add the lemon juice, drop in the artichokes and bring back to the boil. Cook uncovered for 35–40 minutes. When cooked, the leaves will pull out easily. Remove and drain upside down in a colander. Set aside to keep hot. Mix the mustard and water together. Gradually, drop by drop, whisk in the oil to make a creamy sauce. Add the salt, pepper and parsley and serve with the artichokes.

# Tomatoes with assorted fillings

Preparation time: 30 minutes
Serves: 6

**24 small ripe tomatoes**
*shrimp filling*
**2 cans shrimps**
**4 tablespoons thick mayonnaise**
**2 teaspoons tomato sauce**
*cheese filling*
**125 g./4 oz. feta or cream cheese**
**2 tablespoons cream**
*tuna filling*
**1 200-g./7-oz. can tuna**
**2 tablespoons chopped parsley**
**2 tablespoons chopped spring onion**
**1 tablespoon finely chopped capers**
**2 tablespoons vinegar**
**1 teaspoon salt**
**pinch freshly ground black pepper**
*garnish*
**4 anchovies**
**1 jar lumpfish caviar**
**3 tablespoons chopped parsley**
**ivy leaves or watercress**

Using a sharp knife, carefully and thinly slice off the very top and bottom of each tomato. Remove the pulp from inside, using a small teaspoon. (Use this in a stew or sauce.) Drain the shrimps thoroughly; place in a bowl and mix gently with the mayonnaise and tomato sauce. Fill one-third of the tomatoes with this mixture.

Mix the cheese with the cream. Fill half of the remaining tomatoes with the cheese mixture. Blend the tuna in a bowl with its own oil, the parsley, spring onion, capers, vinegar, salt and pepper. Fill remaining tomatoes with the tuna mixture. Slice each anchovy in half. Form each half into a roll and place one on top of each tuna-filled tomato. Spoon a little caviar on the top of each shrimp-filled tomato and sprinkle a little chopped parsley on each cheese-filled tomato. Arrange the tomatoes in close circles on a bed of ivy leaves or watercress on a round flat tray.

# Mushroom kebabs

Preparation time: 10 minutes
Cooking time: 6–8 minutes
Serves: 6–8

**900 g./2 lb. button mushrooms**
**3 tablespoons/1½ oz. butter, melted**
**4 tablespoons salad oil**
**2 tablespoons lemon juice**
**1 teaspoon salt**
**¼ teaspoon freshly ground black pepper**
**pinch dried rosemary**

Wash the mushrooms well and remove the stems (they can be used for soup). Place the mushrooms on skewers. Combine the melted butter, salad oil, lemon juice, salt, pepper and rosemary in a bowl. Whisk for 1 minute. Brush the skewered mushrooms with three-quarters of the mixture. Place under a preheated grill and cook, turning the mushrooms to brown on all sides, for 6–8 minutes. Baste during cooking with the remaining mixture.

# Cheese fondue

Preparation time: 10 minutes
Cooking time: about 10 minutes
Serves: 4–6

**250 ml./½ pint dry white wine**
**2 cloves garlic, crushed**
**500 g./1 lb. Gruyère cheese**
**6 tablespoons milk**
**½ teaspoon salt**
**pinch freshly ground black pepper**
**1½ tablespoons brandy**
**about 2 teaspoons/scant ½ oz. butter**

Bring the wine and crushed garlic cloves to the boil in a saucepan and allow to reduce slightly. Cut the cheese into small thin pieces and place in a saucepan. Add the milk and stir continuously over a low heat until the cheese is creamy. Stir in the salt, pepper, white wine, brandy and butter. Heat the mixture, then serve immediately with crusty bread.

# Pâté in a crock

Preparation time: 15 minutes, plus chilling time
Cooking time: about 10 minutes
Serves: 4–6

**1 kg./2 lb. chicken livers**
**2 large onions**
**4 tablespoons salad oil**
**1 clove garlic, crushed**
**¼ teaspoon freshly ground black pepper**
**1 teaspoon salt**
**1 teaspoon dry mustard**
**¼ teaspoon ground cloves**
**¼ teaspoon grated nutmeg**
**2 tablespoons/1 oz. butter, melted**
**2 teaspoons medium-sweet sherry**
**clarified butter (see below)**

Trim the chicken livers, wash well and dry with absorbent paper. Peel and dice the onions. Heat the oil in a saucepan, add the onions and crushed garlic together with the pepper, salt, mustard, cloves and nutmeg. Cook until golden brown. Add the livers and cook for a further 6–8 minutes, until the livers are cooked, but not well browned. Cool slightly then place in a blender or press through a sieve until puréed. Blend in the butter and sherry. Pack the pâté into a crock and cover the top with clarified butter. Chill for 1 hour before serving. The clarified butter keeps the pâté moist and may be removed just before serving. To serve place the crock in the centre of a large flat dish and surround with triangles of crisp buttered toast.

**Note** Another way of serving pâté is to hollow out a small crusty white loaf of bread and fill with the pâté. Slice as required.

**Clarified butter** Melt 3 tablespoons (1½ oz.) butter in a small saucepan. Remove from the heat and carefully pour off the clear fat, leaving behind the milky sediment that settles at the bottom. Use as required.

# Savoury crêpe batter

Preparation time: few minutes
Makes: 16–18 crêpes

**125 g./4 oz. flour**
**3 eggs**
**250 ml./½ pint milk**
**4 tablespoons water**
**½ teaspoon salt**
**1 tablespoon oil**

Place all the ingredients in a blender. Turn to highest speed and blend for a few seconds. Using a rubber spatula, scrape the batter down to the bottom of the blender. Turn on and blend for another minute, to make batter thick and creamy. This batter may also be made by hand, or with an electric mixer. When mixing by hand use the same method as for basic pancake batter (see page 122). Refrigerate for 1 hour before using. Before making the crêpes give the batter a final beat with an egg whisk. The consistency of the batter should be like medium-thick cream. If too thick, add 1–2 teaspoons cold water, beating it well into the batter. Cook as for basic pancake batter (see page 122).

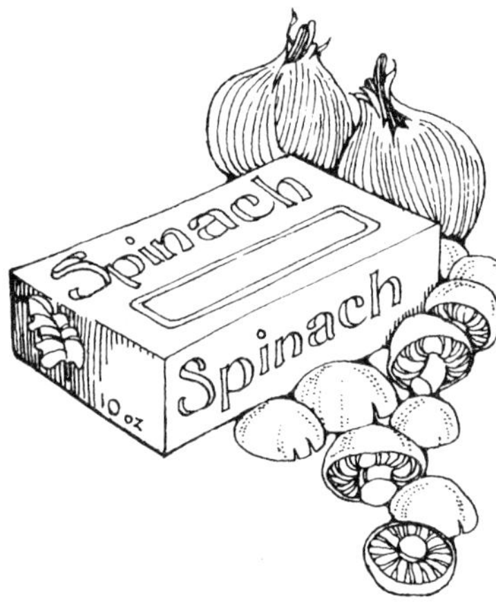

# Crêpes with spinach and mushroom filling

Preparation time: 30 minutes
Cooking time: about 20 minutes
Oven temperature: moderate (350°F., 180°C., Gas Mark 4)
Serves: 6 as a main dish

**16–18 crêpes, using crêpe batter or basic pancake batter (see above or page 122)**
*filling*
**2 260-g./10-oz. packets frozen spinach**
**little butter**
**2 medium-sized onions, finely sliced**
**500 g./1 lb. small black mushrooms**
**125 ml./¼ pint cream**
**3 teaspoons salt**
**1 teaspoon freshly ground black pepper**
**½ teaspoon nutmeg**
*savoury sauce*
**4 tablespoons/2 oz. butter**
**4 tablespoons flour**
**500 ml./1 pint chicken stock, or 2 chicken cubes dissolved in 500 ml./1 pint water**
**½ teaspoon freshly ground black pepper**
**½ teaspoon marjoram**
*topping*
**1 tablespoon chopped parsley**
**3 tablespoons grated Parmesan cheese**

Cook the spinach in 2 tablespoons water until soft. Melt a little butter in a frying pan, add the onion and lightly brown. Add the mushrooms and fry gently. When cooked pour in the cream, add salt, pepper and nutmeg, mix with the spinach and blend well.

To make the sauce, melt the butter in a saucepan, add the flour and mix together until smooth. Gradually add the chicken stock, stirring until the sauce thickens and is creamy and smooth. Remove and add the pepper and marjoram.

Place 2–3 tablespoons of the spinach mixture down the centre of each crêpe and fold over the edges to form a roll. Place in an ovenproof dish and pour over the savoury sauce. Sprinkle with parsley and cheese and bake in a moderate oven for 10–15 minutes. Brown under a preheated grill during the last 5 minutes of cooking time.

# Basic pickled herrings

*Illustrated on page 21*
Preparation time: 5 days, including marinating time
Serves: 12

**6 salted herrings**
**3 onions**
**6 bay leaves**
**12 peppercorns**
**500 ml./1 pint vinegar**
**4 tablespoons water**
**125 g./4 oz. sugar**
**250 ml./$\frac{1}{2}$ pint cream**

Soak the herrings overnight in a large bowl of water. The next morning rinse them thoroughly and fillet. Cut the fillets into $2\frac{1}{2}$-cm. (1-inch) pieces, or slice in half and roll up, securing with a toothpick or cocktail stick. (For dinner-party fare, leave fillets whole.) Slice the onions thinly, layer alternately with the herrings, bay leaves and peppercorns in a bowl, jar or flat dish. Pour over the vinegar, water and sugar mixture. Cover with a double thickness of foil or a tight-fitting lid. Allow to marinate in the refrigerator for 3–4 days. A few hours before serving, remove the herring (with a few of the onion rings), place on a platter and pour over the cream. If herring roes are available, mash one and blend with the cream to make a smooth sauce. A few tablespoons of the marinade may be added to the cream sauce for a more piquant flavour. If liked sprinkle with paprika pepper.

# Pickled herrings with mandarin oranges

*Illustrated on page 21*
Preparation time: 5 minutes
Serves: 8

**4 whole pickled herring fillets**
**2 cans mandarin oranges**
**125 ml./$\frac{1}{4}$ pint double cream (optional)**
**$\frac{1}{2}$ teaspoon freshly ground black pepper**
**1 tablespoon chopped spring onion**

Place the herring fillets on an oval platter, or in a deep dish. Drain the mandarins and reserve the syrup. Place the mandarin oranges around the edge of the dish. If using the cream, mix it with 2 tablespoons of the mandarin syrup and pour over the fillets. Sprinkle with pepper and chopped spring onion.

# Hot mushroom and salami dip

Preparation time: 10 minutes
Cooking time: few minutes
Serves: 4–6

**125 g./4 oz. fresh black mushrooms**
**2 tablespoons/1 oz. butter**
**2 dessertspoons flour**
**500 ml./1 pint milk**
**$\frac{1}{2}$ teaspoon salt**
**$\frac{1}{4}$ teaspoon freshly ground black pepper**
**1 tablespoon chopped parsley**
**6 slices spicy salami**
**1 dessertspoon oil**

Wash and slice the mushrooms. Melt the butter in a saucepan, add the mushrooms and cook for 2–3 minutes. Sprinkle over the flour and blend with a wooden spoon; very gradually add the milk, stirring constantly until the mixture is smooth. Add the seasoning. Bring just to the boil, mix in the parsley and remove from the heat. Cut the salami into thin strips. Heat the oil in a pan. Add the salami and fry until crisp. Fold into the mushroom mixture and serve piping hot with fried whole black mushrooms and little grilled pork sausages on sticks.

# Tuna and caper dip

*Illustrated opposite*
Preparation time: few minutes
Serves: 6–8

**2 200-g./7-oz. cans tuna**
**8 anchovy fillets**
**250 ml./½ pint thick mayonnaise**
**2 tablespoons chopped capers**
**2 tablespoons lemon juice**
**125 ml./¼ pint cream**
**1 clove garlic**
**1 teaspoon salt**
**¼ teaspoon freshly ground black pepper**
**parsley**
**paprika pepper (optional)**

Place the tuna, tuna oil and anchovy fillets in a bowl with the mayonnaise, capers, lemon juice and cream. Crush the garlic and add, together with the seasoning. Mix gently until all the ingredients are well blended to a fairly coarse mixture. (Alternatively, the tuna mixture can be puréed in a blender to form a smooth dip.) Place in a shallow bowl, garnish with parsley and paprika pepper, if liked, and a rolled anchovy fillet. Serve with radishes, celery, spring onions, carrots, cucumber slices, mushrooms and olives.

# Anchovy cream dip

*Illustrated opposite*
Preparation time: few minutes
Serves: 6

**250 ml./½ pint thick sour cream**
**1 can anchovy fillets**
**2 tablespoons chopped spring onion**
**4 tablespoons chopped pickled cucumber**
**1 teaspoon salt**
**½ teaspoon freshly ground black pepper**
**1 teaspoon prepared mustard**
**chopped hard-boiled egg and parsley to garnish**

Beat the sour cream lightly until it forms very soft peaks. Mash the anchovies or purée in a blender. Fold into the cream with the spring onion, cucumber, salt, pepper and mustard. Blend well and spoon into a bowl. Sprinkle with chopped hard-boiled egg and parsley. Serve with small pieces of any firm-fleshed fish such as kabeljou, Cape salmon, steenbras or haddock, coated in batter and deep fried, olives and gherkins.

# Fluffy asparagus omelets

Preparation time: 10 minutes
Cooking time: few minutes
Serves: 4

*filling*
**1 small can asparagus**
**1 tablespoon/½ oz. butter**
**1 heaped teaspoon flour**
**3 tablespoons milk**
**½ teaspoon salt**
**¼ teaspoon white pepper**

**4 large eggs**
**1 tablespoon water**
**½ teaspoon salt**
**¼ teaspoon white pepper**
**2 tablespoons/1 oz. butter**

Drain the asparagus and reserve the juice. Place the butter in a small saucepan over a moderate heat. When melted, add the drained asparagus, sprinkle over the flour and mix gently. Gradually add about 4 tablespoons of the asparagus juice, stirring constantly. Add the milk, salt and pepper and bring to the boil. Remove from the heat. This filling can be made well in advance and reheated while you are making the omelets. (To reheat, stir well over a moderate heat.)

Separate the egg yolks from the whites and beat the whites until stiff. Add the water and seasoning to the yolks. Place half the butter in a 12–13-cm. (5-inch) frying pan. While the butter is heating to a golden brown, lightly fold together a quarter of the yolk mixture and a quarter of the beaten white. Add to the pan. When cooked on one side – about 2 minutes – place a dessertspoonful of the filling in the centre of the omelet. Fold over the one side to cover the filling and allow to cook for 1 minute longer. Make three more omelets and serve immediately. (If you have an electric frying pan or burner these can be made at the serving table in the dining room.)

*Anchovy cream dip, tuna and caper dip (see opposite)*

# Baked eggs

*Illustrated on page 32*
Preparation time: few minutes
Cooking time: about 15 minutes
Oven temperature: moderate (350°F., 180°C., Gas Mark 4)
Serves: 6

**125 ml./$\frac{1}{4}$ pint cream**
**6 teaspoons grated Parmesan cheese**
**6 eggs**
**1 teaspoon salt**
**$\frac{1}{4}$ teaspoon freshly ground black pepper**
**2 teaspoons/scant $\frac{1}{2}$ oz. butter**
**chopped parsley to garnish**

Pour 1 tablespoon of the cream into each of six individual ovenproof pots. Sprinkle 1 teaspoon of the Parmesan cheese over the cream. Break an egg into each pot. Sprinkle with salt and freshly ground black pepper. Lightly dot with butter. Place uncovered in a moderate oven until set, 12–15 minutes. Remove and serve garnished with chopped parsley.

# Eggs in curry cream

*Illustrated on page 33*
Preparation time: few minutes
Serves: 6

**1 cucumber**
**6 large hard-boiled eggs**
**2 teaspoons curry powder**
**6 tablespoons thick mayonnaise**
**3 tablespoons whipped cream**
**3 tablespoons chopped parsley**
**$\frac{1}{4}$ teaspoon salt**
**$\frac{1}{4}$ teaspoon freshly ground black pepper**
**paprika pepper, parsley and small tomatoes to garnish**

Slice the cucumber thinly and arrange on individual dishes. Cut a very thin slice off one side of each egg so that it balances and arrange an egg on each dish. Blend the curry powder, mayonnaise, whipped cream, parsley, salt and freshly ground black pepper together. Just before serving spoon a little over each egg. Sprinkle with paprika pepper and garnish with parsley and small tomatoes. Serve with thin well-buttered triangles of wholewheat bread.

# Buttered cheese eggs in nests

*Illustrated on page 32*
Preparation time: 10 minutes
Cooking time: about 12 minutes
Oven temperature: moderate (350°F., 180°C., Gas Mark 4)
Serves: 6

**6 5-cm./2-inch thick slices bread**
**2 tablespoons/1 oz. butter**
**4 tablespoons salad oil**
**6 eggs**
**1 teaspoon salt**
**$\frac{1}{4}$ teaspoon freshly ground black pepper**
**2 teaspoons/scant $\frac{1}{2}$ oz. butter**
**6 tablespoons grated cheese**
**6 tablespoons milk**
**2 tablespoons freshly chopped parsley**

Hollow out the centres of the bread slightly – enough to form a nest for the eggs. Place the 2 tablespoons butter and the salad oil in a large frying pan. Heat until the butter turns golden brown. Add the bread nests. Cook until crisp and brown on both sides. Remove, drain on absorbent paper and place in an ovenproof dish. Break an egg into each. Sprinkle with salt and pepper and dot with butter. Bake in a moderate oven for about 12 minutes, until the whites are set. Combine the cheese and milk in a saucepan. Cook, stirring until the cheese melts. Pour over egg toasts and brown under the grill until the cheese is puffed and golden brown.

Alternatively, the nests can be lined with grated cheese and an egg placed on top, dotted with butter, seasoning and freshly chopped parsley.

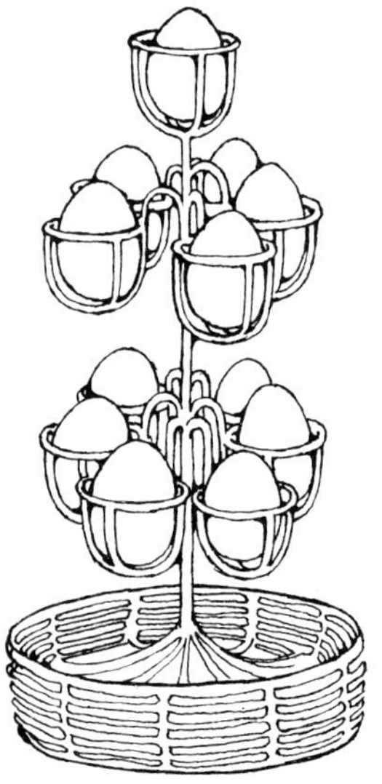

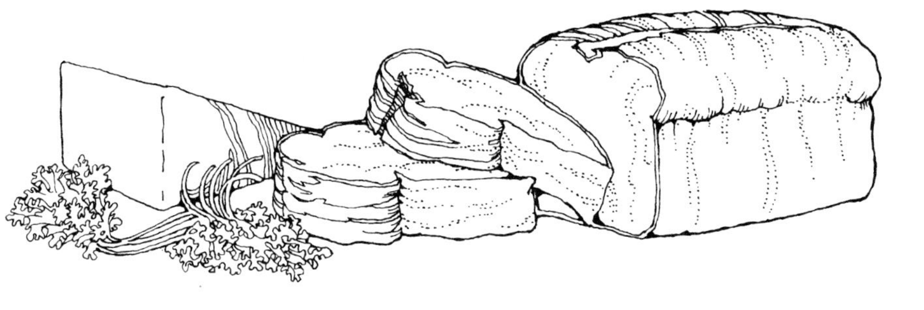

# Avocado mousse

*Illustrated on page 36*
Preparation time: 15 minutes, plus chilling time
Serves: 4–6

**2 small avocados, mashed**
**1 teaspoon salt**
**$\frac{1}{4}$ teaspoon freshly ground black pepper**
**2 tablespoons lemon juice**
**1 teaspoon chopped chives**
**125 ml./$\frac{1}{4}$ pint double cream**
**8 tablespoons thick mayonnaise**
**8 tablespoons hot water**
**1 tablespoon gelatine**
**paprika pepper**
**chopped parsley**
**sprigs leafy celery or watercress and lemon slices to garnish**

Place the mashed avocado in a bowl. Add the salt, pepper, lemon juice and chopped chives. Whip the cream, fold in with the mayonnaise, using a spatula. Put the hot water in a cup and sprinkle on the gelatine. Stir until dissolved. Fold into the mashed avocado mixture. Turn the mousse into a rinsed 1-litre (2-pint) mould and chill for 3–4 hours. Unmould onto a chilled dish. Sprinkle the mousse with paprika pepper and chopped parsley and garnish with leafy celery or watercress and lemon slices. Serve with thin slices of crisp toast.

# Grapefruit with preserves

*Illustrated on page 20*
Preparation time: few minutes, plus chilling time
Serves: 4–6

**3 whole grapefruit**
**6 slices preserved fruit (figs, ginger or mandarins), or any fresh fruit**
**about 2 teaspoons orange liqueur**

Cut the grapefruit in half and loosen segments completely, using a grapefruit knife. Slice the preserved fruit finely. Place on top of the grapefruit segments. Sprinkle with the liqueur. Chill thoroughly before serving.
**Note** Fruits, such as melon, grapefruit, pawpaw, go well with preserved fruits in syrup, or dried fruit soaked in a little liqueur or fruit juice. Almost any variation is good: dried figs, bananas, apricots or glacé pineapple.

# Pawpaw with litchis

*Illustrated on page 20*
Preparation time: 5 minutes, plus chilling time
Serves: 4–6

**2 small pawpaw or ogen melons**
**125 ml./$\frac{1}{4}$ pint orange juice**
**250 g./8 oz. fresh or canned litchis**
**4 pieces preserved ginger or 2 green figs in syrup**

Halve the pawpaws. Remove the pips and peel. Sprinkle with orange juice; pile the litchis into the pawpaw halves. Slice the ginger finely and place thin slices between the litchis. Spoon over a little ginger syrup. Chill thoroughly before serving.

# Parma ham with iced pineapple

Preparation time: 5 minutes, plus chilling time
Serves: 4

**Parma ham**
**1 medium-sized pineapple**
**$\frac{1}{4}$ teaspoon freshly ground black pepper**

Place slices of ham in overlapping circles on a flat dish. Remove the pineapple skin and thinly slice the fruit. Arrange around the ham in overlapping circles. Sprinkle both ham and pineapple with freshly ground black pepper. Chill before serving.
**Note** Parma ham may be bought either freshly sliced from a local delicatessen, or canned, where each slice is separated by greaseproof paper.

*Pawpaw with litchis, grapefruit with preserves* *(see page 19)*

*Basic pickled herrings, pickled herrings with mandarin oranges (see page 15)*

# Soups

## Thick minestrone

Preparation time: 30 minutes, plus overnight soaking of beans
Cooking time: about 2½ hours
Serves: 10–12

**500 g./1 lb. dried haricot beans**
**6 tablespoons salad oil**
**2 cloves garlic, crushed**
**1 onion, chopped**
**4 stalks celery, diced**
**4 carrots, diced**
**1 sprig fresh rosemary or ¼ teaspoon dried rosemary**
**2 tablespoons chopped bacon**
**2 tablespoons tomato purée**
**2 tablespoons hot water**
**1 teaspoon sugar**
**1 dessertspoon lemon juice**
**1 small cabbage, finely shredded**
**4 leeks, finely sliced**
**4 courgettes, diced (optional)**
**pinch basil**
**1 tablespoon chopped parsley**
**1 clove**
**1 dessertspoon salt**
**¼ teaspoon freshly ground black pepper**
**1½ litres/3 pints boiling water**
**50 g./2 oz. noodles**

Soak the beans overnight, covered. Cook the beans in a saucepan with the water in which they were soaked until tender, 1–1½ hours. Cool slightly, sieve half or purée in a blender and drain the rest. Heat the oil in a large saucepan. Gently sauté the garlic, onion, celery, carrots, rosemary and bacon until they begin to turn a light golden brown. Dilute the tomato purée in a cup with the hot water, sugar and lemon juice. Add to the pan together with the cabbage, leeks, courgettes, basil, parsley, clove, salt and pepper. Add the whole and puréed beans to the soup together with the boiling water. Add the noodles and simmer, covered, for 40–50 minutes. Serve in a hot tureen and pass around a bowl of grated Parmesan cheese and hot garlic rolls.

## Fresh green pea soup

*Illustrated on page 25*
Preparation time: 15 minutes
Cooking time: 25–30 minutes
Serves: 4–6

**1 kg./2¼ lb. fresh young green peas**
**3 tablespoons/1½ oz. butter**
**4 spring onions**
**3 tablespoons flour**
**1 chicken stock cube**
**500 ml./1 pint boiling water**
**1 litre/1¾ pints milk**
**1 teaspoon salt**
**¼ teaspoon freshly ground black pepper**
**4 tablespoons double cream**
**fresh mint leaves to garnish (optional)**

Shell the peas. Melt the butter in a medium-sized saucepan. Finely sliver all the spring onions including the green sections. Add all but 2 tablespoons of the spring onions to the butter. Cook for about 5 minutes. Sprinkle on the flour and stir in with a wooden spoon. Dissolve the stock cube in the boiling water. Gradually add to the pan, stirring constantly. Add all but 3 tablespoons of the peas and simmer for 8–10 minutes. Add the milk, salt and pepper, cover and simmer for a further 5–10 minutes, until the peas are completely soft. Sieve the soup into a bowl, pressing the vegetables through (or purée in a blender). Return to the rinsed pan. Add the remaining peas and spring onions and simmer for 8–10 minutes. Pour into a heated soup tureen. Whip the cream lightly and just before serving, swirl into the soup and lightly blend. If liked, garnish with fresh mint leaves.

# Fresh tomato soup

*Illustrated on page 69*
Preparation time: 10 minutes
Cooking time: about 1 hour
Serves: 6–8

**4 large carrots**
**3 medium-sized potatoes**
**6 large ripe tomatoes**
**3 tablespoons/1½ oz. butter**
**2 litres/3½ pints boiling water**
**2 teaspoons salt**
**¼ teaspoon freshly ground black pepper**
**pinch tarragon**
**pinch marjoram**
**2 tablespoons finely chopped parsley**
**2 tablespoons chopped spring onion**
**3 tablespoons sour cream (optional)**
**chopped hard-boiled egg and parsley to garnish**

Peel, wash and chop the carrots and potatoes. Skin the tomatoes by putting them into boiling water for 2 minutes, then remove skins. Chop coarsely. Melt the butter in a large heavy pan and add the prepared vegetables. Cook for 4 minutes, stirring constantly. Add the boiling water, salt, pepper, tarragon, marjoram and parsley. Cover and simmer for 1 hour. Remove from the heat and rub through a sieve or purée in a blender. Chill thoroughly. Add the spring onion and swirl sour cream on the top; serve sprinkled with chopped hard-boiled egg and parsley.

# Steaming onion soup

*Illustrated on page 25*
Preparation time: 5 minutes
Cooking time: about 1 hour
Serves: 4–6

**4 large onions**
**2 tablespoons bacon fat or oil**
**¾ tablespoon flour**
**1 teaspoon salt**
**¼ teaspoon freshly ground black pepper**
**2 cloves garlic**
**3 tablespoons chopped parsley**
**pinch thyme**
**pinch tarragon**
**1 tablespoon lemon juice**
**2 chicken stock cubes dissolved in 2 litres/3½ pints water**
**6 slices crusty French bread**
**chopped parsley to garnish**

Peel and finely slice the onions. Sauté in a saucepan with the bacon fat or oil. Sprinkle over the flour, salt and pepper. Peel and crush the garlic. Add to the pan together with parsley, thyme, tarragon and lemon juice. Stir gently. Gradually add the chicken stock, stirring constantly. Simmer for 1 hour, until soup has reduced to about 1½ litres (3 pints). Place a slice of bread in the bottom of each soup cup. Fill cups with soup, sprinkle with parsley and serve immediately.

# Cream of avocado soup

*Illustrated on page 37*
Preparation time: 5 minutes
Cooking time: few minutes
Serves: 4–6

**3 large avocados**
**2 tablespoons lemon juice**
**1 litre/1¾ pints chicken stock, or 2 chicken stock cubes dissolved in 1 litre/1¾ pints boiling water**
**125 ml./¼ pint cream**
**2 teaspoons grated onion**
**¼ teaspoon freshly ground black pepper**
**½ teaspoon finely grated lemon rind**
**chopped parsley to garnish**

Halve and remove the stones from the avocados. Mash the flesh (or purée in a blender), reserving half an avocado. Dice the avocado half and toss in lemon juice; reserve for the garnish. Place the avocado purée in a saucepan with the chicken stock and heat until the mixture just reaches boiling point. Remove and cool for 2–4 minutes. Stir in the cream, onion, pepper and lemon rind. Chill for 3–4 hours in an airtight container. Just before serving, stir in the diced avocado and sprinkle with chopped parsley.

# Creamy leek and potato soup

Preparation time: 5 minutes
Cooking time: about 1 hour
Serves: 4

**4 large leeks**
**2 medium-sized potatoes**
**1 medium-sized onion**
**4 tablespoons/2 oz. butter**
**1 teaspoon salt**
**$\frac{1}{4}$ teaspoon freshly ground black pepper**
**2 chicken stock cubes**
**1 litre/1$\frac{3}{4}$ pints boiling water**
**125 ml./$\frac{1}{4}$ pint cream**
**chopped chives to garnish**

Wash the leeks, remove roots and discoloured leaves. Cut into 2$\frac{1}{2}$-cm. (1-inch) pieces. Wash and peel the potatoes and slice thinly. Slice the onion. Melt the butter in a saucepan. Add the leeks and onion and fry gently for 10 minutes, or until soft but not coloured. Add the salt, pepper and potatoes. Dissolve the stock cubes in the boiling water. Add to the vegetables. Cover the pan and bring to boiling point. Reduce the heat and simmer for 40 minutes, or until the vegetables are tender. Press the soup through a sieve, using a wooden spoon, or purée in a blender. Reheat for 5 minutes. Stir in the cream and serve sprinkled with chopped chives. Serve with wholewheat bread.

# Cream of celery soup

Preparation time: 5 minutes
Cooking time: 15 minutes
Serves: 4

**3 tablespoons/1$\frac{1}{2}$ oz. butter**
**3 tablespoons finely chopped onion**
**220 g./8 oz. leafy celery, chopped**
**2 tablespoons flour**
**750 ml./1$\frac{1}{2}$ pints milk**
**1 tablespoon finely chopped parsley**
**2 tablespoons cream**
**1 teaspoon salt**
**$\frac{1}{4}$ teaspoon freshly ground black pepper**

Melt the butter in a saucepan, add the onion and cook until golden brown – about 3 minutes. Add the celery and cook for 6–8 minutes, stirring gently with a wooden spoon. Sprinkle over the flour and cook for a further 1–2 minutes. Gradually add the milk, stirring constantly; bring to the boil, lower the heat and simmer until the celery is cooked. Add the parsley, cream, salt and pepper. Pour into a heated soup tureen and serve.

# Curried lentil soup

Preparation time: few minutes, plus soaking time
Cooking time: 2$\frac{3}{4}$ hours
Serves: 4–6

**460 g./1 lb. lentils**
**2 beef cubes dissolved in 1 litre/1$\frac{3}{4}$ pints boiling water**
**1 ham bone**
**6 stalks leafy celery**
**3 cloves garlic, crushed**
**$\frac{1}{2}$ teaspoon cumin seed**
**4 tablespoons curry powder**
**8 tablespoons sour cream**
**125 g./4 oz. ham, finely chopped**

Soak the lentils in water to cover for 2 hours. Drain and place in a saucepan with fresh water to cover. Bring to the boil. Cover and simmer for 10–12 minutes. Drain. Place in a large saucepan together with the beef stock, ham bone and celery. Add the garlic and cumin seed. Cover the pan and bring to the boil; simmer for 2$\frac{1}{2}$ hours. Discard the ham bone. Purée the soup in a blender, or rub through a sieve using a wooden spoon. Mix the curry powder and cream in a small bowl. Pour into the soup and return to the heat. Simmer for a further 6–8 minutes. Stir the ham into the soup then pour into a tureen. Cover and chill for 2 hours before serving.

*Steaming onion soup, fresh green pea soup, velvet chicken soup* *(see pages 23, 22, 26)*

# Cream of hake soup

*Illustrated on page 61*
Preparation time: 10 minutes
Cooking time: about 20 minutes
Serves: 4

**250 g./8 oz. hake**
**2 large onions, finely chopped**
**4 tablespoons/2 oz. butter**
**2 tablespoons flour**
**750 ml./1$\frac{1}{2}$ pints milk**
**2 tablespoons sour cream**
**2 teaspoons dry mustard**
**2 tablespoons chopped parsley**
**2 tablespoons chopped chives**
**1 teaspoon salt**
**freshly ground black pepper to taste**
**paprika pepper or rose paprika and chopped parsley to garnish**

Wash the hake and cut into small pieces. Place the onions in a saucepan with the butter. Cook gently until the onions are translucent. Place the hake on the onions and cook gently until very soft. Sprinkle over the flour and blend in. Gradually pour in the milk, sour cream mixed with the mustard powder, parsley, chives, salt and pepper. Stir constantly until smooth and thickened. Serve hot, poured over toasted cheese rounds. Sprinkle with paprika pepper and chopped parsley.

# Basic chicken stock

Preparation time: few minutes
Cooking time: 3–4 hours
Makes: 4–5 litres (about 8$\frac{1}{2}$ pints)

**1 3-kg./6$\frac{1}{2}$-lb. boiling chicken**
**2 large onions, chopped**
**1 large bay leaf**
**few sprigs parsley**
**2 cloves**
**2$\frac{1}{2}$ teaspoons salt**
**3 peppercorns**

Wash and dry the chicken. Place in a large heavy saucepan with the onions, bay leaf, parsley, cloves, salt, peppercorns and 5 litres (8$\frac{1}{2}$ pints) water. Bring to the boil. Cover and cook over a low heat for 3–4 hours, until the liquid is slightly reduced. Remove the chicken, strain and chill the broth. Remove any fat. Pour into ice trays and freeze. Remove frozen cubes and pack into polythene bags. Use for dishes that need a good home-made chicken stock, such as delicate soups and sauces.
**Note** The meat may be removed from the chicken and used for any dish with cooked chicken, or sliced and served cold.

# Velvet chicken soup

*Illustrated on page 25*
Preparation time: 5 minutes
Cooking time: 15 minutes
Serves: 4–6

**1 litre/1$\frac{3}{4}$ pints clear chicken soup, either home-made or canned**
**5 tablespoons minute tapioca**
**1 egg yolk**
**125 ml./$\frac{1}{4}$ pint cream**
**4 tablespoons dry sherry**
**$\frac{1}{4}$ teaspoon salt**
**pinch freshly ground black pepper**
**2 slices ham**
**chopped parsley to garnish**

Bring the chicken soup to the boil. Gradually add the tapioca, stirring constantly, and simmer for 10 minutes. Whisk the egg yolk in a cup. Slowly add a few teaspoons of the hot soup and blend. Stir the egg mixture back into the soup, together with the cream, sherry, salt and pepper. Slice the ham into long thin strips and add. Cook, stirring constantly over a low heat until soup slightly thickens – do not allow to boil. Serve in heated soup bowls and sprinkle with chopped parsley.

# Chilled curry soup

*Illustrated on the front cover*
Preparation time: 15 minutes
Cooking time: 4 hours
Serves: 4–6

**1 kg./2 lb. chicken giblets (excluding livers)**
**1 dessertspoon cooking salt**
**½ teaspoon freshly ground black pepper**
**4 carrots, sliced**
**2 stalks celery, chopped**
**2 large onions, sliced**
**1 chicken breast**
**2 egg yolks**
**2½ teaspoons cornflour**
**3 teaspoons curry powder**
**125 ml./¼ pint cream**
**1 tablespoon chopped chives**
**2 green-skinned apples, thinly sliced**

Wash and dry the giblets. Place in a large heavy saucepan with 1½ litres (3 pints) water, the salt, pepper, carrots, celery and onions. Bring to the boil. Skim the surface of the stock to remove any foam. Cover the pan and reduce heat. Simmer for 3–4 hours, adding chicken breast during last 30 minutes. Remove and reserve the chicken breast. Strain the stock into a saucepan and discard vegetables. Beat the egg yolks in a bowl with the cornflour and most of the curry powder. Add 2–3 tablespoons of warm chicken stock. Whisk well, slowly add to remaining stock. Place over medium heat. Allow to thicken, stirring constantly. Remove and pour in the cream. Chill well before serving. Slice the chicken breast into thin slivers. Add to the soup with the chives and slices of apple. Sprinkle with remaining curry powder. (If liked, a few apple slices may be reserved and used to garnish the soup.)

# Chilled cream of cucumber soup

*Illustrated on page 144*
Preparation time: 10 minutes
Cooking time: 20 minutes
Serves: 12

**6 large cucumbers**
**3 tablespoons/1½ oz. butter**
**3 tablespoons flour**
**1½ litres/2½ pints chicken stock**
**500 ml./1 pint milk**
**12 thin slices onion**
**8 tablespoons cream**
**2 teaspoons salt**
**½ teaspoon white pepper**
**2 tablespoons chopped chives**
**1 small cucumber**

Peel and slice the large cucumbers, removing seeds. Melt the butter in a pan and add the cucumbers. Cook gently for 10 minutes. Stir in the flour and gradually add the chicken stock, stirring constantly. Scald the milk with the onion. Strain. Add this milky liquid to the cucumber mixture, bring to the boil and simmer for 10 minutes; cool slightly and either purée in a blender or rub through a fine sieve. Just before serving add the cream and seasoning and blend gently. Serve in chilled soup tureens and sprinkle with chopped chives. Score the small cucumber, slice thinly and float the slices on top of the soup.

**Note** When catering for a reception, increase the ingredients, then make the soup in two or three batches. It may be made weeks ahead and frozen. (If freezing the soup, omit the cream and stir it in at the reheating stage.) Defrost the evening before it is served, then pour into large white soup tureens.

# Fish

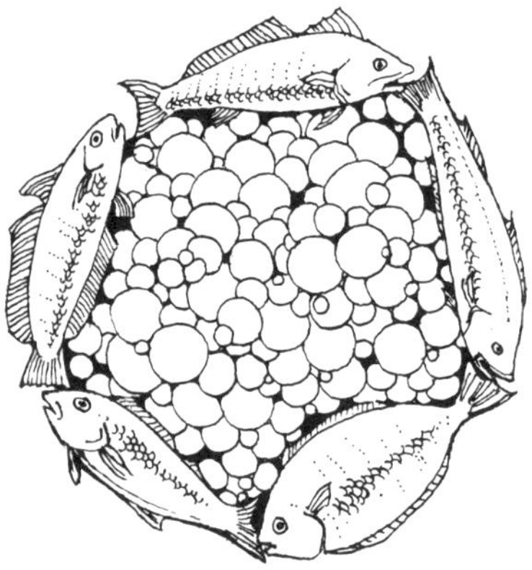

Fish is an excellent less expensive food. It is nourishing and appetising and there are endless varieties available to us with the aid of modern transport and refrigeration. The virtues of fish are by no means inferior to those of meat. For one thing, it is more easily digested and is also an excellent source of protein and minerals.

Fish must be absolutely fresh – the eyes should be bright, the gills bright red, and the flesh firm, but elastic enough to spring back when lightly pressed. If the fish has been pre-cut, freshness is determined by general appearance. Again, the flesh should be firm, elastic, moist to the touch, and have a fresh smell.

Fish is a food valuable in its own right and some varieties have a deservedly high reputation as delicacies. If you have never known anything but fried fish – with or without chips – then a whole new field of delicious experience awaits you.

## Crisp filleted fish

*Illustrated opposite*
Preparation time: 20 minutes, plus chilling time
Cooking time: few minutes
Serves: 6

**500 g./1 lb. Cape salmon or plaice**
**500 g./1 lb. kob**
**500 g./1 lb. steenbras**
**2 tablespoons flour**
**$\frac{1}{2}$ tablespoon salt**
**pinch white pepper**
**vegetable oil for frying**

*batter*
**125 g./4 oz. flour**
**$\frac{3}{4}$ teaspoon salt**
**2 eggs**
**8 tablespoons milk**
**2 tablespoons water**

*garnish*
**watercress**
**lemon slices**

To make the batter, sift the flour and salt into a bowl. Make a well in the centre. Whisk the eggs and half the milk together until smooth. Add the remaining milk and water. Continue whisking for 1 minute. Set aside. Cut the fish into 5-cm. (2-inch) pieces. Wash and pat dry with absorbent paper. (Fish will not fry perfectly if it is wet.) Mix the 2 tablespoons flour with the salt and pepper and dust the fish pieces with the seasoned flour, then dip into the batter. Allow to rest in the refrigerator. Pour enough oil into a frying pan until half full. Heat to 185°C. (360°F.); test by dropping a cube of bread into the oil, which should be golden brown in just under 1 minute. Remove the fish from the refrigerator. Fry until golden brown and crisp and drain on absorbent paper. When cool, arrange on a serving dish and garnish with watercress and lemon slices. Serve with a lemon mayonnaise (see page 151).
**Note** Any firm-fleshed white fish may be substituted for kob and steenbras.

*Crisp filleted fish* (see opposite)

# Baked red roman

Preparation time: 5 minutes
Cooking time: about 10 minutes per ½ kg. (1 lb.)
Oven temperature: moderate (350°F., 180°C., Gas Mark 4)
Serves: 6–8

**1 1.8-kg./about 3½-lb. red roman or mullet**
**1–2 tablespoons salt**
**½ teaspoon freshly ground black pepper**
**3 bay leaves**
**6 peppercorns**
**2 tablespoons lemon juice**
**140 ml./generous ¼ pint white wine**

Clean the fish and dry carefully with absorbent paper. Sprinkle inside and out with the salt and pepper. Put the bay leaves and peppercorns in the cavity, together with lemon juice. Place in well-oiled foil and pour over the white wine. Wrap tightly and bake in a moderate oven for 8–10 minutes per ½ kg. (1 lb.). Remove from the oven, unwrap and cool. Serve with green mayonnaise (see page 151).

# Fish in red wine

Preparation time: 30 minutes
Cooking time: about 30 minutes
Serves: 6–8

**3 kg./6 lb. assorted fish, sliced (kob, red stumpnose, Cape salmon, steenbras, hake, haddock or cod)**
**1 kg./2 lb. fishbones and heads**
**2 teaspoons salt**
**4 bay leaves**
**6 peppercorns**
**10 tablespoons vegetable oil**
**2 cloves garlic**
**4 tablespoons chopped onion**
**500 g./1 lb. tomatoes**
**8 tablespoons red wine**
**½ teaspoon freshly ground black pepper**
**2 tablespoons chopped parsley**
**2–3 teaspoons grated lemon rind**
**pinch rosemary**
**pinch thyme**
**1 tablespoon paprika pepper or rose paprika**
**pinch chilli powder**
**6 slices bread**

Wash the fish slices, bones and heads and dry with absorbent paper. Place the bones and heads in a large saucepan with water to cover with 1 teaspoon salt, 2 bay leaves and 3 peppercorns. Cover and bring to the boil. Reduce the heat and simmer for 30 minutes. Heat 6 tablespoons of the oil in a saucepan. Peel and crush the garlic cloves, add to the pan with the onion. Chop the tomatoes coarsely. Add and stir well. Pour in the wine, add the remaining salt, and peppercorns, the pepper, parsley, lemon rind, rosemary and thyme. Cook for 10–15 minutes, until slightly reduced. Stir in 125 ml. (¼ pint) of the strained fish stock, the paprika and chilli powder. Add the fish, simmer gently for a few minutes; add another 125 ml. (¼ pint) fish stock. Cover and simmer gently for a further 15–20 minutes. Fry the bread slices in a pan with the remaining oil until crisp. Cut into fingers and place at the bottom of hot soup bowls. To serve, spoon over the fish and sauce.

# Grilled snoek with lemon cream

Preparation time: 15 minutes
Cooking time: about 25 minutes
Oven temperature: moderately hot (400°F., 200°C., Gas Mark 6)
Serves: 4–6

**1.5 kg./3 lb. snoek or turbot, in one piece**
**2 tablespoons/1 oz. butter**
**6 tablespoons lemon juice**
**6 tablespoons cream**
**½ teaspoon coarsely crushed black peppercorns**
**1 teaspoon cooking salt**
**2 tablespoons chopped parsley**
**pinch thyme**

Wash the fish and pat dry with absorbent paper. Place on a piece of oiled foil. Cream the butter and lemon juice together in a bowl. Add the cream, peppercorns, salt, parsley and thyme and blend well. Smooth over the fish with a spatula. Close the foil and place on a baking sheet. Bake in a moderately hot oven for 14–16 minutes per kg. (2 lb.). About 5 minutes before end of the cooking time open the foil and allow the fish to brown lightly. Remove the foil and place the fish on a heated dish. Pour over the juices and serve surrounded by baked piped potatoes and little tomato halves filled with peas.

# Baked kingklip

*Illustrated on page 64*
Preparation time: 15 minutes
Cooking time: about 35 minutes
Oven temperature: moderate (350°F., 180°C., Gas Mark 4)
Serves: 4–6

**1.5 kg./3 lb. kingklip or turbot fillets**
**2 teaspoons salt**
**½ teaspoon freshly ground black pepper**
**6 tablespoons finely chopped spring onion**
**6 tablespoons chopped parsley**
**6 tablespoons/2½ oz. butter**
**1 teaspoon prepared mustard**
**1 tablespoon tomato purée**
**1 tablespoon lemon juice**
**1 teaspoon sugar**
**1 clove garlic**
**½ teaspoon vinegar**
**125 ml./¼ pint white wine**
**1 egg yolk**
**8 mushrooms, sliced**
**2 tablespoons fine breadcrumbs**

Cut the fish into neat pieces as in the picture. Layer in an ovenproof dish and sprinkle with half the salt and pepper and all but 1 teaspoon of the spring onion and parsley. Melt 4 tablespoons of the butter in a small saucepan. Blend in the mustard, tomato purée, lemon juice and sugar. Peel and crush the garlic. Add together with the vinegar and white wine, remaining parsley and spring onion. Pour over the fish, cover and bake in a moderate oven for 20–25 minutes. Drain the liquor into a bowl. Lightly beat the egg yolk in a small bowl. Add a little of the hot liquor and blend well. Pour into the remaining sauce, stirring constantly. Lightly fry the mushrooms in a pan with the remaining butter for 3–5 minutes. Arrange the fish on an ovenproof dish, pour over the sauce and arrange a few mushroom slices on each piece of fish. Sprinkle the breadcrumbs over the mushrooms and brown lightly under the grill. If liked, arrange a pile of boiled new potatoes in the centre of the fish and sprinkle with chopped parsley.

# Fish mayonnaise

Preparation time: 10 minutes
Serves: 4

**1 kg./2 lb. cold poached steenbras, hake or kabeljou**
**3 tablespoons grated onion**
**3 tablespoons lemon juice**
**½ tablespoon capers**
**1 cucumber, chopped**
**3 tablespoons mayonnaise**
**2 tablespoons cream**
**2 tablespoons chopped parsley**
**2 teaspoons salt**
**¼ teaspoon freshly ground black pepper**
**6 lettuce leaves**
**2 lemons**

Flake the fish and mix with the grated onion, lemon juice, capers, cucumber, mayonnaise, cream and parsley. Add the salt and pepper. Blend well and place on a long narrow dish. Shred the lettuce leaves finely and cover the fish completely. Slice the lemons thinly and place in an overlapping line down the centre of the dish.

*Buttered cheese eggs in nests, baked eggs (see page 18)*

*Eggs in curry cream (see page 18)*

# Golden haddock

*Illustrated on page 65*
Preparation time: 10 minutes
Cooking time: about 15 minutes
Serves: 4

**1 kg./2 lb. smoked haddock**
**250 g./8 oz. new potatoes, cooked**
**125 ml./$\frac{1}{4}$ pint cream**
**250 ml./$\frac{1}{2}$ pint milk**
**2 tablespoons/1 oz. butter**
**2 tablespoons chopped spring onion**
**1 egg yolk**
**1 teaspoon cornflour**
**freshly ground black pepper to taste**
**$\frac{1}{4}$ teaspoon freshly ground coriander**
**$\frac{1}{2}$ teaspoon curry powder**
**125 g./4 oz. mushrooms, sliced**
**chopped parsley to garnish (optional)**

Cut the haddock into neat slices. Pour boiling water, to cover, over the haddock, then drain immediately. Place in a large pan with the potatoes, cream, milk, butter and onion and cook for 5–6 minutes. Beat the egg yolk and cornflour with a fork. Spoon a little of the hot milk onto the egg mixture and blend. Pour into the pan and add the spices and sliced mushrooms. Cook gently for 5–8 minutes, stirring the sauce carefully with a wooden spoon – do not allow to boil. Place the haddock, potatoes and mushrooms on a heated dish. Pour over the sauce. If liked garnish with chopped parsley and serve immediately with a green salad and soft white cheese-topped rolls.

# Baked steenbras with capers

Preparation time: 5 minutes
Cooking time: 10 minutes per $\frac{1}{2}$ kg. (1 lb.)
Oven temperature: moderate (350°F., 180°C., Gas Mark 4)
Serves: 6–8

**1.6–1.8 kg./about 3$\frac{1}{2}$ lb. steenbras or haddock**
**110 g./4 oz. ripe tomatoes, peeled and chopped**
**about 2 teaspoons capers**
**40 g./1$\frac{1}{2}$ oz. chopped parsley**
**8 spring onions**
**2 cloves garlic**
**2 bay leaves**
**1 teaspoon oregano**
**$\frac{1}{4}$ teaspoon dried basil**
**1 teaspoon salt**
**$\frac{1}{4}$ teaspoon freshly ground black pepper**
**3 tablespoons olive or salad oil**

Place the fish on a piece of oiled foil. Spread with a mixture of the tomatoes, capers, parsley, chopped onions, crushed garlic and seasonings and pour over the olive or salad oil. Close tightly and bake in a moderate oven allowing 10 minutes per $\frac{1}{2}$ kg. (1 lb.). When cooked, open the foil and remove the bay leaves. Serve with tiny boiled potatoes.

# Mustard herrings with potato rounds

Preparation time: 20 minutes, plus overnight soaking
Cooking time: 12 minutes
Oven temperature: moderate (350°F., 180°C., Gas Mark 4)
Serves: 6

**6 salted or fresh herrings**
**6 boiled potatoes**
**250 ml./$\frac{1}{2}$ pint cream**
**2 tablespoons prepared mustard**
**1 teaspoon freshly ground black pepper**
**2 tablespoons chopped parsley**
**1 tablespoon paprika pepper**

Soak the herrings overnight. Clean and take out the backbone, but leave as whole fillets. Place in a casserole. Slice the potatoes and place these in overlapping layers down the length of the dish. Mix the cream, mustard, pepper and parsley, and pour over the herrings. Sprinkle with paprika pepper. Cover and bake in a moderate oven for 12 minutes.

# Pink prawns in white wine

Preparation time: 15 minutes
Cooking time: about 5 minutes
Serves: 4–6

**12 large prawns**
**125 g./4 oz. flour**
**1 teaspoon salt**
**¼ teaspoon freshly ground black pepper**
**pinch piri-piri or chilli powder**
**4 tablespoons/2 oz. butter**
**4 tablespoons oil**
**125 ml./¼ pint white wine**
**2 tablespoons chopped parsley**

Shell and vein the prawns. Wash well and pat dry with absorbent paper. Mix the flour, salt, pepper and piri-piri or chilli powder in a bowl. Dip each prawn in the flour mixture to coat. Heat the butter and oil in a large frying pan. When hot but not smoking, add the prawns. Allow to turn golden, 3–4 minutes. Gradually pour over the white wine and stir in the parsley. Serve in heated individual dishes, on a bed of rice.

# Salmon quiche

Preparation time: 30 minutes
Cooking time: about 30 minutes
Oven temperature: hot (450°F., 230°C., Gas Mark 8), reducing to moderately hot (400°F., 200°C., Gas Mark 6), reducing to moderate (350°F., 180°C., Gas Mark 4)
Serves: 6–8

**250 g./8 oz. shortcrust pastry**
**2 eggs**
**250 ml./½ pint milk**
**½ teaspoon salt**
**¼ teaspoon freshly ground black pepper**
**170 g./6 oz. sharp Cheddar cheese, grated**
**2 medium-sized cans salmon**

Turn the dough onto a lightly floured board and roll with quick light strokes into a circle, 3 mm. (⅛ inch) thick and 28 cm. (11 inches) in diameter. Fit the pastry loosely into a 23-cm. (9-inch) tin and trim with a pair of scissors, leaving a 2½-cm. (1-inch) margin over the edge of the tin. Fold a little of this edge under to make a standing rim. Flute with your fingers along the edge. Prick the pastry case with a fork. Chill for 10 minutes and bake in a hot oven until the case is lightly browned. Reduce the temperature to moderately hot. Set aside to cool before filling. Whisk the eggs in a bowl, add the milk, salt, pepper and grated cheese. Drain the salmon and flake lightly with a fork. Fold into the egg mixture. Place the pastry case on a large sheet of foil and spoon in the filling. Bake in the moderately hot oven for 10 minutes, then reduce the heat to moderate and continue baking for about 20 minutes, until the filling is golden brown and set.

To freeze, cool on the foil, then wrap completely in foil and freeze. To reheat, remove from the freezer, place in a moderate oven, still wrapped, for 10 minutes, then open the foil and bake for a further 20 minutes. Remove, place on a plate and serve.

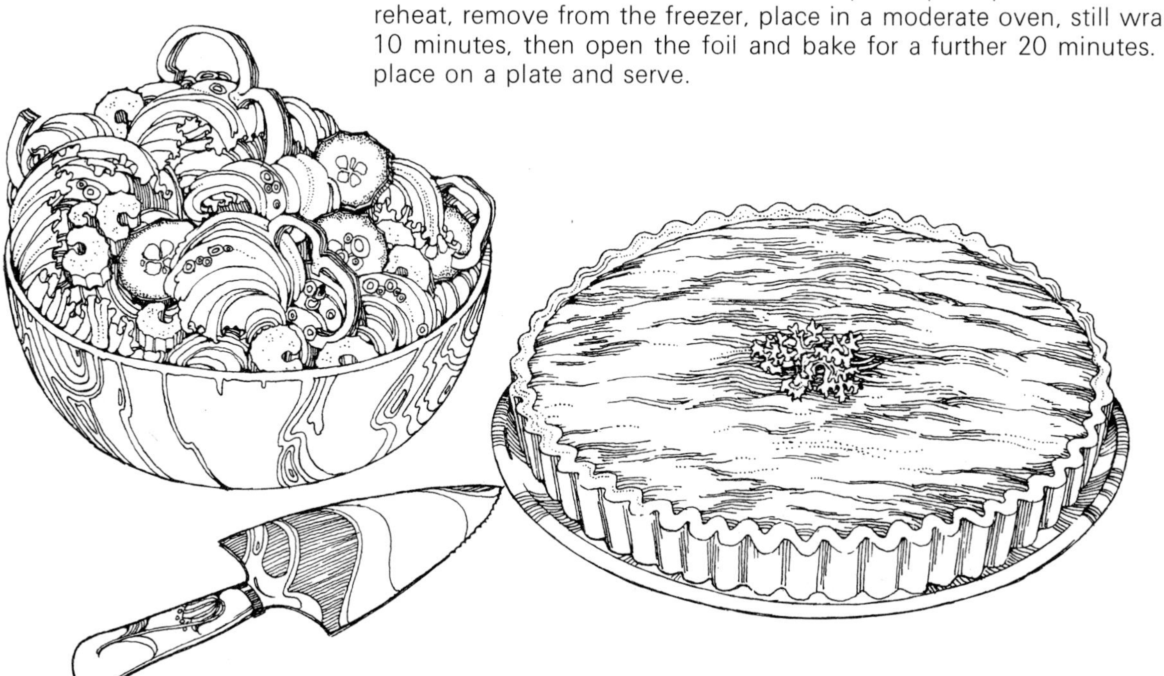

*Avocado mousse, stuffed avocado* (see pages 19, 78)

*Cream of avocado soup (see page 23)*

# Main dishes

The main course is the pivot around which the menu revolves, your very first consideration to build around for the best balance. If you intend serving a hearty main dish, follow with a light sweet. A less substantial main course should be followed by a filling dessert. Most of our day-to-day planning goes into what to serve as our main dish. It must be generous enough to satisfy. If on a budget, shop around for the best daily buys. Never allow yourself to become trapped by a weekly routine of familiar dishes. Try to change these as much as possible; there really are a hundred ways with mince, and chicken dishes by the score. Make the best possible use of rice, pasta, vegetables, herbs and spices to add interest and flavour.

Good-looking dishes to have: deep oven-to-table casseroles, large, medium and small, in warm colours; a large flat platter for meat and vegetables combined; a spiked wooden board for carving joints.

## Meat

### Marinated flank in red wine

Preparation time: 10 minutes, plus overnight marinating
Cooking time: about 3 hours
Serves: 8

**1 2-kg./4½-lb. piece thick beef flank, leg or silverside**
**1 large onion**
**3 bay leaves**
**6 cloves**
**¼ teaspoon powdered ginger**
**6 peppercorns, crushed**
**brown or malt vinegar**
**3 thick slices bacon**
**4 tablespoons/2 oz. butter**
**1 teaspoon salt**
**250 ml./½ pint dry red wine**
**500 ml./1 pint beef stock**
**1 tablespoon flour**
**2 teaspoons brown sugar**

Place the meat in a bowl with the halved onion, one of the bay leaves, the cloves, ginger and peppercorns. Cover with the vinegar and marinate for 24 hours, turning twice during this time. Drain and dry the meat with absorbent paper, reserving the onion. Make little slits in the meat and lard it with strips of bacon. Melt half the butter in a heavy saucepan and brown the meat evenly on all sides. Add the reserved onion and the salt and brown together with the meat. Add the remaining bay leaves, the wine and stock. Cover and simmer slowly for 2–3 hours, until the meat is tender. Remove the meat and set aside the stock. Add the remaining butter to the pan and brown with the flour. Gradually add stock to the pan and stir until the sauce thickens, then add the brown sugar. Slice the meat to serve, pour over a little gravy and serve the remainder in a sauceboat.

# Steak and kidney pie

Preparation time: 20 minutes
Cooking time: about 1 hour
Oven temperature: moderately hot (400°F., 200°C., Gas Mark 6), reducing to moderate (350°F., 180°C., Gas Mark 4)
Serves: 4–6

**1 kg./2 lb. topside**
**250 g./8 oz. calf's kidneys**
**1½ teaspoons salt**
**½ teaspoon freshly ground black pepper**
**4 tablespoons flour**
**3 tablespoons chopped beef suet**
**125 g./4 oz. mushrooms, thinly sliced**
**3 tablespoons chopped onion**
**250 ml./½ pint water**
**2 tablespoons sherry**
**1 tablespoon finely chopped parsley**
**¼ teaspoon thyme**
**¼ teaspoon Worcestershire sauce**
**250 g./8 oz. puff pastry**
**1 egg yolk**

Cut the topside and kidneys into 2½-cm. (1-inch) cubes. Pat dry with absorbent paper. Sprinkle with 1 teaspoon salt and half the pepper. Toss the meat with the flour in a bowl to coat evenly. Heat the suet in a large frying pan until it splutters. Brown the meat, adding a little more suet to the pan if necessary. Place the browned meat in a heavy casserole or pie dish. Add the mushrooms and onion to the remaining fat in pan. Cook over a moderate heat, stirring constantly, for 2–3 minutes. Add to the casserole. Pour the water into the frying pan and bring to the boil, scraping in any brown bits. Pour over the meat. Add the sherry, parsley, thyme, Worcestershire sauce and remaining salt and pepper. Stir together gently and leave aside to cool. Roll out the pastry on a lightly floured board to a rough rectangle about 6 mm. (¼ inch) thick and cut two strips 30 cm. (12 inches) long and 1¼ cm. (¾ inch) wide. Place the strips end to end around the edge of casserole and press into place. Moisten with a little water using a pastry brush. Cover with the remaining pastry; trim off the excess and crimp the edges with the prong of a fork. Make two slits in centre of the pie and brush with beaten egg. Bake in a moderately hot oven for 30 minutes. Reduce heat to moderate and bake for an additional 30 minutes, until the crust is golden brown. Serve immediately.

# Pot roast beef with prunes

*Illustrated on page 45*
Preparation time: 10 minutes, plus overnight soaking of prunes
Cooking time: about 4 hours
Serves: 8

**24 prunes**
**2 kg./4½ lb. middle-cut brisket**
**4 tablespoons flour**
**2 onions**
**3 tablespoons salad oil**
**2 bay leaves**
**¼ teaspoon nutmeg**
**¼ teaspoon cinnamon**
**¼ teaspoon salt**
**freshly ground black pepper to taste**
**1 litre/1¾ pints chicken stock**
**4 carrots, thinly sliced**
**2 potatoes, sliced**
**juice of 3 large lemons**
**2 tablespoons golden syrup**

Soak the prunes overnight until well puffed. Dust the meat with flour. Slice the onions into rings. Heat the oil in a heavy saucepan, add the onion rings and cook until golden. Remove. Add the meat and brown on all sides. Add the onion rings, bay leaves, nutmeg, cinnamon, salt and pepper. Pour over the stock. Cover tightly and simmer for 3–4 hours, until the meat is tender. Remove the meat to a deep serving dish; cover with foil and keep warm. Add the drained prunes, carrots, potatoes, lemon juice and golden syrup to the pan. Cook gently for 10–15 minutes. Place the prunes, carrots and potatoes with the meat and pour over the sweet-sour gravy. If liked, serve with potato dumplings (see page 76).

**Note** This dish can be prepared and cooked the day before serving and reheated.

# Peppered sirloin

*Illustrated opposite*
Preparation time: few minutes
Cooking time: about 1 hour
Oven temperature: moderately hot (400°F., 200°C., Gas Mark 6)
Serves: 6–8

**2 tablespoons dry mustard**
**1 1.5-kg./3-lb. piece well-hung rolled sirloin**
**2 tablespoons oil**
**1 tablespoon lemon juice**
**1 teaspoon chopped garlic**
**2 tablespoons freshly ground black pepper**

Press the mustard over the sirloin. Blend the oil, lemon juice, garlic and pepper. Smooth over the sirloin. Place in a roasting tin and cook in a moderately hot oven, allowing 36 minutes to the kg. (2 lb.). To serve hot, place on a heated dish and serve immediately with a choice of pickled walnuts, horseradish sauce or mustard. To serve cold, cut into thin slices and serve with a selection of salads. For the best flavour, do not serve the meat straight from the refrigerator – allow it to reach room temperature.

# Savoury sliced brisket with beans

Preparation time: 20 minutes, plus overnight soaking of beans
Cooking time: about 4 hours
Oven temperature: moderately hot (400°F., 200°C., Gas Mark 6)
Serves: 6–8

**500 g./1 lb. haricot beans**
**1 beef stock cube dissolved in 500 ml./1 pint boiling water**
**4 tablespoons salad oil**
**6 onions**
**1 2-kg./4½-lb. piece middle-cut brisket or silverside**
**250 ml./½ pint red wine**
**1 litre/1¾ pints water**
**4 bay leaves**
**4 large cloves garlic**
**¼ teaspoon rosemary**
**8 large ripe tomatoes**
**1 small can tomato purée**
**¼ teaspoon thyme**
**2 tablespoons lemon juice**
**1 tablespoon brown sugar**

Soak the beans in water overnight. Drain and place in a saucepan with the boiling stock. Cook covered over a medium heat until just tender, about 3–4 hours, adding extra water as necessary. Meanwhile heat the oil in a heavy saucepan. Peel and thinly slice the onions and add half to the pan; fry until golden brown. Add the meat and brown on both sides. Lower the heat and add the red wine, water and two of the bay leaves. Peel half the garlic, add together with half the rosemary. Cover and cook for about 3–4 hours, until the meat is tender. Remove. Allow the liquid to cool and skim off the fat. Peel the tomatoes by placing in boiling water for 1 minute. Add to the pan with the remaining onion, the tomato purée, remaining bay leaves and rosemary and the thyme, lemon juice and sugar. Crush the remaining garlic cloves and add; cover and cook for 15–20 minutes until quite soft. Sieve, pressing the vegetables through. Mix the drained beans with the tomato mixture in a saucepan. Add the skimmed cooking liquid and simmer over a low heat for 10–15 minutes. Slice the brisket very thinly. Place in a deep ovenproof dish. Spoon over the beans and gravy. Reheat in a moderately hot oven and serve.

**Note** This is an ideal party dish as it can be prepared completely the day before and heated just before serving. It is equally good served with potatoes, buttered noodles or rice.

*Peppered sirloin (see opposite)*

# Oxtail in Burgundy

*Illustrated on page 48*
Preparation time: 15 minutes
Cooking time: 4 hours
Oven temperature: moderate (325°F., 170°C., Gas Mark 3)
Serves: 4–6

**2 kg./4$\frac{1}{2}$ lb. oxtail**
**125 g./4 oz. flour**
**2 teaspoons salt**
**$\frac{1}{2}$ teaspoon freshly ground black pepper**
**4 tablespoons vegetable oil**
**1 beef stock cube**
**250 ml./$\frac{1}{2}$ pint boiling water**
**$\frac{1}{2}$ bottle Burgundy**
**1 clove garlic**
**pinch sage**
**2 bay leaves**
**12 small onions**
**3 cloves**
**18 new potatoes**
**12 young carrots**
**8 mushrooms, sliced**
**250 g./8 oz. fresh peas**

Wash the oxtail thoroughly and trim. Mix the flour, salt and pepper together on wax or greaseproof paper. Lightly flour the meat. Heat the oil in a flameproof casserole and brown the oxtail. Drain off all the fat. Dissolve the beef stock cube in boiling water. Add to the casserole together with the Burgundy, crushed garlic, sage, bay leaves, peeled onions and cloves. Cover and cook in a moderate oven for 3$\frac{1}{2}$ hours. Remove and add the scraped potatoes, carrots, peeled and cut into sticks, mushrooms and peas. Cover and return to the oven for a further 30 minutes. (The oxtail should be meltingly tender.) Serve in warm deep earthenware bowls.
**Note** If possible, plan to cook oxtail for 3$\frac{1}{2}$ hours the day before serving. Leave overnight then skim off any fat and complete the cooking on day of serving.

# Spiced beef casserole

Preparation time: 20 minutes, plus marinating time
Cooking time: about 2 hours
Oven temperature: moderate (325°F., 170°C., Gas Mark 3)
Serves: 4–5

**1 kg./2 lb. beefsteak or braising steak**
**250 g./8 oz. small onions**
**1 large green pepper**
**1 medium-sized orange**
**1 clove garlic**
**2 teaspoons prepared mustard**
**2 teaspoons Worcestershire sauce**
**2 tablespoons wine vinegar**
**1 teaspoon salt**
**$\frac{1}{4}$ teaspoon freshly ground black pepper**
**250 g./8 oz. salt pork or streaky bacon**
**about 3 tablespoons oil**
**1 tablespoon flour**
**1 bay leaf**
**250 ml./$\frac{1}{2}$ pint beef stock or $\frac{1}{2}$ beef stock cube dissolved in 250 ml./$\frac{1}{2}$ pint water**
**1 large can new potatoes**
**2 tablespoons chopped parsley**

Trim the meat and cut into cubes. Place in a large mixing bowl. Peel the onions and add whole to the meat. Wash the green pepper, removing stalk, white pith and seeds. Slice and add to the meat and onions. Coarsely grate the orange rind into a cup, avoiding the white pith. Cover with water and set aside. Squeeze the juice from the orange. Peel the garlic, slice thinly and place in the orange juice with the mustard, sauce and vinegar. Add to meat. Season and cover the bowl. Leave in the refrigerator for at least 2 hours, or overnight, turning over occasionally. When ready to cook, pour the marinade into a casserole. Cut the salt pork or bacon into pieces, removing the rind. Heat the oil until hot in a frying pan and cook the pork or bacon until crisp. Drain and place in the casserole. Toss the drained meat and vegetables in the flour. Add to the frying pan. Cook quickly for 10–12 minutes, turning occasionally until brown all over. Add to the casserole with the bay leaf and stock. Cover and bake in a moderate oven for 1$\frac{1}{2}$ hours, or until the meat is tender. Add the potatoes and bake for a further 30 minutes. Drain the orange rind and before serving, garnish the meat with chopped parsley and rind.

# Stuffed fillet of beef

Preparation time: 10 minutes
Cooking time: about 1¼ hours
Oven temperature: moderately hot (400°F., 200°C., Gas Mark 6)
Serves: 6

**1 1.8-kg./3¼-lb. piece beef fillet**
**2¼ teaspoons salt**
**1¼ teaspoons freshly ground black pepper**
**4 tablespoons/2 oz. butter**
**90 g./3 oz. mushrooms, chopped**
**45 g./2 oz. onion, chopped**
**2 tablespoons chopped parsley**
**4 chicken livers**

Make a deep cut lengthwise along the fillet and spread the meat out on wax or greaseproof paper. Season with 2 teaspoons salt and 1 teaspoon pepper. Place half the butter in a roasting tin in a moderately hot oven and when brown add the fillet and cook for 1–2 minutes on each side, just long enough to brown the surface. Sauté the mushrooms, onion and parsley in remaining butter and spread over the surface of the meat. Using the same pan, sauté the chicken livers and add the remaining salt and pepper. Cook for 2–3 minutes. Remove, cool slightly then chop coarsely. Spread on top of vegetable stuffing. Roll up the fillet and tie with twine at 5-cm. (2-inch) intervals. Roast in a moderately hot oven for 18 minutes per ½ kg. (1 lb.) for rare steak. Serve sliced, with roast potatoes and creamed spinach (see page 70).

# Brisket with beer

Preparation time: 15 minutes
Cooking time: about 3 hours
Oven temperature: cool (300°F., 150°C., Gas Mark 2)
Serves: 4

**1 1.5-kg./3-lb. piece middle-cut brisket, silverside or topside**
**4 tablespoons flour**
**4 tablespoons salad oil**
**1 clove garlic**
**2 teaspoons salt**
**¼ teaspoon freshly ground black pepper**
**2 bay leaves**
**125 g./4 oz. green beans**
**8 prunes**
**250 g./8 oz. sweet potatoes**
**8 small onions**
**250 ml./½ pint beer**
**2 tablespoons honey**
**6 tablespoons water**
**¼ teaspoon freshly ground nutmeg**

Wipe the meat with a cloth soaked in vinegar. Sprinkle with flour. Heat the oil in a flameproof casserole and brown the brisket on all sides. Peel and crush the garlic and add to the dish with the salt, pepper, bay leaves, green beans and prunes. Peel the potatoes and onions. Place in the dish together with the beer, honey, water and nutmeg. Cover and bake in a cool oven for 2–3 hours, until the meat is tender and the vegetables are very soft, almost forming thick gravy.

# Minute steaks in French brandy sauce

Preparation time: few minutes
Cooking time: few minutes
Serves: 4

**2 cloves garlic**
**2 teaspoons freshly ground black pepper**
**8 minute steaks**
**2 tablespoons/1 oz. butter**
**2 tablespoons brandy**
**1 tablespoon French mustard**
**2 teaspoons salt**
**3 tablespoons cream**

Crush the garlic and mix with the pepper. Pat into the steaks. Heat the butter in a frying pan and quickly fry the steaks on both sides, for 3 minutes in all. Remove to a hot dish. Add the brandy to the pan and ignite. When the flames have died down, add the mustard, salt and cream and stir together well. Heat, but do not boil, then pour over the steaks.

# Paprika beef steaks

Preparation time: 15 minutes
Cooking time: about 1¾ hours
Oven temperature: moderate (325°F., 170°C., Gas Mark 3)
Serves: 6

**12 6-mm./¼-inch thick beef steaks**
**4 tablespoons flour**
**6 tablespoons salad oil**
**2 onions**
**¼ teaspoon freshly ground black pepper**
**pinch rosemary**
**pinch marjoram**
**2 bay leaves**
**1 teaspoon salt**
**1 beef stock cube dissolved in 250 ml./½ pint boiling water**
**125 ml./¼ pint white wine**
**2 tablespoons rose paprika or paprika pepper**
**125 ml./¼ pint sour cream**
**2 tablespoons capers**
**2 tablespoons finely chopped parsley**

Wipe the beef steaks with a damp cloth. Sprinkle the flour on a piece of wax or greaseproof paper and lightly coat each steak. Heat the oil in a large pan and fry the steaks lightly. Remove to a casserole. Peel and dice the onions. Add to the pan and cook until golden. Add the pepper, rosemary, marjoram, bay leaves and salt. Put with the steaks, cover with the stock and wine and cook, covered, in a moderate oven for 1½ hours, or until the meat is tender when pierced with a metal skewer. Remove the lid, add the paprika pepper, cream, capers and parsley. Stir gently. Return to the oven, covered, for a further 10 minutes. Serve from the casserole.
**Note** This is a good dish to prepare in advance.

# Tournedos in pastry

Preparation time: 20 minutes
Cooking time: about 15 minutes
Oven temperature: moderately hot (400°F., 200°C., Gas Mark 6)
Serves: 4

**4 4-cm./1½-inch thick tournedos**
**1 teaspoon freshly ground black pepper**
**3 tablespoons/1½ oz. butter**
**1½ teaspoons salt**
**4 small slices ham**
**250 g./8 oz. frozen puff pastry**
**1 egg yolk, beaten**
*chicken liver sauce*
**2 tablespoons oil**
**1 onion, coarsely chopped**
**500 g./1 lb. chicken livers**
**125 ml./¼ pint chicken stock**
**4 tablespoons cream**
**2 tablespoons sherry**
**¼ teaspoon freshly ground black pepper**
**½ teaspoon salt**

Sprinkle the tournedos with pepper. Heat the butter in a frying pan and when moderately hot, gently sauté the tournedos for 3 minutes on each side. Sprinkle with 1 teaspoon of the salt. Remove and cool. Place a slice of ham on the top of each steak. Roll out the puff pastry and cut into four squares, each large enough to completely enfold a tournedo. To fold, damp the edges, draw up the points of the square to the centre of the tournedo. Pinch the openings closed and cut out two pastry leaves for each little case from the remaining dough. Dampen slightly and press onto the tops of each pastry case. Place on a baking sheet, brush with a little beaten egg and bake in a moderately hot oven for 12–15 minutes, until the pastry is well puffed and crisp.

To make the chicken liver sauce, add the oil to the frying pan and gently fry the onion. Add the chicken livers and sauté for 5–8 minutes. When brown add the chicken stock, cream, sherry and seasoning. Scrape the bottom of the pan to stir in all the brown bits. Heat thoroughly (but do not boil) and serve with the tournedos.
**Note** The chicken liver sauce can be prepared in advance and refrigerated. The puff pastry can be cut into squares and refrigerated, wrapped, separately, in wax or greaseproof paper. Sauté the tournedos 2 hours before use, remove to a cool place, cover but do not refrigerate. Complete preparation 30 minutes before serving.

*Pot roast beef with prunes (see page 39)*

# Rounds of lamb

Preparation time: 15 minutes
Cooking time: about 20 minutes
Serves: 4–6

**8 4-cm./1½-inch thick loin lamb chops**
**8 large mushrooms**
**2 tablespoons/1 oz. butter**
**1½ teaspoons salt**
**¼ teaspoon freshly ground black pepper**
**2 tablespoons salad oil**
**2 tablespoons white wine**
**4 tablespoons water**
**2 tablespoons chopped parsley**

Ask the butcher to trim away the long bone on each chop leaving on the outer layer of fat. Wrap this fat around the meat forming a round shape. Tie each one with string. Wash the mushrooms, trim off the stalks at the base of the mushrooms and slice a very thin sliver off the top of each mushroom to enable them to stand firmly. Heat the butter in a frying pan and when hot add the mushrooms, ½ teaspoon salt and the pepper. Fry gently until just soft, 8–10 minutes. Remove and keep warm. Heat the oil in another pan. When hot add the lamb chops and brown on all sides. Sprinkle with salt. Reduce the heat slightly and cook for a further 6–8 minutes, for rare chops. Remove and place each lamb round on a mushroom. Add the white wine to the pan together with the water, parsley and remaining salt. Stir in all the brown bits. Reduce slightly by rapid boiling and pour over the chops.

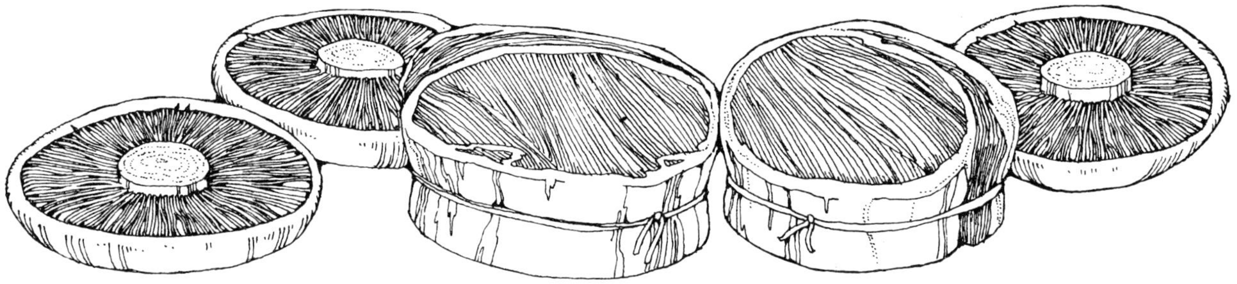

# Lamb boulangère

Preparation time: 20 minutes, plus time to make the stock
Cooking time: 1 hour 20 minutes
Oven temperature: moderately hot (400°F., 200°C., Gas Mark 6)
Serves: 6

**2 kg./4½ lb. shoulder of lamb, boned**
*stock*
**lamb bones**
**water**
**1 stalk celery**
**1 onion**
**2 carrots**
**1 teaspoon cooking salt**
**freshly ground black pepper to taste**
*stuffing*
**2½ teaspoons/about ½ oz. dripping**
**4 teaspoons chopped onion**
**125 g./4 oz. soft breadcrumbs**
**2 tablespoons chopped parsley**
**grated rind of ½ lemon**
**1 teaspoon salt**
**freshly ground black pepper to taste**
**1 egg, beaten**
**1 tablespoon/½ oz. butter**
**1 kg./2 lb. potatoes**
**1 kg./2 lb. onions**

Wipe the lamb with a vinegar-soaked cloth. To make the stock, place the bones which have been removed from the shoulder in a saucepan, barely cover with water and add the celery, peeled onion, carrots, salt and pepper. Bring to the boil, cover and simmer for 1 hour.

Melt the dripping in a pan. Add the chopped onion and soften over a gentle heat. Add the breadcrumbs, parsley, lemon rind, salt, pepper and beaten egg. Blend thoroughly – the stuffing should be rather firm. Open the boned shoulder, spread with the stuffing, roll up and tie securely with twine. Spread the top of the lamb with butter. Peel and slice the potatoes and onions and place in a casserole. Put the meat on top of the vegetables. Pour over the strained stock. Bake in a moderately hot oven for 1 hour 20 minutes, adding 125 ml. (¼ pint) extra water or stock if necessary. The cooked lamb should be faintly pink.

# Stuffed leg of lamb with raisins

Preparation time: 20 minutes
Cooking time: about 2 hours
Serves: 8–10

**1 2-kg./4½-lb. leg of lamb**
**2 cloves garlic**
**6 tablespoons oil**
**1 onion, chopped**
**125 g./4 oz. long-grain rice**
**450 ml./about ¾ pint beef broth**
**25 g./1 oz. pine nuts or slivered blanched almonds**
**3 tablespoons seedless raisins**
**¼ teaspoon each powdered all-spice, nutmeg, cinnamon**
**1 teaspoon salt**
**½ teaspoon freshly ground black pepper**

Ask the butcher to bone the lamb and cut out about 230 g. (8 oz.) of meat from the inside of the leg. Mince this meat and set it aside. Slice 1 clove garlic and push slivers of it into the leg of lamb. Melt 4 tablespoons of the oil in a saucepan and brown the onion. Add the rice, remaining garlic clove, crushed, and the minced lamb and cook for 10 minutes. Add a quarter of the broth, the nuts and raisins. Season with spices, salt and pepper and simmer for 10–12 minutes. Cool and stuff the lamb with this mixture and sew up or close the join with skewers on all sides. Heat the remaining oil in a pan and brown the stuffed lamb on all sides. Add the remaining broth and simmer, closely covered, for 1½–2 hours. Skim the cooking liquor and strain before serving.

# Marinated chops and spicy sausages

Preparation time: 10 minutes, plus marinating time
Cooking time: about 10 minutes
Serves: 6–8

**1 kg./2 lb. loin lamb chops**
**1 kg./2 lb. beef sausages**
**125 ml./¼ pint lemon juice**
**125 ml./¼ pint white wine**
**2 tablespoons vinegar**
**2 tablespoons salad oil**
**2 tablespoons smooth apricot jam**
**1 tablespoon curry powder**
**2 cloves garlic**
**¼ teaspoon freshly ground black pepper**
**1 teaspoon salt**
**3 bay leaves**
**¼ teaspoon chopped rosemary**

Trim the loin chops and arrange in a flat dish together with the beef sausages. Prick each sausage with a fork. Combine the lemon juice, white wine, vinegar, salad oil, apricot jam and curry powder in a bowl. Peel and crush the garlic. Add together with the freshly ground black pepper and salt. Whisk until creamy. Pour over the chops and sausages. Place the bay leaves on top of the chops and sprinkle with rosemary. Marinate for 2–3 hours. Remove from the marinade and cook the chops and sausages on each side under a heated grill. Brush with the marinade during cooking.

# Barbecued spareribs

Preparation time: 5 minutes, plus marinating time
Cooking time: 30 minutes
Oven temperature: moderate (350°F., 180°C., Gas Mark 4)
Serves: 4

**1.5 kg./3 lb. pork spareribs**
**125 ml./¼ pint soy sauce**
**2 tablespoons honey**
**1 tablespoon sherry**
**1 clove garlic, crushed**

Wash the spareribs and remove excess fat and gristle. Place the whole rack (or individual ribs) in a roasting tin. Mix the soy sauce, honey, sherry and garlic together. Pour the mixture over the spareribs and leave to marinate 1 hour; turn the meat over and marinate for another hour. Drain, reserving the marinade. Brush the spareribs with the marinade and bake in a moderate oven for 20 minutes on each side; cook under a preheated grill, brushing or basting both sides of ribs, for a further 10 minutes. (If a higher glaze is desired, brush lightly with honey before placing under the grill.)

Oxtail in Burgundy (see page 42)

*Country casserole* *(see page 50)*

# Roast leg of pork with oranges

Preparation time: 15 minutes
Cooking time: about 4½ hours
Oven temperature: moderate (350°F., 180°C., Gas Mark 4)
Serves: 12–14

**1 3-kg./6½-lb. leg of pork**
**3 cloves garlic**
**2 teaspoons black peppercorns**
**4 onions**
**2 bay leaves**
**250 ml./½ pint water**
**2 teaspoons salt**
**1 small can apricot juice**
**250 g./6–8 oz. brown sugar**
**2 large oranges**

Score the pork skin in a diamond pattern and rub with one of the cloves of garlic. Place in a roasting tin with the remaining garlic, crushed, and the crushed peppercorns. Slice the onions and place with the pork. Add the bay leaves, half the water and the salt. Cover with foil and roast for 1 hour. Remove the foil, add the apricot juice and baste well. Return to the oven and continue roasting, allowing 60 minutes per kg. (2 lb.), until tender and well done. (Pork requires very long, slow cooking. The meat should be white with no pinky tinge.) Boil the sugar and remaining water for 5 minutes. Slice the unpeeled oranges thinly and place all over the pork and secure with toothpicks or cocktail sticks. Pour over the sugar syrup and roast for a further 5–8 minutes, uncovered. Then place under the grill for 5–8 minutes, until glazed. Remove the toothpicks and serve hot with a crisp green salad platter – lettuce, cucumber, green peppers and spring onions.

# Country casserole

*Illustrated on page 49*
Preparation time: 10 minutes, plus overnight soaking of beans
Cooking time: 3 hours
Oven temperature: moderate (325°F., 170°C., Gas Mark 3)
Serves: 4

**500 g./1 lb. haricot beans**
**7 small onions**
**3 tablespoons oil**
**2 bratwurst (smoked sausages)**
**500 g./1 lb. thick gammon steaks or rashers**
**2 bay leaves**
**2 cloves garlic**
**¼ teaspoon freshly ground black pepper**
**½ teaspoon salt**
**2 teaspoons dry mustard**
**1 chicken stock cube**
**500 ml./1 pint boiling water**
**3 tablespoons white wine**
**chopped parsley to garnish**

Soak the beans in water overnight. Peel the onions. Heat the oil in a heavy casserole and when just hot, add the onions and brown. Add the thickly sliced sausages and chunks of gammon to the casserole with the bay leaves, garlic, pepper, salt and mustard. Dissolve the stock cube in the boiling water. Stir into the casserole together with the drained beans and white wine. Cover and bake in a moderate oven for 3 hours, adding extra water if necessary. Remove garlic cloves, serve in deep bowls, and sprinkle with chopped parsley.

**Note** For a more economical dish use pork or lamb knuckles or shank end in place of the gammon.

# Veal stew with sour cream

Preparation time: 10 minutes
Cooking time: about 1¼ hours
Serves: 6–8

**1.5 kg./3 lb. boned veal shoulder**
**250 ml./½ pint boiling water**
**1 bay leaf**
**2 teaspoons salt**
**5–6 peppercorns**
**pinch thyme**
**1 tablespoon paprika pepper**
**2 medium-sized onions**
**6 carrots**
**2 sprigs parsley**
**125 g./4 oz. celery, thinly sliced**
**125 ml./¼ pint sour cream**

Cut the veal into 5-cm. (2-inch) pieces. Wipe with a damp cloth and place in a heavy saucepan; pour over the boiling water. Add the bay leaf, seasonings and paprika pepper. Cover and simmer gently for 45 minutes. Add the chopped onions, diced carrots, parsley and celery, cover and continue cooking for about 30 minutes, or until the meat and vegetables are tender. Just before serving, stir in the cream.

# Veal in caper sauce

Preparation time: 5 minutes, plus chilling time
Cooking time: 3½ hours
Oven temperature: moderate (350°F., 180°C., Gas Mark 4) reducing to cool (300°F., 150°C., Gas Mark 2)
Serves: 8–10

**1 2.3-kg./5-lb. loin of veal**
**2 onions**
**2 stalks leafy celery**
**1 carrot**
**1 clove garlic**
**3 tablespoons/1½ oz. butter**
**1 medium-sized can tuna**
**280 ml./generous ½ pint chicken stock**
**2 teaspoons salt**
**1 teaspoon freshly ground black pepper**
**280 ml./generous ½ pint white wine**
**280 ml./generous ½ pint thick mayonnaise**
**1 small jar capers**

Wipe the veal with a damp cloth and place in a roasting tin. Surround with the whole onions, celery stalks and carrot. Chop the garlic and add. Rub top of the veal with butter, seal the tin with foil and roast in a moderate oven for 1½ hours. Remove the foil completely. Flake the tuna and place it around the meat, pour the chicken stock into the pan and add the salt, pepper and white wine. Reduce the temperature to cool. Continue roasting for 2 hours, basting from time to time. Cover the dish and allow the veal to cool in the liquid. Strain the liquid, discarding the vegetables and fish, and add 3 tablespoons to the mayonnaise. Slice the veal and place in overlapping slices on a dish. Pour mayonnaise in a broad band down the centre. Drain the capers, mix with remaining liquid, pour over meat and chill lightly, covered with foil.

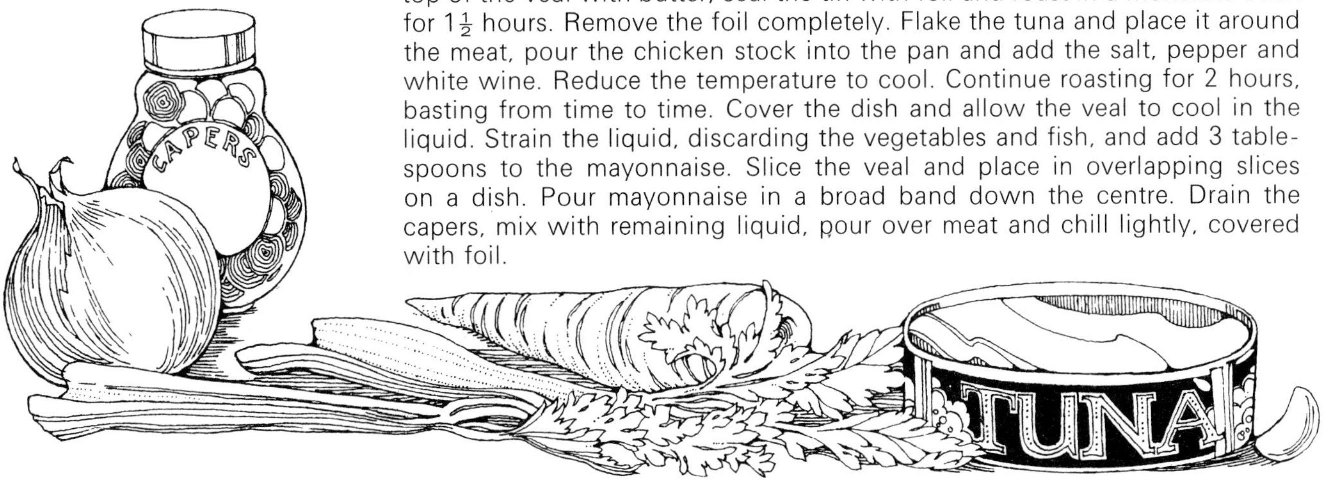


# Roast veal with rum and bananas

Preparation time: 5 minutes
Cooking time: about 2¼ hours
Oven temperature: moderate (325°F., 170°C., Gas Mark 3) increasing to moderately hot (400°F., 200°C., Gas Mark 6)
Serves: 6

**2 kg./4½ lb. veal shoulder**
**3 tablespoons/1½ oz. butter**
**3 tablespoons vegetable oil**
**1 chicken stock cube dissolved in 250 ml./½ pint boiling water**
**250 ml./½ pint white wine**
**2 teaspoons salt**
**¼ teaspoon freshly ground black pepper**
**125 ml./¼ pint cream**
**2 tablespoons rum**
**1 teaspoon grated orange rind**
**¼ teaspoon freshly grated nutmeg**
**6 ripe bananas**

Ask the butcher to bone and tie the veal for roasting. Heat the butter and oil in a flameproof casserole. Brown the meat on all sides. Pour over a quarter of the stock and white wine. Cover and cook in a moderate oven for 1 hour. Remove and pour over the remaining stock and wine. Replace and continue cooking for a further 1¼ hours, until the veal is tender. Increase the oven temperature to moderately hot. Leave the veal for 15–20 minutes, then cut into slices. Sprinkle with salt and pepper and place in overlapping layers on an ovenproof dish. Add the cream to the juices in the casserole and simmer for 5–8 minutes to reduce slightly. Add the rum, orange rind and nutmeg. Peel and slice the bananas, in rounds, slantwise. Add to the rum mixture and cook for 2–3 minutes. Spoon the bananas around the braised veal and pour the sauce over the meat. Cover and reheat in a moderately hot oven for 8–10 minutes.

**Note** When serving this dish at a dinner party, cook the meat until tender and leave in the casserole; 20 minutes before serving slice the veal and finish the sauce.

*Duck braised with apples* *(see page 63)*

Chicken with peaches (see page 58)

## Veal scallops in sherry

Preparation time: 10 minutes
Cooking time: about 15 minutes
Serves: 4–6

**12 thin slices veal**
**4 tablespoons flour**
**1 teaspoon salt**
**$\frac{1}{4}$ teaspoon freshly ground black pepper**
**6 large mushrooms**
**3 tablespoons/$1\frac{1}{2}$ oz. butter**
**1 tablespoon oil**
**4 tablespoons medium-sweet sherry**
**6 tablespoons cream**

Remove any transparent skin left on the veal scallops. Place between two sheets of wax or greaseproof paper and pound for 1 minute – the scallops should be 6 mm. ($\frac{1}{4}$ inch) thick. Cut little slits at intervals around each scallop to prevent them curling. Mix the flour with salt and pepper on a sheet of wax or greaseproof paper. Dip each scallop in the seasoned flour. Wash the mushrooms well, dry and slice very thinly. Heat the butter and oil in a frying pan. Add the veal and cook lightly on both sides for 5–6 minutes in all. Remove to a heated dish. Add the mushrooms to the pan and cook for 5–8 minutes. Stir in the sherry and cook for about 5 minutes to slightly reduce. Add the cream and heat to just boiling point. Pour over the veal scallops and serve immediately with very young peas.

## Veal kidneys on croûtons

Preparation time: 10 minutes
Cooking time: about 6 minutes
Serves: 4–6

**6 pairs veal kidneys**
**3 tablespoons flour**
**1 teaspoon salt**
**$\frac{1}{4}$ teaspoon freshly ground black pepper**
**3 tablespoons/$1\frac{1}{2}$ oz. butter**
**8 tablespoons vegetable oil**
**2 tablespoons tomato purée**
**$2\frac{1}{2}$ teaspoons lemon juice**
**$\frac{1}{2}$ teaspoon sugar**
**4 tablespoons red wine**
**2 tablespoons chopped parsley**
**4–6 slices French bread, cubed**

Wash, trim and slice the kidneys. Mix the flour, salt and freshly ground black pepper together on wax or greaseproof paper. Lightly coat the kidneys with the seasoned flour. Heat the butter and 2 tablespoons of the oil in a frying pan and fry the kidneys gently. Stir in the tomato purée, lemon juice, sugar, red wine and parsley. Cook stirring gently for 5–6 minutes. Heat the remaining oil in another pan. Fry the French bread cubes until golden brown, drain and place in a hot dish. To serve, spoon the kidneys and sauce over the croûtons.

## Lambs' tongues sweet and sour

Preparation time: 5 minutes
Cooking time: about $1\frac{3}{4}$ hours
Serves: 4–6

**12 lambs' tongues**
**2 onions, sliced**
**6 tablespoons oil**
**1 small can tomato purée**
**2 tablespoons lemon juice**
**4 tablespoons vinegar**
**250 ml./$\frac{1}{2}$ pint red wine**
**1 tablespoon sugar**
**1 tablespoon golden syrup**
**1 teaspoon salt**
**$\frac{1}{4}$ teaspoon crushed peppercorns**
**2 bay leaves**
**2 tablespoons sultanas**
**2 apples, unpeeled and thinly sliced**

Wash the tongues thoroughly. Dry and place in a heavy saucepan with a quarter of the onions and water to barely cover. Cover and simmer for 1–$1\frac{1}{2}$ hours. Remove and peel skins off the tongues and trim off any bones. Heat the oil in a saucepan. Add the remaining onions and fry until golden. Add the tomato purée, lemon juice, vinegar, red wine, sugar, golden syrup, salt, crushed peppercorns, bay leaves and sultanas. Add the tongues and cook gently for 15 minutes. Add the apple slices and cook for a further 3–5 minutes. Serve in a heated dish surrounded with herbed rice.
**Note** This dish can be prepared in the morning, or even the day before, and refrigerated, covered. The apples should be added just before serving.

# Pot roast tongue with brandied apricots

Preparation time: 5 minutes
Cooking time: about $3\frac{1}{2}$ hours
Serves: 8

**2 kg./$4\frac{1}{2}$ lb. fresh ox tongue**
**1 litre/$1\frac{3}{4}$ pints chicken stock**
**4 tablespoons oil**
**3 onions, sliced**
**3 carrots, sliced**
**3 bay leaves**
**4 peppercorns**
**1 teaspoon salt**
**$\frac{1}{2}$ teaspoon freshly ground black pepper**
**1 tablespoon finely chopped celery**
**1 large can apricots**
**250 ml./$\frac{1}{2}$ pint apricot syrup**
**2 teaspoons cornflour**
**2 tablespoons brandy**
**125 g./4 oz. shelled walnuts**

Wash the tongue thoroughly and place in a heavy saucepan. Cover with the chicken stock and simmer gently until tender, about 3 hours. Remove and skin the tongue. (The stock may be kept for a chicken soup.) Add the oil to the pan and lightly brown the onions and carrots. Add the tongue, bay leaves, peppercorns, seasoning and celery. Cook until golden brown. Remove the tongue and vegetables to a dish and cover with foil. Add the apricots and syrup to the pan. Mix the cornflour with a little water until smooth. Add to the pan, stir until the sauce thickens. Add the brandy and walnuts. Return tongue and vegetables to the pan and reheat. Serve whole on a platter with the apricots and place the sauce in a heated sauceboat.

# Liver with apples

Preparation time: few minutes
Cooking time: about 10 minutes
Serves: 4–6

**6 slices calf's liver**
**2 tablespoons flour**
**2 teaspoons salt**
**$\frac{1}{4}$ teaspoon freshly ground black pepper**
**2 cooking apples**
**3 tablespoons/$1\frac{1}{2}$ oz. butter**
**2 tablespoons vegetable fat**
**2 tablespoons lemon juice**
**3 tablespoons apple juice**
**about 2 teaspoons brandy**
**2 teaspoons chopped parsley**
**lemon slices to garnish**

Sprinkle each slice of liver with flour and half the salt and pepper. Peel, core and slice the apples very thinly. Heat two frying pans. Place butter in one, vegetable fat in the other. Cook the apples gently in the butter for 10–12 minutes and the liver in the vegetable fat, allowing 3–5 minutes on each side. Sprinkle with lemon juice and remaining salt and pepper and place on a heated dish. Pour the apple juice over the apples and add the brandy and parsley. Spoon the apple slices onto the liver and pour over the juice. Serve garnished with lemon slices.

# Grilled chipolatas with baby tomatoes on skewers

Preparation time: 5 minutes
Cooking time: about 20 minutes
Serves: 4–6

**500 g./1 lb. chipolatas**
**6 tablespoons lemon juice**
**4 teaspoons French mustard**
**2 teaspoons sugar**
**$\frac{1}{2}$ teaspoon salt**
**$\frac{1}{4}$ teaspoon freshly ground black pepper**
**6 baby tomatoes**

Roll the chipolatas in a dish with 4 tablespoons of the lemon juice. Mix the remaining juice with the mustard, sugar, salt and pepper. Brush each tomato thoroughly with the mustard mixture. Thread the sausages onto one long skewer and the tomatoes onto another. Place, three racks down, under a preheated grill and cook for 8–12 minutes. Then raise one rack higher for a further 5 minutes to crisp the sausage and brown the tomatoes slightly.

# Grilled bacon and sausage twists

Preparation time: few minutes
Cooking time: about 12 minutes
Serves: 4–6

**6 beef sausages**
**juice of 1 lemon**
**6 rashers bacon**
**¼ teaspoon freshly ground black pepper**

Place the sausages on a board and sprinkle with lemon juice. Twist a rasher of bacon around each sausage and sprinkle with freshly ground black pepper. Place, three racks down, under a preheated grill and cook for 8–10 minutes then put directly under the heat to crisp the bacon. (As the bacon cooks it flavours the sausage.) Serve in a heated dish.

# Crisped salami with mushrooms

Preparation time: 10 minutes
Cooking time: 5 minutes
Serves: 4–6

**500 g./1 lb. mushrooms**
**3 tablespoons/1½ oz. butter**
**1 tablespoon flour**
**1 teaspoon salt**
**pinch marjoram**
**1 tablespoon chopped parsley**
**pinch rosemary**
**250 ml./½ pint milk**
**¼ chicken stock cube**
**¼ teaspoon freshly ground black pepper**
**1 teaspoon dry mustard**
**2 teaspoons Worcestershire sauce**
**12 slices spicy salami**

Wash the mushrooms well in a colander under running water. Dry and slice thinly then place in a saucepan with the butter. Cook uncovered for 5–8 minutes. Sprinkle with the flour, salt and herbs. Blend with a wooden spoon; gradually add the milk and then the stock cube. Continue cooking, stirring, until the mixture thickens and comes to the boil. Add the freshly ground black pepper, mustard and Worcestershire sauce. Slice the salami into thin strips. Cook in a hot greased frying pan for 5 minutes, until crisp. Spoon the mushroom mixture into a hot dish and cover with salami strips.

# Poultry

# Cold turkey with cherry sauce

Preparation time: 10 minutes
Cooking time: about 2½ hours
Oven temperature: moderate (350°F., 180°C., Gas Mark 4)
Serves: 10–12

**1 4-kg./9-lb. turkey**
**4 tablespoons/2 oz. soft butter**
**3 teaspoons salt**
**1 teaspoon freshly ground black pepper**
**½ teaspoon freshly ground coriander**
**2 onions**
**1 lemon**
**2 bay leaves**
**4 black peppercorns**

*cherry sauce*
**1 large can cherries**
**juice of 1 lemon**
**¼ teaspoon cinnamon**
**4 tablespoons strawberry cordial or fruit juice**
**2½ teaspoons custard powder**
**1½ tablespoons water**

Rub the turkey with the butter and sprinkle with salt, pepper and coriander, both inside and out. Place the onions and halved lemon inside the cavity of the turkey. Oil a large piece of foil and wrap the turkey in it, together with the bay leaves and peppercorns. Place in a roasting tin and roast in a moderate oven for 40 minutes per kg. (2 lb.).

Drain and stone the cherries, reserving the liquid. Place the cherry liquid, lemon juice and cinnamon in a saucepan with the fruit juice. Mix the custard powder with water to a smooth paste and add to the juices. Stir over a medium heat and bring to the boil; add the cherries and cook for 2 minutes. Chill before serving with the cold turkey.

*Orange baked chicken* *(see page 59)*

# Roast turkey with pine nut stuffing

Preparation time: 15 minutes
Cooking time: 4¼ hours
Oven temperature: cool (300°F., 150°C., Gas Mark 2)
Serves: 20

**1 5-kg./11-lb. turkey**
**½ lemon**
*stuffing*
**4 tablespoons/2 oz. butter**
**110 g./4 oz. spring onions, finely chopped**
**1 teaspoon dried crushed tarragon**
**1 teaspoon salt**
**½ teaspoon freshly ground black pepper**
**450 g./1 lb. fresh white breadcrumbs**
**2 teaspoons finely grated lemon rind**
**30 g./1 oz. pine nuts**
**4 tablespoons chopped parsley**
**125 g./4 oz. soft butter**
**2 teaspoons salt**
**½ teaspoon freshly ground black pepper**
**125 ml./¼ pint water**

Wash the turkey inside and out. Reserve the giblets and dry completely with absorbent paper. Rub the cavity with the cut side of the lemon. Melt the butter in a saucepan. Add the onions and fry gently over a medium heat until just limp. Spoon into a bowl together with the juices. Add the tarragon, salt, pepper, breadcrumbs, lemon rind, pine nuts and parsley. Blend together until thoroughly mixed. Stuff the cavity lightly. Crumble a piece of aluminium foil into the opening of the vent to prevent the stuffing from spilling out during roasting. Close the vent with metal skewers and sew together. Truss with twine and rub the turkey all over with the soft butter. Sprinkle with salt and pepper. Line a shallow roasting tin with aluminium foil. Place the turkey, breast up, on a rack in the tin. Take a second sheet of foil that is larger than the turkey. Crease it in the centre. Place over the turkey like a tent. Press down slightly in between the drumsticks to secure. Roast in a cool oven for 4¼ hours (about 50 minutes per kg., 2 lb.). Remove the turkey from the roasting tin and keep warm wrapped in foil. Pour off all but 3 tablespoons of the fat from the tin. Pour in the water and stir gently, using a wooden spoon to blend in all juices which have accumulated. Place the turkey on a serving dish and serve the gravy in a sauceboat.
**Note** If a slightly thicker gravy is preferred, either reduce the gravy by rapid boiling, or thicken with 1–2 teaspoons blended cornflour.

# Chicken with peaches

*Illustrated on page 53*
Preparation time: 5 minutes
Cooking time: about 3½ hours
Oven temperature: moderate (325°F., 170°C., Gas Mark 3)
Serves: 4–6

**1 2-kg./4½-lb. chicken**
**3 tablespoons/1½ oz. butter**
**2 teaspoons honey**
**2 teaspoons salt**
**¼ teaspoon freshly ground black pepper**
**1 teaspoon ginger**
**2 bay leaves**
**6 fresh pink peaches**
**1 teaspoon sugar**
**250 ml./½ pint apple juice**
**2 tablespoons frozen orange concentrate**
**3 tablespoons cream**
**parsley to garnish**

Clean, wash and dry the chicken. Cream the butter and honey together until soft and fluffy. Smooth all over the chicken. Sprinkle with salt, pepper and ginger. Wrap in foil together with the bay leaves and place in a roasting tin. Roast in a moderate oven for 1 hour. Remove the foil and baste the chicken with the buttery juices. Roast for a further 2 hours then remove to an oven-proof dish and keep warm, wrapped in foil. Dip the unpeeled peaches into boiling water for 1 minute. Remove and peel off the skins and sprinkle with sugar. Place in the roasting tin and pour over the apple juice. Cook for a further 7–10 minutes. Set the peaches aside to keep hot. Reduce the liquid in the roasting tin until slightly thickened – stir in all the brown bits using a wooden spoon. Add the orange concentrate and cream and stir well. Heat, but do not boil. Cut the chicken into serving portions. Replace in the roasting tin with the sauce. Baste with the juices and cook for a further 8–10 minutes. Lift out onto the same dish as the peaches and spoon over the juices. Garnish with parsley and serve with fried rice and pine nuts.

# Devilled chickens

Preparation time: 5 minutes
Cooking time: about 30 minutes
Oven temperature: moderately hot (400°F., 200°C., Gas Mark 6)
Serves: 2

**2 750-g./1½-lb. baby chickens**
**2 teaspoons salt**
**¼ teaspoon freshly ground black pepper**
**6 tablespoons/3 oz. butter**
**3 teaspoons dry mustard**
**1 tablespoon Worcestershire sauce**
**pinch cayenne pepper**
**180 g./6 oz. fresh white breadcrumbs**

Split the chickens in half down the back. Wash and dry well. Sprinkle with half the salt and pepper. Melt half the butter in a small pan and brush over the chickens. Place them, cut side down, on a rack in a roasting tin. Cook in a moderately hot oven for 15 minutes, or until chickens are a light golden colour. Mix together the remaining butter, salt, pepper, the mustard, Worcestershire sauce and cayenne pepper. Stir in the breadcrumbs and mix well. Spread the skin-side of the chickens with the crumb mixture, using a spatula to spread thickly. Brown under the grill for about 15 minutes. Remove and leave to cool. Serve cold with thick, sliced, boiled potatoes tossed in sour cream with chopped chives.

# Chicken in red wine

Preparation time: 15 minutes
Cooking time: about 3 hours
Oven temperature: cool (300°F., 150°C., Gas Mark 2)
Serves: 4–6

**1 2-kg./4½-lb. chicken**
**3 rashers streaky bacon**
**10 button onions**
**125 g./4 oz. button mushrooms**
**2 tablespoons/1 oz. butter**
**2 tablespoons oil**
**1 clove garlic**
**1 bay leaf**
**sprig thyme**
**2 teaspoons salt**
**½ teaspoon freshly ground black pepper**
**3 tablespoons flour**
**2 tablespoons brandy**
**500 ml./1 pint red wine**

Rinse the chicken under running water and wipe the body cavity with a clean cloth. Remove rind and cut bacon into 1¼-cm. (¾-inch) strips. Peel the onions but leave whole. Wash the mushrooms and leave whole (if large, peel and cut into quarters). Melt half the butter with the oil in a large frying pan. Add the bacon and onions and fry for 5 minutes, or until the onion is clear. Add the mushrooms, cover and fry for a further 5 minutes. Remove and keep warm in a large casserole. Skin and finely chop the garlic and add to the casserole with the herbs and half the salt and pepper. Coat the chicken with the flour, seasoned with the remaining salt and pepper, shaking off excess. Fry the chicken in the remaining butter and oil, turning occasionally until golden brown. Pour the brandy over the chicken and ignite when warm, then add the wine. Turn into the casserole and cook in a cool oven for 3 hours.

# Orange baked chicken

*Illustrated on page 57*
Preparation time: 20 minutes
Cooking time: about 30 minutes
Oven temperature: moderate (350°F., 180°C., Gas Mark 4)
Serves: 3–4

**1 1.2-kg./2¾-lb. chicken**
**4 tablespoons flour**
**2 teaspoons salt**
**¼ teaspoon freshly ground black pepper**
**pinch rosemary**
**pinch basil**
**6 tablespoons oil**
**2 tablespoons orange marmalade**
**500 ml./1 pint orange juice**
**2 tablespoons blanched almonds**
**orange slices to garnish**

Wash and dry the chicken. Cut into quarters and lightly dust with flour. Sprinkle with salt, pepper, rosemary and basil. Heat the oil in a large frying pan. Add the chicken and brown on all sides, 8–10 minutes. Remove and drain on absorbent paper then place in an ovenproof casserole. Add the marmalade and orange juice. Cover and bake in a moderate oven for 30 minutes, until tender. Arrange the chicken portions on a serving dish and spoon over the sauce, thickened, if liked with flour. Sprinkle with blanched almonds and serve garnished with orange slices. Serve with fluffy fried rice.

# Crispy pie

Preparation time: 20 minutes
Cooking time: about 2 hours
Oven temperature: moderate (350°F., 180°C., Gas Mark 4) increasing to moderately hot (400°F., 200°C., Gas Mark 6)
Serves: 4–6

**1 2-kg./4$\frac{1}{2}$-lb. chicken**
**2 tablespoons water**
**500 g./1 lb. button mushrooms**
**4 tablespoons chopped bacon**
**3 hard-boiled eggs**
**about 250 ml./$\frac{1}{2}$ pint chicken stock**
**125 ml./$\frac{1}{4}$ pint port**
**1 teaspoon grated onion**
**sprig thyme or pinch dried thyme**
**4 tablespoons orange juice**
**2 teaspoons lemon juice**
**$\frac{1}{4}$ teaspoon grated orange rind**
**2 teaspoons salt**
**$\frac{1}{4}$ teaspoon freshly ground black pepper**
**2 tablespoons/1 oz. butter**
**2 teaspoons flour**
**4 potatoes**
**1 onion**
**1 tablespoon cream**
**2 tablespoons milk**
**2 tablespoons chopped parsley**

Wash the chicken but do not dry. Place it with the 2 tablespoons of water in a double piece of oiled foil. Wrap up completely, place in a roasting tin and bake in a moderate oven for 1$\frac{1}{2}$ hours. Remove and pour the stock and fat from the foil into a jug. Reserve and cool to allow the fat to rise to the top and set. Cut the chicken into serving pieces. Arrange in a casserole. Wash and slice the mushrooms. Skim off the cooled chicken fat, and place 3 tablespoons in a saucepan with the mushrooms and bacon. Cook over high heat for 3–5 minutes, until the bacon browns and the mushrooms are lightly browned. Drain and add to the chicken. Quarter the hard-boiled eggs and add. Pour the stock into a saucepan and stir in port, grated onion, thyme, orange and lemon juices, orange rind, salt and pepper. Boil the mixture to reduce by half. Strain and reserve. Melt half the butter in a small saucepan. Add the flour and cook for 2 minutes. Stir the port mixture gradually into the roux. Simmer the sauce, stirring constantly until slightly thickened. Pour into the casserole. Peel and slice the potatoes and onion very thinly and arrange over the chicken to cover completely. Dot with the remaining butter. Combine the cream, milk and parsley and pour over. Bake in a moderately hot oven, uncovered, for 20–25 minutes, until the potato topping is crisp and golden.

# Barbecued chicken

Preparation time: 20 minutes
Cooking time: about 40 minutes
Oven temperature: moderate (350°F., 180°C., Gas Mark 4)
Serves: 6

**2 1.5-kg./3-lb. chickens**
**125 ml./$\frac{1}{4}$ pint white wine**
**125 ml./$\frac{1}{4}$ pint water**
**2 teaspoons salt**
**2 bay leaves**
**250 ml./$\frac{1}{2}$ pint tomato sauce**
**3 teaspoons dry mustard**
**4 tablespoons peach chutney**
**juice of 2 lemons**
**2 cloves garlic**
**2 tablespoons Worcestershire sauce**
**$\frac{1}{2}$ teaspoon freshly ground black pepper**

Clean, wash and joint the chickens. Put in an ovenproof dish and add the white wine, water, half the salt and the bay leaves. Cover and bake in a moderate oven for 15–20 minutes. Remove the chicken. (The wine stock may be reserved for use in soups.) Place the tomato sauce, dry mustard, chutney and lemon juice in a bowl. Peel and crush garlic. Add together with Worcestershire sauce, remaining salt and the pepper. Brush over the chicken pieces until well coated. Place on the rack over the barbecue and cook until well browned on both sides, 10–12 minutes. Place any remaining sauce in a flameproof dish. Add the barbecued chicken and place back over the heat for 5–6 minutes to absorb the extra sauce and cook in its own juice. Serve immediately.

*Cream of hake soup, fish salad (see pages 26, 165)*

# Pot roast chicken in orange gravy

Preparation time: 5 minutes
Cooking time: about 2 hours
Serves: 4

**1 1.8-kg./3¼-lb. chicken**
**2 teaspoons salt**
**1 teaspoon freshly ground black pepper**
**2 tablespoons flour**
**3 tablespoons/1½ oz. butter**
**110 g./4 oz. onion, chopped**
**2 bay leaves**
**4 peppercorns**
**½ teaspoon marjoram**
**500 ml./1 pint orange juice**
**2 tablespoons orange marmalade**
**4 tablespoons lemon juice**
**3 tablespoons cream**
**4 oranges**

Rub the chicken with salt and pepper and dust lightly with flour. Heat the butter in a flameproof casserole until moderately hot and lightly brown the onion. Add the chicken and cook turning on all sides until golden. Add the bay leaves, peppercorns and marjoram. Pour over the orange juice and add the orange marmalade and lemon juice. Cook covered until tender, about 2 hours. Remove the chicken and keep warm. Skim off any fat from the juices, add the cream, stir well and scrape in all the brown bits. Slice the peeled oranges into segments and heat in sauce. Place around chicken and serve the orange gravy in a sauceboat.

# Stuffed chicken breasts

Preparation time: 20 minutes
Cooking time: 8 minutes
Serves: 4–6

**6 chicken breasts, boned**
**4 tablespoons sultanas**
**2 tablespoons dry sherry**
**2 tablespoons/4 oz. soft butter**
**2 tablespoons cooked, finely diced ham**
**1 tablespoon chopped parsley**
**grated rind of ½ orange**
**7 tablespoons fine breadcrumbs**
**salt and pepper**
**2 tablespoons flour**
**1 teaspoon paprika pepper**
**½ teaspoon garlic salt**
**1 egg, beaten**
**90 g./3½ oz. breadcrumbs**
**oil for deep frying**

Wash the chicken breasts and dry with absorbent paper. Soak the sultanas in sherry for about 3 minutes. Blend the butter with the soaked sultanas, ham, parsley, orange rind, fine breadcrumbs, salt and pepper. Lay the chicken breasts skin-sides down on a board. Divide the stuffing equally between them. Form into rolls, secure with toothpicks or cocktail sticks and roll each breast in a mixture of flour, paprika pepper and garlic salt. Dip each into beaten egg and breadcrumbs. Heat the oil in a deep saucepan until hot but not smoking. Fry the chicken breasts for 8 minutes, drain on absorbent paper and serve with green salad.

# Chicken suprêmes

Preparation time: 10 minutes, plus chilling time
Cooking time: 8 minutes
Serves: 2–4

**4 chicken breasts**
**250 g./8 oz. cooked ham**
**125 g./4 oz. sweetmilk or Gruyère cheese**
**pinch dried or fresh tarragon**
**1½ teaspoons salt**
**¼ teaspoon freshly ground black pepper**
**4 tablespoons flour**
**1 large egg**
**4 tablespoons fine dry breadcrumbs**
**oil for deep frying**

Place the chicken breasts between sheets of wax or greaseproof paper. Pound with the flat side of a cleaver until they are about 6 mm. (¼ inch) thick. Cut the ham and cheese into eight strips each. Place two strips of ham and two of cheese on each breast. Sprinkle with tarragon, salt and pepper. Roll up the breasts; secure with toothpicks. Coat the breasts in flour. Beat the egg in a bowl. Dip the chicken rolls into the egg, then into breadcrumbs. Chill for 1 hour. Deep fry in heated oil for 8 minutes, until golden brown and tender. Drain on absorbent paper and arrange on a hot dish. Serve with sauté potatoes and young peas.

# Chicken with spiced sausage filling

Preparation time: 15 minutes
Cooking time: about $3\frac{3}{4}$ hours
Oven temperature: moderate (325°F., 170°C., Gas Mark 3)
Serves: 4–6

**1 2-kg./$4\frac{1}{2}$-lb. chicken**
**1 teaspoon salt**
**$\frac{1}{4}$ teaspoon freshly ground black pepper**
**1 kg./2 lb. sausagemeat**
**250 g./8 oz. stale French breadcrumbs**
**125 ml./$\frac{1}{4}$ pint milk**
**1 chicken liver**
**2 tablespoons oil**
**2 onions, chopped**
**2 eggs**
**pinch dried rosemary**
**pinch dried marjoram**
**pinch dried thyme (or use fresh herbs)**
**2 tablespoons diced bacon (optional)**
**2 teaspoons grated lemon rind**

Clean, wash and dry the chicken well with absorbent paper. Rub with salt and black pepper. Place the sausagemeat in a bowl and break it up slightly. Add the breadcrumbs and milk. Dice the chicken liver. Heat the oil in a small saucepan. Add the liver and chopped onions. Fry until golden brown. Mix together with the sausage mixture. Blend in the eggs, rosemary, marjoram, thyme, bacon and lemon rind; mix thoroughly. Stuff the chicken with about $1\frac{1}{2}$ cups of the mixture, bearing in mind that stuffing swells during cooking. Close with small skewers and sew with thread. Truss. Wrap completely in oiled foil and place in an ovenproof dish. Roast in a moderate oven for about 3 hours. Remove the foil, baste with the juices and continue cooking for about 30 minutes, until the chicken browns. Form the remaining stuffing into a roll and place beside the chicken. Cover with foil and cook for 10–12 minutes; remove the foil and cook for a further 10–12 minutes. Remove and leave to cool, together with the chicken. To serve, place the chicken on a dish. Slice the stuffing and place alongside the chicken. In between, arrange sprigs of watercress or leafy celery.

# Duck braised with apples

Preparation time: 10 minutes
Cooking time: about 3 hours
Oven temperature: moderate (325°F., 170°C., Gas Mark 3)
Serves: 4

**1 2-kg./$4\frac{1}{2}$-lb. duck**
**3 tablespoons/$1\frac{1}{2}$ oz. soft butter**
**2 teaspoons salt**
**1 teaspoon freshly ground black pepper**
**1 onion**
**1 stalk celery**
**2 tablespoons olive oil**
**6 large apples**
**1 piece orange rind**
**3 teaspoons sugar**
**$\frac{1}{2}$ teaspoon salt**
**$\frac{1}{4}$ teaspoon nutmeg**
**1 tablespoon lemon juice**
**250 ml./$\frac{1}{2}$ pint apple juice**

Clean and wash the duck thoroughly. Pat dry with absorbent paper and rub inside with a damp vinegar-soaked cloth. Smooth over 1 tablespoon of the butter and sprinkle with salt and pepper inside and out. Place the onion, celery and orange rind in the cavity of the duck. Heat the remaining butter and the oil in a large saucepan until moderately hot. Brown the duck and drain thoroughly. Slice the apples thinly and place in the bottom of a lightly buttered flameproof casserole. Sprinkle with sugar, salt, nutmeg and lemon juice. Place the duck on the apples, cover tightly with foil and the lid. Cook in a moderate oven for $2\frac{1}{2}$–3 hours. Remove the duck to a dish and keep warm wrapped in foil. Blend the apple juice into the liquid in the casserole and reduce slightly by boiling. Carve the duck and arrange portions on a heated dish, spoon over the apple sauce and serve with red cabbage.

**Variation** *(Illustrated on page 52)*
Roast the duck as described above, omitting the apple slices. Instead cut each peeled apple into half. Sprinkle with sugar, salt and nutmeg and brush with honey. Roast around the duck for the last 35 minutes of the cooking time. Place the whole duck (removing the onion, celery and orange rind from inside) on a heated serving dish and surround with the apples. If liked, top each apple with a walnut half.

*Baked kingklip* (see page 31)

*Golden haddock (see page 34)*

# Duck with plums

Preparation time: 5 minutes
Cooking time: overnight plus 25 minutes
Oven temperature: very cool (250°F., 130°C., Gas Mark $\frac{1}{2}$) increasing to moderately hot (400°F., 200°C., Gas Mark 6)
Serves: 4–6

**1 2.4-kg./4$\frac{3}{4}$-lb. duck**
**2 teaspoons salt**
**$\frac{1}{4}$ teaspoon freshly ground black pepper**
**1 teaspoon powdered ginger**
**$\frac{1}{4}$ teaspoon freshly ground nutmeg**
**1 tablespoon honey**
**2 tablespoons salad oil**
**1 tablespoon flour**
**$\frac{1}{2}$ chicken stock cube**
**250 ml./$\frac{1}{2}$ pint water**
**250 g./6–8 oz. sugar**
**12 large ripe red plums**
**500 ml./1 pint concentrated berry fruit juice extract**
**3 tablespoons lemon juice**

Clean the duck thoroughly. (Some ducks still need additional plucking.) Wash well and pat dry with absorbent paper. Rub the skin with salt, pepper, ginger, nutmeg and honey. Wrap completely in foil. Place in roasting tin and cook in a very cool oven overnight, as the larger ducks tend to be a little tough. Cooking a duck this way will make it tender and give it a brown skin. Allow to cool. Pour off the juices, cool then spoon off the fat. Heat the oil in a saucepan, add the flour and stir until bubbling. Gradually add the skimmed juices (about 250 ml./$\frac{1}{2}$ pint) and stock cube. Stir continually until the sauce thickens and comes to the boil. Remove from the heat. Bring the water to the boil in a saucepan. Add the sugar, bring back to the boil and add the plums and fruit extract. Cook for 5–8 minutes, until the plums are just soft but not falling apart. Remove the plums, boil the fruit juice to reduce slightly. Add the reduced juice and lemon juice to the thickened sauce. Cut the cooled duck in serving portions and place in an ovenproof dish. Pour over the plum sauce. Cover with the lid or foil and reheat in a moderately hot oven for 12–15 minutes, until piping hot. Spoon the plums over the top and return to the oven, covered, for a further 8–10 minutes. Serve with layered casseroled potatoes and fresh peas.

# Vegetables, rice and pasta

When you buy vegetables, look for the youngest, freshest and crispest in season; the whitest cauliflower, the smallest baby marrows, the crunchiest celery. To clean, pare as little as possible. To slice, use a sharp knife. To cook, spare the water unless you are blanching green vegetables. To flavour, use butter, cream, herbs, lemon and spices. Vegetables are versatile – they can be baked in a casserole, wrapped in foil and cooked in glowing embers, or skewered and grilled. Handled with care, they are a delight to start the menu, to serve as an accompaniment or to eat as the main dish.

Rice and pasta dishes also make good meal starters and accompaniments, or they can be served on their own.

**To cook green vegetables**
It takes careful cooking – and not a pinch of bicarbonate of soda – to maintain the colour and flavour of spring vegetables. Here are three simple methods that will bring good results.

**Standard** For vegetables that are not extra-young. Use 250 ml. ($\frac{1}{2}$ pint) water, 1 teaspoon salt to 1 kg. (2 lb.) vegetables. The water must be fast boiling when the vegetables are added, then brought to boiling point again as soon as possible. Cook uncovered until just tender. Drain, season and serve.

**Steaming** This takes a little longer than the standard method (above) but preserves the colour and nutrients more completely. Place the vegetables in a perforated pan over boiling water. Cover and steam until just tender. Toss with salt, pepper, butter or cream; serve.

**Blanching and refreshing** For particularly young vegetables and for vegetables that are to be cooked well in advance of being served. Use 3 litres (5 pints) water, 1 dessertspoon salt to 1 kg. (2 lb.) vegetables; bring the water to a rapid boil. Cook beans for 10–15 minutes, peas about 8 minutes, spinach 5–7 minutes. Remove and drain. Plunge immediately into cold water to stop the cooking process. This sets the colour and preserves the texture. Just before the meal, either simmer the vegetables in butter for 3–4 minutes to heat them, or boil rapidly in a few tablespoons of water. Do not keep cooked greens for long periods of time as this will ruin both the flavour and appearance.

*Green beans with glazed onions (see page 71)*

*Fresh tomato soup (see page 23)*

# Cauliflower with buttered crumbs

*Illustrated on page 73*
Preparation time: 5 minutes
Cooking time: about 12 minutes
Serves: 4–6

**1 large cauliflower with a firm white head**
**about 2 teaspoons cooking salt**
**250 ml./$\frac{1}{2}$ pint milk**
**4 tablespoons/2 oz. butter**
**2 tablespoons white crumbs**
**1 hard-boiled egg (optional)**
**4 tablespoons chopped parsley**
**$\frac{1}{4}$ teaspoon salt**
**sprinkling freshly ground black pepper**

Divide the cauliflower into flowerettes by cutting off the stem close to the head. (Do not throw away the glossy green leaves and stalk, they can be used for a cream soup with onions.) Cut small slits in any thick stems for quicker cooking. Wash the cauliflowerettes very well under running water. Bring 3 litres (5 pints) of water to the boil with the cooking salt in a large saucepan and add the milk to the water. This helps to maintain the whiteness of the cauliflower. Drop the flowerettes into the boiling liquid. Bring back to the boil as quickly as possible. Cook uncovered for 10–12 minutes, or until a knife pierces the stem easily. Remove and place in a colander if you are not serving immediately. Allow cold water to run over the flowerettes; this stops the cooking at once. When ready to serve, place in a covered colander and steam over boiling water for 4–5 minutes.

To prepare the buttered crumbs, melt the butter in a saucepan and allow to brown lightly. Add the crumbs, blending them into the butter. Chop the hard-boiled egg (if used) and add the parsley, salt and pepper. Blend together. Add to the butter and crumbs. Heat for 1 minute, then spoon over the top of the cauliflower.

# Creamed spinach

Preparation time: 10 minutes
Cooking time: about 15 minutes
Serves: 6

**2 kg./4$\frac{1}{2}$ lb. spinach**
**1 freshly boiled potato**
**3 tablespoons/1$\frac{1}{2}$ oz. butter**
**4 tablespoons cream**
**$\frac{1}{4}$ teaspoon freshly ground nutmeg**
**$\frac{1}{4}$ teaspoon freshly ground black pepper**
**2 teaspoons salt**
**4 tablespoons grated Parmesan cheese**

Wash the spinach thoroughly to remove any traces of sand. Trim off the thick stalk leaving the leaves. Bring 3 litres (5 pints) of water to the boil in a large saucepan. Add the spinach and allow to cook for 3–5 minutes. Remove and plunge into a basin of cold water. Drain thoroughly in a colander, pressing out all the water with the back of a wooden spoon. Place in a saucepan with potato, butter, 3 tablespoons of the cream, the nutmeg, pepper and salt. Using a hand mixer, blend together until well mashed. Heat for 5–8 minutes, stirring well. Spoon into an ovenproof dish and sprinkle with grated Parmesan cheese. Spoon the remaining cream into the centre of the cheese and place under a preheated grill until the cheese is golden brown and the cream bubbling.

# Peas with ham

Preparation time: 15 minutes
Cooking time: about 15 minutes
Serves: 6

**3$\frac{1}{2}$ litres/about 5 pints water**
**1.5 kg./3 lb. shelled tender young peas**
**4 slices ham**
**2 tablespoons/1 oz. butter**
**$\frac{1}{2}$ teaspoon salt**
**$\frac{1}{4}$ teaspoon freshly ground black pepper**
**1 teaspoon finely chopped spring onion**

Bring the water to the boil. Add the peas. Bring back to the boil as quickly as possible and cook for 8–10 minutes, then drain. Cut the ham into strips. Melt the butter, add the peas, ham, salt, pepper and onion and cook for 5–6 minutes. Spoon into a hot dish and serve immediately.

# Broccoli with butter

Preparation time: 5 minutes
Cooking time: about 10 minutes
Serves: 4–6

**1 kg./2 lb. green, fresh broccoli**
**about 2 teaspoons cooking salt**
**2 tablespoons/1 oz. butter**
**1 tablespoon lemon juice**
**1 teaspoon grated lemon rind**
**$\frac{1}{2}$ teaspoon salt**
**$\frac{1}{4}$ teaspoon freshly ground black pepper**

Divide the broccoli into flowerettes. Peel the thin green skin off the stalks. Cut $2\frac{1}{2}$ cm. (1 inch) off the end of each stalk. Place in a metal colander. Bring 3 litres (5 pints) of water and the cooking salt to the boil in a large saucepan. Lower the colander into the boiling water and cook for 8–10 minutes. Remove and plunge into a basin of cold water. Remove and allow to stand while preparing the butter. Cream the butter, lemon juice, lemon rind, salt and freshly ground black pepper in a bowl. Place in a saucepan and heat, whisking, for 1–2 minutes until the butter looks creamy. Just before serving, add the broccoli and heat for 4–5 minutes.

# Green beans with glazed onions

*Illustrated on page 68*
Preparation time: 20 minutes
Cooking time: about 40 minutes
Serves: 6

**250 g./8 oz. small onions**
**125 ml./$\frac{1}{4}$ pint white wine**
**1 teaspoon salt**
**$\frac{1}{4}$ teaspoon freshly ground black pepper**
**2 tablespoons/1 oz. butter**
**1 tablespoon chopped parsley**
**1 kg./2 lb. young fresh green beans**
**about 2 teaspoons cooking salt**
**chopped parsley to garnish**

Peel the onions by placing in rapidly boiling water for 5–10 minutes, long enough for the skins to loosen. Plunge them into cold water. Remove and cut off both the top and bottom ends. Slip off the top skin and first layer of the onion using your fingers. Cut a cross at the root end to avoid bursting during cooking. (This is one way to peel onions without tears.) Place the onions in a flameproof casserole with the white wine, half the salt, half the pepper, half the butter and all the parsley. Cover and simmer very slowly for about 40 minutes. If the liquid evaporates during cooking, add 2–4 tablespoons extra white wine. During the last 20 minutes of cooking time, prepare the beans. Trim and remove the strings on the beans by snapping off the tips and drawing them down the length of one side of the bean. Leave whole. Place 3 litres (5 pints) of water in a large saucepan, add cooking salt and bring to the boil. Gradually add beans and cook for 10–12 minutes. Remove and plunge in a basin of cold water. This stops the cooking process instantly and retains the colour of the beans. Place in a pan with the remaining butter, salt and pepper. Cook for an additional 4–6 minutes, while the onions finish cooking. To serve, arrange the beans in one half of a large flat dish. Place the onions in the other half and pour any remaining juices over the beans; sprinkle the onions with chopped parsley.

**Note** Both these vegetables can be prepared in advance if you are having a buffet supper; the beans to all but the last stage of cooking. The onions may be completed well in advance, to be reheated at the last minute.

# Potatoes

The humdrum potato we take so much for granted can be cooked in many ways. It can be simply boiled and dressed with butter and freshly chopped parsley, or cut into thin rounds and shallow fried as in the picture opposite. Cook them in the skins as often as possible to keep the full nutritional value; bake, boil or steam.

**How to buy and cook perfect potatoes**

Select potatoes which are firm, smooth, clean and regular in shape and size. The eyes should be shallow to avoid wastage in peeling. If buying in bulk, you are going to have to live with the same batch for some time, so remember different varieties have different cooking properties. Floury potatoes are best for baking, chips and purées. The waxy variety makes excellent scalloped potatoes and potato salad or any dish where the vegetable should maintain firmness without being hard or boiling away to nothing.

Peel potatoes with a potato peeler as thinly as possible as the mineral salts lie directly under the skin.

Bake the perfect potato by pricking with a fork before cooking and, just before serving, cut a cross on each potato top, pinch to spread the opening and allow the steam to escape before returning to the oven to dry for a few moments.

Prevent potatoes from bursting out of their skins during boiling by paring a thin strip from the centre.

Soak old potatoes (peeled) in cold water for an hour before cooking to prevent them discolouring.

## Perfect mash

Preparation time: 5 minutes
Cooking time: about 25 minutes
Serves: 4–6

**1 kg./2 lb. floury potatoes**
**1 teaspoon coarse salt**
**250 ml./½ pint milk**
**4 tablespoons/2 oz. butter**
**1 teaspoon fine salt**
**¼ teaspoon freshly ground black pepper**

Peel and quarter the potatoes. Place in a saucepan with boiling water to cover and add the coarse salt. Simmer uncovered for 20–25 minutes, until tender. Test by inserting a knife blade. Drain the potatoes thoroughly in a large sieve. Using a wooden spoon, sieve into the saucepan. Heat the milk in a small saucepan. Cook the sieved potato over a low heat with the butter. Beat with a whisk, gradually adding the hot milk. Season with salt and pepper and serve at once in a heated dish.

## Creamy potato cake

Preparation time: 5 minutes
Cooking time: about 1 hour
Oven temperature: hot (450°F., 230°C., Gas Mark 8) then moderately hot (400°F., 200°C., Gas Mark 6)
Serves: 6

**8 large baking potatoes**
**4 tablespoons/2 oz. butter**
**1 teaspoon salt**
**¼ teaspoon freshly ground black pepper**
**4 tablespoons double cream**
**2 tablespoons grated Parmesan cheese**
**1 teaspoon chopped fresh or freeze-dried chives**

Bake the unpeeled potatoes in a hot oven for 45–50 minutes, until cooked. Lower the heat to moderately hot. Halve and scoop out the potato from the cases. Heat the butter in a saucepan, add the scooped-out potato and cook for 5–6 minutes. Sprinkle with salt and pepper. Place in a buttered ovenproof dish and smooth the top with a spatula so the mixture resembles a cake. Pour over the cream, sprinkle with Parmesan cheese and chives. Bake in a moderately hot oven for 8 minutes, then cook under a preheated grill until the cheese is bubbly and golden brown. Serve immediately.

*Cauliflower with buttered crumbs, thin potato rounds, grilled baby tomatoes (see pages 70, 75, 83)*

# Potatoes in lemon butter

Preparation time: 5 minutes
Cooking time: about 20 minutes
Serves: 6

**12 medium-sized potatoes**
**2 tablespoons lemon juice**
**2 tablespoons/1 oz. butter, melted**
**1 teaspoon salt**
**$\frac{1}{4}$ teaspoon freshly ground black pepper**
**2 tablespoons chopped parsley**

Peel the potatoes. Bring to the boil in water to cover and cook until softened. Drain thoroughly. Whisk the lemon juice, butter, salt, freshly ground black pepper and parsley together in a small bowl. Pour over the potatoes and simmer for 2 minutes. Spoon into a hot earthenware dish and serve.

# Crisp potato cakes

Preparation time: 15 minutes
Cooking time: few minutes
Serves: 4–6

**6 medium-sized potatoes**
**2 onions**
**2 eggs**
**1 teaspoon salt**
**$\frac{1}{4}$ teaspoon freshly ground black pepper**
**oil for shallow frying**

Peel and grate the potatoes onto a wooden board using the coarse side of grater. Peel and grate the onions. Spoon both into a bowl. Press out any liquid using a spoon. Add the eggs to the bowl and blend. Add the salt and pepper. Heat the oil in a frying pan. When hot, place teaspoonfuls of the potato mixture in the oil. Fry until brown on one side. You will see the edges crisping. Turn and complete cooking until golden brown on the second side. Remove and drain on absorbent paper. If you make these in advance, they may be kept warm, uncovered, in a dish over boiling water until ready to serve.

# Baby potato balls

Preparation time: 15 minutes
Cooking time: about 15 minutes
Serves: 4

**5 large potatoes**
**1 teaspoon salt**
**2 tablespoons/1 oz. butter**
**2 tablespoons oil**

Scoop balls out of large peeled potatoes with a special scoop. Soak in cold water until needed. (Reserve the remaining potatoes which can be boiled and mashed for another meal.) Put the balls into a saucepan, barely cover with cold water and sprinkle on a little salt. Bring the potatoes to the boil and simmer for 5–6 minutes. Remove and drain. Heat the butter and oil in a pan. Gently tip in the potatoes and cook over a very gentle heat, shaking the pan often until the potatoes are completely cooked through and an even golden brown on the outside; be very careful, however, not to break any. Drain on absorbent paper and serve.

# Swirled baked potatoes

Preparation time: 10 minutes
Cooking time: about 1 hour
Oven temperature: moderately hot (400°F., 200°C., Gas Mark 6) then moderate (325°F., 170°C., Gas Mark 3)
Serves: 6

**6 large potatoes**
**1 tablespoon/$\frac{1}{2}$ oz. butter**
**125 ml./$\frac{1}{4}$ pint milk**
**1 teaspoon salt**
**$\frac{1}{4}$ teaspoon freshly ground black pepper**
**2 tablespoons finely grated Cheddar cheese**
**1 teaspoon melted butter**

Scrub and place the unpeeled potatoes in a moderately hot oven. Bake for about 1 hour. Remove and halve each potato; scoop out the potato into a bowl, leaving the shell. Add the butter, milk, salt, pepper and Cheddar cheese. Mix and press thoroughly through a wire sieve. Spoon into an icing bag and swirl into each shell. Place on a baking sheet. Brush melted butter on the top of each potato swirl, then place in a moderate oven for 5–6 minutes before serving.

# Thin potato rounds

*Illustrated on page 73*
Preparation time: 5 minutes
Cooking time: about 8 minutes
Serves: 4–6

**8 small potatoes**
**oil for shallow frying**
**cooking salt**

Peel, wash and slice the potatoes into paper-thin rounds. Heat the oil in a frying pan. When hot but not smoking, add the potato rounds. Allow to cook until transparent and golden brown, about 8 minutes. Remove and place on absorbent paper to drain. Sprinkle with cooking salt and arrange in a mound on a heated flat platter. Prepare in advance if necessary, leaving the potatoes in a bowl of water until just before frying. *Dry thoroughly with absorbent paper before frying.*

# Ham bake

Preparation time: 15 minutes
Cooking time: about 1 hour
Oven temperature: hot (450°F., 230°C., Gas Mark 8) then moderately hot (400°F., 200°C., Gas Mark 6)
Serves: 4

**4 large baking potatoes**
**2 tablespoons/1 oz. butter**
**1½ teaspoons salt**
**¼ teaspoon freshly ground black pepper**
**4 tablespoons cooking oil**
**3 tomatoes**
**1 clove garlic**
**1 tablespoon green pepper strips**
**2 slices ham**
**1 tablespoon chopped parsley**
**4 tablespoons breadcrumbs**
**1 teaspoon oil**

Bake the unpeeled potatoes in a hot oven for 45–50 minutes, until cooked. Lower the heat to moderately hot. Halve lengthwise and scoop out the potato with a tablespoon. Mash in a bowl, working in the butter, 1 teaspoon of salt and the pepper. Heat the oil in a saucepan. Skin tomatoes by placing them in boiling water for 1 minute. Chop. Peel and crush garlic. Add tomatoes, garlic, green pepper, chopped ham, remaining salt and the chopped parsley to the pan. Cook until the vegetables are tender and the liquid reduced, 10–15 minutes. Place a layer of mashed potato in each potato case and fill to the top with the ham mixture. Sprinkle each potato with the breadcrumbs and a few drops of oil. Place in a moderately hot oven for 5 minutes, then place under the grill to crisp the breadcrumbs. Serve immediately.

# Potato puffs

Preparation time: 10 minutes
Cooking time: about 15 minutes
Serves: 6

**6 floury potatoes**
**1½ litres/3 pints rendered beef suet**
**1 teaspoon fine salt**

Peel the potatoes and cut into uniformly thick ovals. Wash in cold water and dry thoroughly on absorbent paper. Half fill a deep saucepan with melted beef suet. (This type of fat is used in preference to any other as it cooks at very high temperatures without burning.) Heat suet to 180°C. (350°F.), using the bread test (see below). Drop the ovals into the fat one at a time. Using a perforated spoon, raise them singly from the fat for a few seconds, then return for about 8 minutes, or until they begin to swell. Drain on absorbent paper and cool for 10 minutes before the final frying. (This second frying can be done several hours later or even the next day.) The ovals deflate, but will puff again during next frying. While standing, leave between absorbent paper. For the final frying, heat the fat to 190°C. (375°F.). At this temperature the surface of the potatoes is transformed into a waterproof skin which swells as the water inside evaporates. Lower the ovals, a few at a time, into the fat. They should puff like balloons. Turn the puffs until well browned on both sides. Remove. Drain on absorbent paper. Sprinkle with salt and serve at once.

**Note** At 180°C. (350°F.) a cube of bread will turn light brown in 60 seconds; at 190°C. (375°F.) the cube will turn light brown in 40 seconds.

# Potato dumplings

Preparation time: 10 minutes
Cooking time: 15 minutes
Serves: 4–6

**5 medium-sized potatoes**
**125 g./4 oz. breadcrumbs**
**3 tablespoons milk**
**2 teaspoons fresh or freeze-dried chives**
**2 eggs**
**about 3 tablespoons flour**
**1 teaspoon salt**
**$\frac{1}{4}$ teaspoon freshly ground black pepper**

Finely grate the raw potatoes into a bowl. Moisten the breadcrumbs with the milk. Add to the bowl together with the chives. Lightly beat the eggs and add to the bowl with 1 tablespoon of the flour, the salt and pepper. Mix thoroughly. Lightly flour your hands with some of the remaining flour. Form small balls with the mixture. Place them in either boiling salted water or broth prepared with a stock cube. Cover tightly and boil for 15 minutes. Drain and serve.

**Note** If you are preparing a dish that has plenty of gravy, cook these dumplings in the liquid for 15 minutes.

# Potato slices in mustard cream

Preparation time: 10 minutes
Cooking time: 25–30 minutes
Serves: 4–6

**6 medium-sized potatoes**
**1 teaspoon salt**
**125 ml./$\frac{1}{4}$ pint salad or olive oil**
**2 teaspoons prepared strong mustard**
**$\frac{1}{2}$ teaspoon salt**
**2 teaspoons vinegar**
**1 clove garlic**
**1 egg yolk**
**4 teaspoons cornflour**
**250 ml./$\frac{1}{2}$ pint water**
**4 tablespoons chopped parsley**
**2 tablespoons chopped spring onion**
**$\frac{1}{4}$ teaspoon freshly ground black pepper**

Scrub the potatoes. Pare a strip, around the centre, off each one to prevent them bursting during cooking. Place in a saucepan with boiling water to cover. Add the salt and cook for 25–30 minutes, until the potatoes are soft. Drain well and return to the pan. Cook for 1 minute to remove any moisture. Cool. Remove the skins. Slice thinly and place in overlapping slices in a bowl. Place the oil, mustard, salt and vinegar in a bowl. Peel and crush the garlic. Add together with the egg yolk. Stir well for 1 minute. Blend the cornflour with a little of the water. Place in a saucepan and add the remaining water. Bring to the boil and simmer for 1–2 minutes. Slowly add to the egg mixture, whisking continuously until creamy and well blended – do not allow to boil. Pour over the potatoes. Chill lightly before serving. Mix the parsley and spring onion together and sprinkle thickly in two sections down the length of the potatoes. Sprinkle with freshly ground black pepper.

# Honeyed orange sweet potatoes

*Illustrated opposite*
Preparation time: 5 minutes
Cooking time: about 30 minutes
Serves: 4

**6 medium-sized sweet potatoes**
**3 tablespoons/1$\frac{1}{2}$ oz. butter**
**3 tablespoons honey**
**$\frac{1}{2}$ teaspoon grated orange rind**
**$\frac{1}{2}$ teaspoon freshly grated nutmeg**
**2 oranges, sliced**
**orange peel to garnish (optional)**

Place the unpeeled sweet potatoes in a saucepan of boiling water to cover. Simmer for 20 minutes. Remove, drain, peel and cut into 1$\frac{1}{4}$-cm. ($\frac{3}{4}$-inch) slices. Reassemble the slices and place in a ovenproof dish. Cream the butter, honey and grated rind in a bowl. Spread a little of the mixture on each sweet potato and sprinkle with nutmeg. Cook under a preheated grill for 10 minutes. Add the orange slices to the dish and cook for a further 1–2 minutes. If liked, garnish with strip of orange peel and serve with a pot roast.

*Honeyed orange sweet potatoes* (see opposite)

# Potato nuts with sour cream

Preparation time: 15 minutes
Cooking time: few minutes
Makes: 50 nuts

**12 medium-sized potatoes**
**4 onions**
**4 eggs**
**2 teaspoons salt**
**$\frac{1}{2}$ teaspoon freshly ground black pepper**
**oil for shallow frying**
**1 litre/1$\frac{3}{4}$ pints sour cream**

Peel and grate the potatoes on a wooden board using the coarse side of the grater. Peel and grate the onions and mix with the potatoes. Press out any liquid using a spoon. Add the eggs and blend with the potato mixture. Add the salt and pepper. Heat the oil in a heavy frying pan. When hot, drop teaspoonfuls of the mixture into the oil. Fry until brown on one side, and crisp at the edges. Turn and complete cooking until golden brown on second side. Remove and drain on absorbent paper. If made in advance, the nuts may be kept warm, uncovered, in a dish over boiling water until ready to serve. Accompany with a dip of sour cream.
**Note** Allow 2–4 nuts per person, so adjust ingredients accordingly. Cook the nuts in several batches. Make well in advance, then keep warm as directed and serve hot.

# Savoury baked potatoes

Preparation time: 10 minutes
Cooking time: about 55 minutes
Oven temperature: moderately hot (400°F., 200°C., Gas Mark 6)
Serves: 4–6

**1 kg./2 lb. large non-floury potatoes**
**2 onions**
**750 ml./1$\frac{1}{2}$ pints reduced meat gravy or 1 beef stock cube dissolved in 750 ml./1$\frac{1}{2}$ pints boiling water**
**2 tablespoons chopped parsley**

Peel the potatoes and slice into paper-thin rounds. Peel and slice the onions. Layer the potatoes with slices of onion in a fairly shallow ovenproof dish. Pour over the stock and bake, covered, in a moderately hot oven for 40 minutes. Remove lid and cook for a further 10–15 minutes. Sprinkle with parsley and serve.

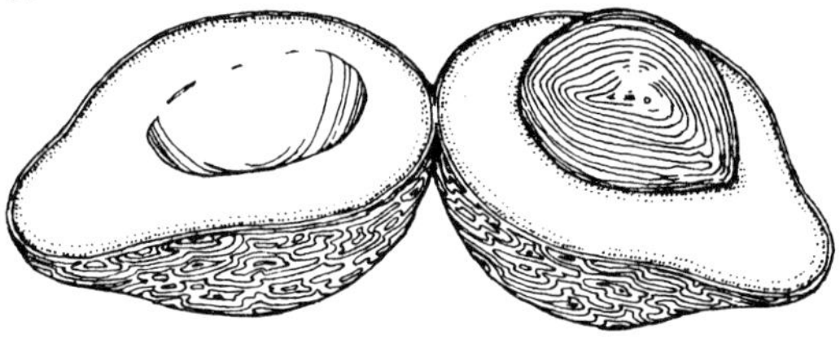

# Avocados

Choose an avocado by holding it in one hand and gently pressing – if it is ready it will give like a packet of slightly soft butter.

Ignore fruit with a spotted, shrivelled or sunken skin.

Select according to taste. The Natal avocado has a thick skin and nutty flavour – the more popular Transvaal variety has a smooth skin and buttery pulp.

Ripen at room temperature – uneaten avocado halves will keep in the refrigerator in an airtight container.

Cut fruit by sliding a knife point down the top of the avocado to the stone – edge the knife over the stone, twist apart by hand.

Sprinkle lemon juice or vinegar over cut fruit to stop the pulp turning black.

Blend avocados with oranges, bananas, apples, grapefruit, pineapple, dried fruit for a sweet mixture, or with chopped chives, spring onions, capers and olives for a tart mixture. If liked, the mixture may be bound with mayonnaise and spooned into an avocado half as in the picture on page 36.

Chill for serving by covering and refrigerating for about 15 minutes – over-chilling spoils the flavour.

Remember avocado is a good source of protein and the vital vitamins A, B, C, D and E.

# Avocado with ham

Preparation time: 15 minutes
Serves: 6–8

**4 avocados**
**3 tablespoons lemon juice**
**200 g./8 oz. cooked ham, chopped**
**4 small oranges**
**1 medium-sized pineapple**
**1 green pepper**
**3 spring onions**
**4 tablespoons orange juice**
**2 tablespoons salad oil**
**½ teaspoon salt**
**¼ teaspoon freshly ground black pepper**
**3 tablespoons chopped celery leaves**

Peel the avocados, remove stones and cut flesh into oblong strips. Sprinkle with lemon juice. Mix with the ham pieces. Peel and segment the oranges and peel and chop the pineapple. Halve, seed and slice the green pepper in strips and chop the spring onions. Mix with the avocado, ham and fruit. Whisk the orange juice, salad oil, salt and pepper and pour over mixture. Sprinkle with the celery. Chill for 10–15 minutes and serve with wholewheat rolls.

# Grapefruit mélange

Preparation time: 5 minutes
Serves: 2

**1 grapefruit**
**1 avocado**
**2 tablespoons oil**
**2 tablespoons lemon juice**
**¼ teaspoon French mustard**
**¼ teaspoon chopped garlic**
**½ teaspoon salt**
**freshly ground black pepper to taste**
**2 lettuce leaves**

Halve the grapefruit and carefully take out the segments; reserve the two shells. Halve the avocado, remove the stone, peel and slice the flesh. Put the grapefruit segments and avocado slices back in the grapefruit shells. Whisk the oil, lemon juice, mustard, garlic, salt and pepper and pour over the filling. Garnish grapefruit cups with lettuce and serve with crisp salty biscuits.

# Baked stuffed avocado

Preparation time: few minutes
Cooking time: 25 minutes
Oven temperature: moderate (325°F., 170°C., Gas Mark 3)
Serves: 4

**2 avocados**
**2 tablespoons lemon juice**
**1 tablespoon butter**
**4 large mushrooms**
**1 teaspoon salt**
**¼ teaspoon freshly ground black pepper**
**2 teaspoons French mustard**
**¼ teaspoon crushed garlic**
**4 tablespoons chopped bacon**

Halve the avocados and remove stones. Sprinkle the cut surfaces with half the lemon juice. Place in a casserole, pour in a little hot water and cook in a moderate oven for 20 minutes. Melt the butter in a saucepan, add the sliced mushrooms, salt, pepper, mustard, garlic and remaining lemon juice. Cook for 5 minutes, then spoon into hot avocado halves. Grill the chopped bacon until crisp then sprinkle over the mushroom filling.

# Hot sweet-and-sour dressing

Preparation time: few minutes
Cooking time: about 20 minutes
Makes: enough for 2 avocados

**1 tablespoon sugar**
**2 tablespoons water**
**2 tablespoons vinegar**
**2 tablespoons tomato sauce**
**1 tablespoon/½ oz. butter**
**½ teaspoon salt**
**¼ teaspoon freshly ground black pepper**

Dissolve the sugar and water in a small saucepan and stir in the remaining ingredients. Cover and cook over low heat for 15–20 minutes, until thickened. To serve, pour a little of the hot dressing over the avocado halves. The dressing may be made in advance and reheated.

*Apples in 'kerchiefs* *(see page 119)*

*Tipsy meringue peaches (see page 106)*

*Plum and orange preserve (see page 156)*

# Piquant egg dressing

Preparation time: few minutes
Makes: enough for 3 avocados

**3 tablespoons chopped parsley**
**3 tablespoons black olives, stoned**
**3 hard-boiled eggs**
**4 tablespoons salad oil**
**6 tablespoons lemon juice**
**1 tablespoon vinegar**
**1 teaspoon salt**
**$\frac{1}{4}$ teaspoon freshly ground black pepper**
**6 lettuce leaves to garnish**

Mix the chopped parsley and black olives in a bowl. Chop the hard-boiled eggs finely. Place a tablespoon of the mixture in each avocado half and place on a lettuce leaf. Pour salad oil, lemon juice, vinegar, salt and pepper into a bowl. Whisk until creamy. Spoon over the avocados.

# Root vegetables

## Young lemon-glazed carrots

Preparation time: 5 minutes
Cooking time: about 15 minutes
Serves: 6–8

**1 kg./2 lb. young carrots**
**250 ml./$\frac{1}{2}$ pint boiling water**
**1 chicken stock cube**
**3 tablespoons brown sugar**
**$\frac{1}{2}$ teaspoon salt**
**$\frac{1}{4}$ teaspoon freshly ground black pepper**
**3 tablespoons/1$\frac{1}{2}$ oz. butter**
**1 tablespoon lemon juice**
**pinch freshly ground nutmeg**
**2 tablespoons finely chopped parsley**

Trim the carrots and scrape using a vegetable peeler. Leave whole. Place the boiling water in a saucepan together with the stock cube. Add the carrots, sugar, salt, pepper and butter. Cover and boil over a medium heat, until the carrots are tender and the liquid has evaporated, leaving a syrup. Allow the carrots to continue cooking for 2–3 minutes by tossing them in the syrup. Add the lemon juice, nutmeg and parsley. Serve in a hot dish with braised lamb.

**Note** As an alternative, omit the brown sugar and nutmeg and add 3 tablespoons cream with the lemon juice etc.

## Creamed onions

Preparation time: 5 minutes
Cooking time: about 45 minutes
Serves: 10

**10 medium-sized onions**
**1 bay leaf**
**pinch mace**
**$\frac{1}{2}$ litre/$\frac{3}{4}$ pint milk**
**4 tablespoons/2 oz. butter**
**2$\frac{1}{2}$ teaspoons flour**
**1 teaspoon paprika pepper**
**pinch ground cloves**
**1 teaspoon salt**
**$\frac{1}{4}$ teaspoon freshly ground black pepper**
**2 tablespoons sherry**
**3 tablespoons cream**
**2 tablespoons chopped parsley**
**paprika pepper to garnish**

Wash the onions, but do not peel. Cover and cook in a double boiler over simmering water for 30–45 minutes, until just tender. Place on a heated serving dish and keep warm. Add the bay leaf and mace to the milk. Slowly bring to just below boiling. Remove from the heat and leave to cool, then strain into a jug. Melt the butter in a saucepan. Remove from the heat and stir in the flour. Return to the heat and cook gently for 1–2 minutes. Gradually stir in milk. Bring to the boil and stir until thickened. Flavour with the paprika pepper, cloves, salt, pepper and sherry. Stir in cream and parsley. Remove skins from onions and top and tail with a pair of scissors. Pour the sauce over onions. Serve immediately, garnished with paprika pepper.

# Glazed turnips

Preparation time: 5 minutes
Cooking time: about 30 minutes
Oven temperature: moderate (350°F., 180°C., Gas Mark 4)
Serves: 4–6

**1 kg./2 lb. young turnips**
**150 ml./¼ pint freshly squeezed orange juice**
**½ teaspoon salt**
**2 tablespoons brown sugar**
**¼ teaspoon ground ginger**
**3 tablespoons/1½ oz. butter, melted**
**1 large orange, peeled and segmented**

Peel the turnips and cut into 2½-cm. (1-inch) pieces. Cook in boiling salted water to cover for about 25 minutes, or until soft. Drain. Place in a bowl and mash. Beat in the orange juice, salt, brown sugar, ginger and melted butter. Put into a buttered ovenproof dish. Garnish with fresh orange segments and bake in a moderate oven for 5–7 minutes.

Alternatively, heat the mashed turnips in a saucepan without orange segments. Put into a serving dish and garnish with orange segments.

# Baby beets with orange sauce

Preparation time: 5 minutes
Cooking time: about 40 minutes
Serves: 4–6

**12 small beetroots**
**2 tablespoons/1 oz. butter**
**3 tablespoons brown sugar**
**250 ml./½ pint orange juice**
**½ teaspoon salt**
**¼ teaspoon freshly ground black pepper**
**1 teaspoon cornflour**
**2 teaspoons water**

Remove the beetroot greens leaving the roots and 2½ cm. (1 inch) of the stem to prevent excessive loss of juice. Scrub the beetroot and place in a saucepan with boiling water to cover. Cook for 25–30 minutes, then drain and peel. Leave to cool. Slice thinly on a wooden board. Melt the butter in a saucepan. Add the brown sugar, orange juice, salt and pepper. Mix the cornflour with 2 teaspoons water in a cup until it forms a smooth paste. Add to the saucepan stirring constantly. Place the sliced beetroot in the saucepan. Bring to the boil. Turn down the heat and simmer for 5–8 minutes. Serve in a heated dish.

## Tomatoes

# Grilled baby tomatoes

*Illustrated on page 73*
Preparation time: few minutes
Cooking time: about 8 minutes
Serves: 6

**6 small tomatoes**
**2 teaspoons brown sugar**
**¼ teaspoon dried basil or 1 sprig fresh**
**½ teaspoon salt**
**¼ teaspoon freshly ground black pepper**
**3 teaspoons lemon juice**
**½ teaspoon butter**
**1 tablespoon chopped parsley**

Halve the tomatoes and place on a piece of foil. Sprinkle each with a little brown sugar, basil, salt, pepper and lemon juice. Dot with the butter. Cook under a preheated grill (two racks down) for 5–8 minutes. Sprinkle with parsley and serve in a heated dish, with the cooking juices poured over.

As an alternative, blend 4 tablespoons cream with 1 tablespoon French mustard. Heat until just hot and pour over the tomatoes before serving. If liked, garnish with mint.

*Orange peel in chocolate, sugared almonds, mocha truffles in walnuts (see pages 158, 159)*

*Noodles with ham and cream cheese* *(see page 90)*

# Baby tomatoes with peas

Preparation time: 10 minutes
Cooking time: about 8 minutes
Oven temperature: moderately hot (400°F., 200°C., Gas Mark 6)
Serves: 4–6

**12 small tomatoes**
**500 g./1 lb. young peas**
**about 2 teaspoons/scant ½ oz. butter**
**1 sprig fresh mint, chopped or ¼ teaspoon dried**
**½ teaspoon salt**
**pinch freshly ground black pepper**

Cut a thin slice off the top of each tomato and an even thinner one from the base of the tomatoes to prevent them falling over. Hollow out the insides. (Reserve the pulp for a sauce.) Place the peas in a saucepan filled with 250 ml. (½ pint) rapidly boiling water. Cook uncovered for 8–12 minutes, then drain. Add the butter, mint, salt and pepper. Spoon into the tomato cases. Arrange in an ovenproof dish and cook in a moderate oven for 5–8 minutes.
**Note** As an alternative, the tomatoes may be filled with creamed spinach (see page 70). Use a quarter of the quantity given in the recipe, sprinkle with Parmesan cheese and brown under the grill.

# Rice and pasta

## Brown rice with raisins

Preparation time: few minutes
Cooking time: about 1 hour
Serves: 4–6

**500 g./1 lb. raw brown rice**
**750 ml./1½ pints boiling water**
**1 chicken stock cube**
**3 tablespoons/1½ oz. butter**
**4 tablespoons seedless raisins**
**2 tablespoons chopped spring onion**
**3 tablespoons pine or hazel nuts**
**¼ teaspoon freshly ground black pepper**

Wash the rice thoroughly and drain. Add to a saucepan with the boiling water and stock cube. Cover and bring back to the boil. Stir once with a fork, then reduce the heat to the lowest possible point and cook, covered, for 45 minutes. Drain the rice and allow to stand covered for 10–12 minutes. Melt the butter in a saucepan. Add the raisins, chopped spring onion, nuts and pepper. Cook for 5–8 minutes, then stir into the rice.

## Herbed rice

Preparation time: about 20 minutes
Cooking time: about 20 minutes
Serves: 4–6

**3 tablespoons/1½ oz. butter**
**3 tablespoons salad oil**
**6 tablespoons chopped parsley**
**6 tablespoons chopped spring onion or chives**
**2 teaspoons salt**
**¼ teaspoon freshly ground black pepper**
**1 teaspoon chopped fresh or dried marjoram**
**500 g./1 lb. cooked long-grain white rice**

Heat the butter and salad oil in a large saucepan. When hot but not smoking, add the parsley, spring onion, salt, pepper and marjoram. Fry gently for 5–8 minutes. Add the rice and fold into the fried mixture. Cook stirring gently for 8–10 minutes. Remove to a heated dish and serve.

# Swedish cabbage rolls

Preparation time: 15 minutes
Cooking time: $1\frac{1}{4}$ hours
Serves: 4

**12 large cabbage leaves**
**100 g./3 oz. cooked carrots, chopped**
**120 g./4 oz. frozen peas**
**115 g./$3\frac{1}{2}$ oz. cooked long-grain rice**
**1 teaspoon finely chopped parsley**
**1 large egg**
**4 tablespoons milk**
**25 g./1 oz. onion, finely chopped**
**2 tablespoons chopped walnuts**
**1 teaspoon salt**
**pinch freshly ground black pepper**
**2 tablespoons vegetable fat**
**2 tablespoons brown sugar**
**1 large can condensed tomato soup**
**125 ml./$\frac{1}{4}$ pint water**
**1 bay leaf**
**4 cloves**

Drop the cabbage leaves into a saucepan of boiling salted water. Parboil for 5 minutes, or until soft. Drain and cut out the thick centre vein. Combine the carrots, peas, rice, parsley, egg, milk, half the onion, the nuts, salt and pepper in a bowl. Place a tablespoon of the mixture on each leaf. Roll up and fasten with toothpicks or cocktail sticks. Melt the vegetable fat in a heavy-bottomed saucepan. Put in the cabbage rolls, add the sugar, soup and water. Add the remaining onion, the bay leaf and cloves. Simmer, covered, for about $1\frac{1}{4}$ hours, adding more water if required. Serve with carrots and buttered potatoes.

# Rice with spiced sausages

Preparation time: 10 minutes
Cooking time: about 1 hour
Oven temperature: moderate (325°F., 170°C., Gas Mark 3)
Serves: 4–6

**500 g./1 lb. white long-grain rice**
**1 litre/$1\frac{3}{4}$ pints boiling water**
**1 chicken stock cube**
**4 tablespoons oil**
**2 medium-sized onions, sliced**
**2 tablespoons finely sliced green pepper**
**3 tablespoons finely chopped parsley**
**1 teaspoon salt**
**$\frac{1}{4}$ teaspoon freshly ground black pepper**
**pinch dried rosemary**
**pinch dried marjoram**
**2 spicy semi-dry sausages**
**1 teaspoon butter**

Wash the rice thoroughly and drain. Mix the boiling water in a jug with the stock cube. Place the rice in an ovenproof dish and pour over the stock. Heat the oil in a frying pan and fry the onion rings until golden brown. Remove to a plate. Add the green pepper slices to the remaining oil in the pan, with the parsley, salt, pepper and herbs. Cook for 5–8 minutes. Return the onion rings to the pan and mix in gently. Spoon the vegetables into the ovenproof dish and mix gently with the rice and stock. Cover and cook in a moderate oven for 1 hour, until the rice is tender. Slice the sausages thinly. Heat the butter in a small frying pan and when it begins to brown add the sausages. Fry for 2–3 minutes and fold into the rice just before serving.

# Savoury rice

Preparation time: 5 minutes
Cooking time: about 10 minutes
Serves: 2

**4 tablespoons/2 oz. butter**
**250 g./8 oz. cooked long-grain rice**
**4 spring onions**
**2 tablespoons walnuts**
**4 tablespoons sultanas**
**2 teaspoons salt**
**freshly ground black pepper to taste**

Melt the butter in a frying pan. Add the rice, heat through gently, stirring occasionally, for 5 minutes. Clean and chop the spring onions and chop the walnuts. Add the onions, walnuts and sultanas to the rice, season and stir. When thoroughly heated through, arrange on a heated serving dish and place kebabs on top.

# Rice nut loaf

Preparation time: 20 minutes
Cooking time: about 30 minutes
Oven temperature: moderately hot (375°F., 190°C., Gas Mark 5)
Serves: 6–8

**335 g./12 oz. long-grain rice**
**1 litre/1¾ pints boiling water**
**2 tablespoons/1 oz. butter**
**2 tablespoons flour**
**½ litre/¾ pint milk**
**2 teaspoons salt**
**¾ teaspoon freshly ground black pepper**
**4 tablespoons chopped onion**
**1 egg**
**165 g./6 oz. mixed chopped walnuts and almonds**
**½ teaspoon poultry seasoning**
**3 tablespoons breadcrumbs**

Wash the rice and add to the boiling water. Cook covered for 18–20 minutes. Rinse in a colander with cold water and drain well. Melt the butter in a saucepan and stir in flour. Cook, stirring, until the mixture bubbles. Remove from the heat. Gradually add the milk, stirring constantly. Return to the heat and continue stirring until the mixture just boils. Remove and add ½ teaspoon of the salt and ¼ teaspoon of the pepper. Stir in the chopped onion and rice. Beat the egg and add to rice mixture, together with the nuts; add seasonings. Grease a 23- by 12-cm. (9- by 5-inch) loaf tin and sprinkle with the crumbs. Spoon in the rice mixture. Bake in a moderately hot oven for about 30 minutes. Turn out and serve with tomato sauce (see page 91).

# Chicken risotto with peas and ham

*Illustrated opposite*
Preparation time: few minutes
Cooking time: about 1 hour
Oven temperature: moderate (350°F., 180°C., Gas Mark 4)
Serves: 4–6

**125 g./4 oz. white long-grain rice**
**3 tablespoons/1½ oz. butter**
**3 tablespoons salad oil**
**250 g./8 oz. very young peas**
**4 tablespoons ham slivers**
**2 tablespoons chopped chives**
**2 tablespoons chopped parsley**
**1 teaspoon salt**
**¼ teaspoon freshly ground black pepper**
**3 cooked chicken breasts, cut into strips**
**1 chicken stock cube dissolved in 1 litre/1¾ pints boiling water, or 1 litre/1¾ pints chicken stock (see page 26)**
**chopped parsley, mint or celery leaves to garnish**

Wash and drain the rice thoroughly. Heat the butter and oil in a saucepan. Add the rice and fry until a light gold, 5–8 minutes. Add the peas, ham, chives, parsley, salt, pepper and chicken strips. Spoon into an ovenproof dish and pour in the chicken stock. Cover and bake in a moderate oven for about 1 hour, until the stock is absorbed and the rice tender. Pile on a hot dish and serve sprinkled with chopped parsley. If liked, garnish with mint or celery leaves.

# Basic noodle dough

Preparation time: about 15 minutes
Cooking time: see individual recipes
Serves: 2–4

This is much simpler than a recipe containing eggs and does not require as much kneading. It is delicate and buttery, lacking the firmness of an egg noodle, but very good none the less.

**4 tablespoons/2 oz. butter**
**250 g./8 oz. flour**
**½ teaspoon salt**
**4–6 tablespoons boiling water**

Cut the butter into pieces, rub into the flour and salt in a bowl with your fingers, until the mixture resembles fine breadcrumbs. Gradually add the boiling water – enough to make a fairly stiff dough. Knead the dough for 5–8 minutes until pliable and smooth. Divide into two, placing a bowl over one half to prevent it from drying out. Roll out very thinly on a floured board. (If your board is not large enough, divide the dough into four.) As you roll the dough keep sprinkling the surface lightly with flour to prevent sticking and turn the pieces over frequently. When each section is rolled, cover with a clean cloth.

*Chicken risotto with peas and ham, mushroom pasta casserole*
*(see opposite and page 90)*

# Ravioli with chicken

Preparation time: 30 minutes
Cooking time: about 10 minutes
Serves: 4

**basic noodle dough (see page 88)**
**2 tablespoons butter**
**3 tablespoons flour**
**125 ml./$\frac{1}{4}$ pint milk**
**2 cooked chicken breasts, finely minced**
**1 egg yolk**
**1 tablespoon cream**
**1 teaspoon salt**
**$\frac{1}{4}$ teaspoon freshly ground black pepper**
**pinch nutmeg**
**2 teaspoons finely chopped parsley**
**chicken stock (see page 26) or water**

Prepare the noodle dough, rolling it out in thin sheets on a board. Make a thick white sauce with the butter, flour and milk. Remove from the heat and blend in the chicken, egg yolk, cream, seasonings and parsley. Place teaspoonfuls of the mixture on a sheet of dough at 5-cm. (2-inch) intervals. When one sheet is completed, cover it with a second layer of dough and press round each mound of filling to seal firmly. (No liquid is necessary for sealing.) Using a pastry wheel or a sharp knife, cut the ravioli out into small squares. Drop them into simmering chicken stock or well salted water and cook for 8–10 minutes, or until tender. Drain and serve with grated cheese and tomato sauce (see page 91).

# Noodles with ham and cream cheese

*Illustrated on page 85*
Preparation time: 5 minutes
Cooking time: about 15 minutes
Serves: 4–6

**250 g./8 oz. ribbon noodles**
**250 g./8 oz. cream cheese**
**1 teaspoon salt**
**$\frac{1}{4}$ teaspoon freshly ground black pepper**
**1 tablespoon/$\frac{1}{2}$ oz. butter**
**6 thin slices ham, chopped**

Cook the noodles as directed. Break up the cream cheese and mix lightly with the drained noodles. Add seasoning. Melt the butter in a saucepan, add the ham and cook until hot. Place the noodles in a warm dish, top with the ham and serve with a green salad.

As an alternative, the noodle mixture can be put into an ovenproof dish, the top sprinkled with grated Parmesan cheese and browned under a hot grill before serving.

# Mushroom pasta casserole

*Illustrated on page 89*
Preparation time: 15 minutes
Cooking time: about 10 minutes
Oven temperature: moderate (350°F., 180°C., Gas Mark 4)
Serves: 6

**250 g./8 oz. noodles or pasta shells**
**125 g./4 oz. mushrooms**
**6 tablespoons/3 oz. butter**
**8 tablespoons flour**
**500 ml./1 pint milk**
**100 g./4 oz. mature Cheddar cheese, grated**
**1 tablespoon finely chopped parsley**
**1 teaspoon salt**
**$\frac{1}{4}$ teaspoon freshly ground black pepper**
**about 2 teaspoons cream**

Parboil the noodles for 10 minutes, then drain. Wash the mushrooms carefully and slice. Sauté in a frying pan with 2 tablespoons of the butter. Make a white sauce with remaining butter, the flour and milk. Remove from the heat and stir in all but 1 tablespoon of the cheese, the parsley and seasoning. Layer the noodles, cheese sauce and mushrooms in a medium-sized casserole. Sprinkle over the remaining cheese and the cream. Bake in a moderate oven for 10–12 minutes, until the top is golden brown and bubbly.

# Two sauces to serve with pasta

## Bolognese sauce

Preparation time: 10 minutes
Cooking time: about 45 minutes
Serves: 6–8, or enough for 500 g. (1 lb.) spaghetti

**125 g./4 oz. ham, finely chopped**
**1 large onion, coarsely chopped**
**1 small carrot**
**4 tablespoons finely chopped celery**
**2 tablespoons/1 oz. butter**
**5 teaspoons salad oil**
**375 g./12 oz. topside, minced**
**125 g./4 oz. pork, finely minced**
**4 tablespoons dry red wine**
**375 ml./generous ½ pint beef stock**
**2 tablespoons tomato purée**
**pinch ground nutmeg**
**2 teaspoons salt**
**¼ teaspoon freshly ground black pepper**

Combine the ham, onion, chopped carrot and celery in a bowl. Melt the butter over a moderate heat in a large heavy frying pan. When melted, add the vegetables and cook for 10 minutes. Remove to a heavy saucepan. Add the oil to the frying pan and lightly brown the beef and pork over a moderate heat, stirring constantly. Pour in the wine, increase the heat and bring to the boil, stirring constantly until all the liquid has boiled away. Add the meat to the vegetables in the saucepan and stir in the stock and tomato purée. Bring to the boil, reduce the heat and simmer, partially covered, for 45 minutes, stirring occasionally. Add the nutmeg and seasoning. Serve hot with buttered spaghetti or noodles.

## Tomato sauce

Preparation time: 5 minutes
Cooking time: about 40 minutes
Serves: 4, or enough for 250 g. (8 oz.) spaghetti

**3 tablespoons olive or salad oil**
**1 clove garlic**
**1 large onion, finely chopped**
**½ large green pepper, finely chopped**
**½ carrot, diced**
**4 tomatoes, skinned and chopped**
**1 bay leaf**
**4 stalks celery, chopped**
**¼ teaspoon thyme**
**½ teaspoon salt**
**¼ teaspoon freshly ground black pepper**

Heat the oil in a large saucepan and add the crushed garlic, onion, green pepper and carrot. Cook, stirring constantly, until the onion begins to brown slightly. Then add the tomatoes, bay leaf, celery, thyme and seasoning. Cook for 40 minutes, until the mixture thickens. Press through a fine sieve, or purée in a blender.

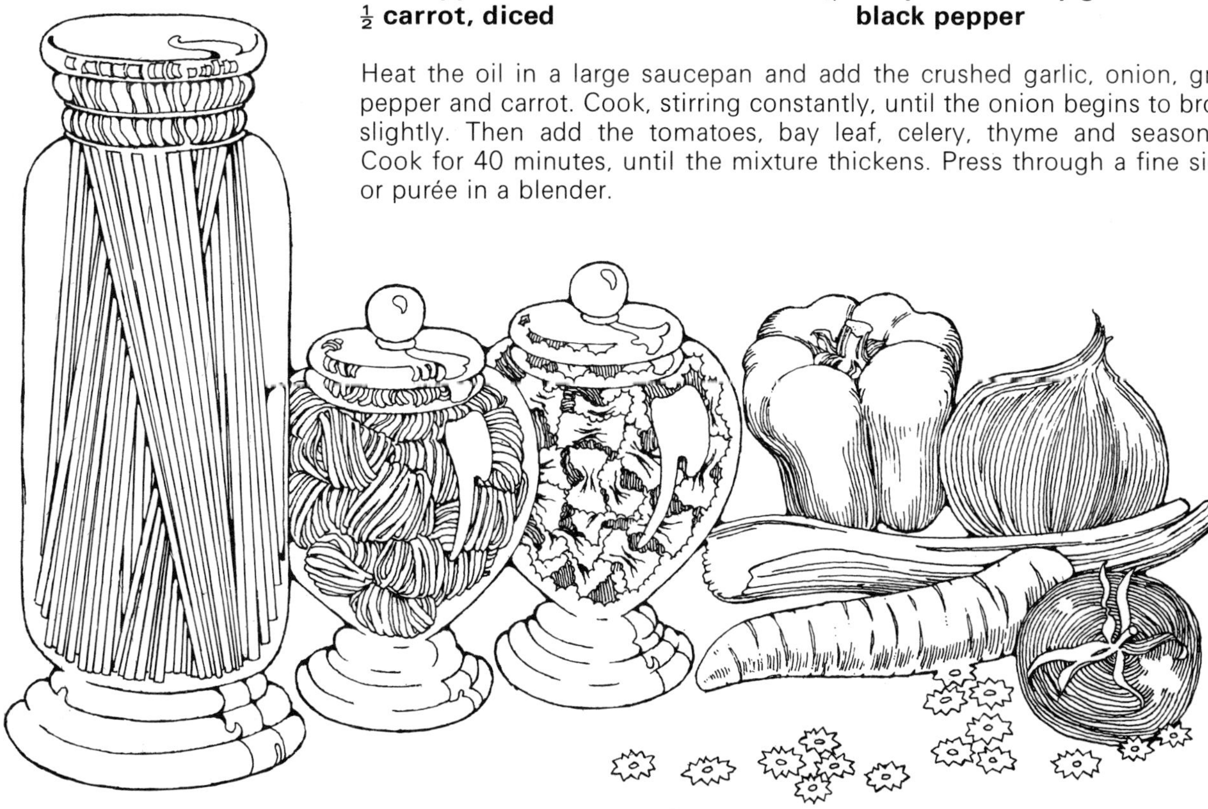

# Salads

A salad can be either light and refreshing and served as an accompaniment, or a meal on its own.

For the classic and best-loved green salad, choose your ingredients with care; pick out the freshest heads of lettuce, the most slender cucumbers, translucent spring onions and the greenest chives and parsley. Use the best oil and a wine vinegar for your basic salad dressings. Ring the changes with these by trying vinegar flavoured with herbs, a touch of mustard and garlic and always freshly ground black pepper.

Delicate leafed salads should only be dressed at the last possible moment before eating. Never drench them with dressing, a light coating is enough. Only more solid salads should be marinated. Experiment with new combinations – the variations in a salad bowl are endless.

Good-looking dishes to have: a large wooden salad bowl; small individual wooden salad bowls; fine glass bowls for delicate salads; one or two plain pottery bowls in clear colours.

## Potato salad with lemon dressing

*Illustrated opposite*
Preparation time: 20 minutes
Serves: 4–6

**6 medium-sized potatoes**
**6 tablespoons lemon juice**
**125 ml./$\frac{1}{4}$ pint hot chicken stock**
**5 tablespoons oil**
**1 tablespoon vinegar**
**1 teaspoon sugar**
**1 teaspoon finely grated lemon rind**
**3 tablespoons thinly slivered spring onion**
**1 teaspoon capers**
**1 teaspoon salt**
**$\frac{1}{4}$ teaspoon freshly ground black pepper**
**2 tablespoons finely diced celery**
**few caraway seeds**
**4 tablespoons thin slivers ham (optional)**
**4 tablespoons cream (optional)**
**paprika pepper, chopped parsley and hard-boiled egg slices to garnish**

Boil the potatoes in their jackets. Peel off the skins and slice thinly into a bowl whilst still hot. Blend the lemon juice, chicken stock, oil, vinegar, sugar, lemon rind, spring onion, capers, salt, pepper, celery and caraway seeds together in a bowl. Whisk for 1 minute. Pour over the potato slices. Allow to cool but do not chill. Serve garnished with paprika pepper, chopped parsley and hard-boiled egg slices. The ham and cream may be added if you are serving this salad as a light luncheon dish.

*Potato salad with lemon dressing, tongue and pasta salad (see opposite and page 102)*

# Marinated mushroom salad

*Illustrated on page 144*
Preparation time: 5 minutes
Serves: 4–6

**1 kg./2 lb. mushrooms**
**4 tablespoons chopped parsley**
**4 tablespoons chopped chives**
**250 ml./$\frac{1}{2}$ pint salad oil**
**125 ml./$\frac{1}{4}$ pint vinegar**
**2 tablespoons lemon juice**
**$\frac{1}{2}$ teaspoon salt**
**$\frac{1}{4}$ teaspoon freshly ground black pepper**
**3 tablespoons slivered salted almonds**

Wash the mushrooms thoroughly, dry and slice very thinly. Layer in a dish with the parsley and chives. Whisk the salad oil, vinegar, lemon juice, salt and pepper together in a bowl. When thick and creamy, pour over the mushroom salad. Lightly fold in the slivered almonds.

# Chicken tuna salad

Preparation time: 15 minutes
Serves: 4–6

**1 1.5-kg./3-lb. cooked chicken**
**1 medium-sized can tuna**
**1 medium-sized can baby clams**
**1 medium-sized can mussels (optional)**
**6 small tomatoes**
**1 small cucumber**
**1 avocado**
**2 tablespoons lemon juice**
**2 tablespoons capers**
**2 tablespoons black olives, halved and stoned**
**4 tablespoons vinegar**
**2 tablespoons salad oil**
**1 teaspoon salt**
**$\frac{1}{4}$ teaspoon freshly ground black pepper**
**3 hard-boiled eggs**
**4 tablespoons chopped parsley**

Remove the chicken meat and dice. Drain and flake the tuna, reserving the oil. Arrange the chicken and tuna on a dish and pour over the tuna oil. Spoon over the baby clams and mussels with their juices. Quarter the tomatoes. Score the unpeeled cucumber with a sharp fork and slice finely. Peel the avocado and slice following the curve of the fruit; sprinkle slices with lemon juice. Arrange the cucumber in overlapping slices at intervals between the chicken and seafood. Add the avocado slices and spoon over the capers and olives. Blend the vinegar, salad oil, salt and pepper, and pour over the salad. Shell and quarter the hard-boiled eggs and arrange on the salad. Sprinkle with parsley.

# Tomatoes with basil

Preparation time: 10 minutes
Serves: 4–6

**8 ripe tomatoes**
**4 spring onions**
**1 sprig fresh basil or $\frac{1}{4}$ teaspoon dried**
**8 anchovies**
**4 tablespoons vinegar**
**3 tablespoons lemon juice**
**4 tablespoons salad or olive oil**
**1 teaspoon sugar**
**2 cloves garlic**
**$\frac{1}{4}$ teaspoon freshly ground black pepper**
**2 tablespoons chopped parsley**
**12 black olives**
**12 sprigs parsley**

Slice the tomatoes thinly using a very sharp knife. Place on a flat dish in overlapping circles. Wash, peel and thinly slice the spring onions. Scatter over the tomatoes. Chop the fresh basil and sprinkle over the salad. (If this is not available, include the dried basil in the dressing.) Mix the anchovies, vinegar, lemon juice, salad oil and sugar in a blender, or use an electric hand mixer. Peel and crush the garlic cloves. Add to the anchovy mixture together with the freshly ground black pepper. Blend until smooth and creamy. Add the chopped parsley and pour over the tomatoes. Place the black olives in a little pyramid in the centre and surround with sprigs of parsley.

# Marinated vegetables

*Illustrated on page 96*
Preparation time: 30 minutes
Serves: 4–6

**2 medium-sized aubergines**
**2 teaspoons salt**
**4 courgettes**
**6 tablespoons oil**
**6 black mushrooms**
**125 g./4 oz. cooked whole green beans**
**8 black olives**
**4 tablespoons vinegar**
**4 tablespoons lemon juice**
**1 teaspoon sugar**
**1 teaspoon salt**
**¼ teaspoon freshly ground black pepper**
**1 teaspoon grated onion**

Slice the unpeeled aubergines in 1¼-cm. (¾-inch) pieces. Sprinkle with salt and allow to stand for 20–30 minutes. Drain off the juices. Trim the courgettes and peel, using a potato peeler. Slice in 1¼-cm. (¾-inch) pieces. Cook the aubergines in a pan with 125 ml. (¼ pint) water for 8–10 minutes. Drain and place in a bowl. Lightly cook the courgettes in a saucepan with 1 tablespoon oil and 2 tablespoons water for 5–6 minutes. Remove and place on top of the aubergines. Wash the mushrooms thoroughly. Slice thinly and layer on top of the courgettes. Cover with the green beans and black olives. Whisk the remaining oil, the vinegar, lemon juice, sugar, salt, pepper and onion together until creamy. Pour over the salad. Allow to stand at room temperature for 2–3 hours before serving.
**Note** Other vegetables, as available, may be used for this recipe. If liked, a bay leaf and a chilli pepper can also be added.

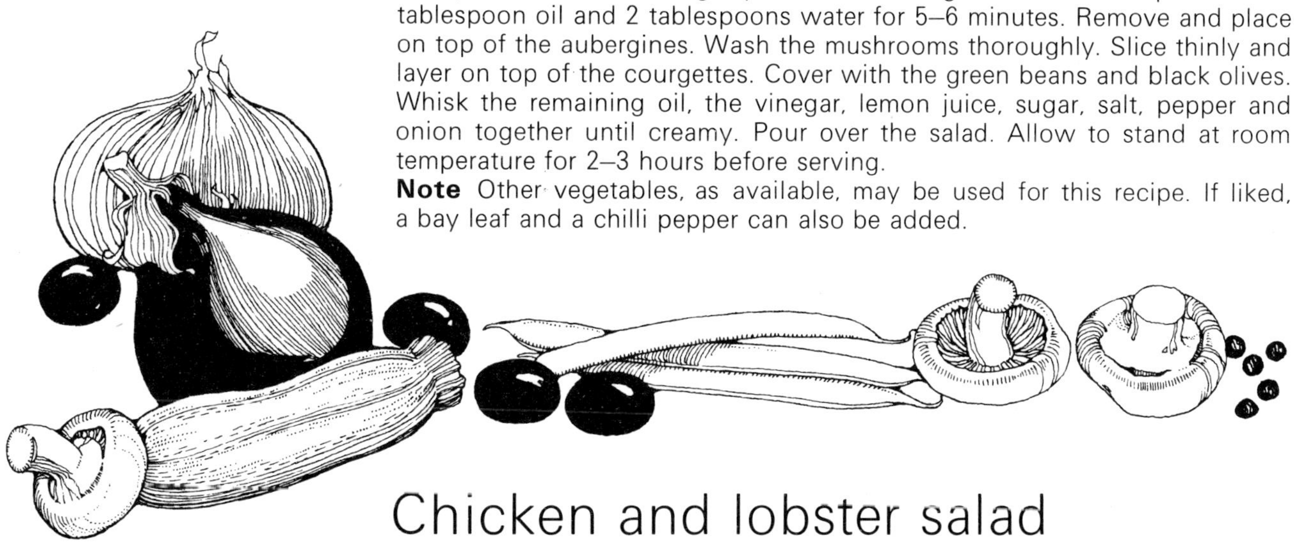

# Chicken and lobster salad

*Illustrated on page 144*
Preparation time: 20 minutes, plus overnight cooking of chicken
Oven temperature: very cool (225°F., 110°C., Gas Mark ¼)
Serves: 4–6

**1 1.5-kg./3-lb. chicken**
**2½ teaspoons salt**
**½ teaspoon freshly ground black pepper**
**1 clove garlic**
**1 large freshly cooked lobster**
**250 ml./½ pint thick mayonnaise**
**4 tablespoons chopped chives**
**2 tablespoons tomato sauce**
**2 teaspoons prepared mustard**
**125 ml./¼ pint cream**
**1 can black olives**
**1 stalk celery**
**4 tablespoons chopped parsley**
**1 cucumber**

Clean the chicken and wash thoroughly. Sprinkle with 2 teaspoons salt and half the pepper. Peel the garlic clove and place inside the chicken. Lightly oil a piece of foil and completely enclose chicken. Place in a roasting tin in a very cool oven overnight. (The very slow heat turns the chicken golden brown; it becomes meltingly tender and provides a jellied gravy.) Allow to cool. Vein and wash the lobster tail. Crack all the claws to remove meat. If there is coral, reserve. Dice all the lobster meat. Remove the chicken meat and cut into medium-sized pieces. Mix the thick mayonnaise in a bowl with chives and tomato sauce. Add the chicken and lobster. Mash the coral, and add with mustard, remaining salt, pepper and the cream. Drain olives, halve and stone; add half to the mayonnaise mixture. Place the chicken and lobster salad in a shallow bowl. Finely dice the celery and sprinkle over, together with parsley. Slice the cucumber very thinly and arrange slices at intervals in overlapping circles on the salad. Place the remaining olives in little mounds on the cucumber sections. Serve slightly chilled.

Alternatively, the chicken and lobster may be arranged on platters as shown in the picture on page 144.

**Note** If this salad is made in advance, cover it with foil before chilling and remove 1 hour before serving.

*Marinated vegetables (see page 95)*

*Duck and orange salad (see page 102)*

# Fruity cabbage salad

Preparation time: 10 minutes
Serves: 6–8

- 1 medium-sized green cabbage
- ½ teaspoon salt
- ¼ teaspoon freshly ground black pepper
- 1 medium-sized sweet melon
- 1 pineapple
- 3 peaches
- 4 tablespoons seedless raisins
- 3 tablespoons walnuts, peanuts or almonds
- 250 ml./½ pint thick mayonnaise
- 4 tablespoons cream
- 2 tablespoons chopped parsley

Wash, dry and shred the cabbage. Place in a wooden salad bowl and add the salt and pepper. Cut open and cube the flesh of the melon. Peel, slice and cube the pineapple; peel and slice the peaches. Add to the cabbage and sprinkle with raisins and nuts. Blend the mayonnaise with the cream, pour over the salad, and mix gently. Sprinkle with chopped parsley.

# Chilled vegetable salad

Preparation time: 15 minutes, plus marinating time
Serves: 4–6

- 1 small cooked cauliflower
- 250 g./8 oz. cooked whole green beans
- 1 stalk celery
- 2 medium-sized tomatoes
- 6 spring onions
- 2 hard-boiled eggs
- 6 anchovy fillets
- 12 black olives
- 8 tablespoons salad oil
- 4 tablespoons lemon juice
- 4 tablespoons vinegar
- 1 teaspoon sugar
- 1 teaspoon dry mustard
- 1 teaspoon salt
- ¼ teaspoon freshly ground black pepper

Break up and arrange the cauliflowerettes amongst the beans in a shallow bowl. Clean and dice the celery and sprinkle in the bowl. Quarter the tomatoes; wash and trim the spring onions but leave uncut. Add to the bowl. Shell and quarter the hard-boiled eggs and add together with anchovy fillets and black olives. Pour salad oil, lemon juice, vinegar, sugar, mustard, salt and pepper into a bowl. Whisk well to combine until creamy. Pour over the salad and allow to marinate in the refrigerator for 15–20 minutes before serving.

# Mediterranean salad

Preparation time: 10 minutes
Serves: 4–6

- 6 tomatoes
- 1 pineapple
- 1 green pepper
- 1 small onion
- 1 avocado
- 2 hard-boiled eggs
- 1 small can black olives
- 125 ml./¼ pint olive or salad oil
- 125 ml./¼ pint vinegar
- 2 tablespoons sugar
- 1 teaspoon salt
- ¼ teaspoon freshly ground black pepper

Quarter the tomatoes. Peel, slice and cube the pineapple. Seed the green pepper and slice finely. Peel and slice the onion into paper-thin rings; peel and cut the avocado into wedges; shell and slice the eggs. Drain the olives; arrange all the prepared ingredients on a flat dish. Mix the oil, vinegar, sugar, salt and pepper, whisk well, and pour over the salad.

# Individual asparagus and leek salads

Preparation time: 10 minutes
Serves: 4–6

**2 large cans asparagus tips**
**1 small lettuce**
**6 hard-boiled eggs**
**6 tablespoons mayonnaise**
**3 tablespoons cream**
**2 tablespoons finely chopped onion**
**½ teaspoon grated lemon rind**
**¼ teaspoon freshly ground black pepper**
**6 tablespoons finely slivered green leeks**

Drain the asparagus. Wash, dry and break the lettuce into thin wedges. Shell and quarter the hard-boiled eggs. Divide the asparagus, lettuce wedges and egg quarters equally between individual dishes. Blend mayonnaise, cream, onion, lemon rind and pepper together. Spoon over each salad. Sprinkle over the leeks.

# Green bean and potato salad

Preparation time: 5 minutes
Serves: 4–6

**500 g./1 lb. cooked green beans**
**4 large cold boiled potatoes**
**4 tablespoons chopped spring onion**
**2 tablespoons black olives**
**2 tablespoons chopped parsley**
**8 tablespoons salad oil**
**6 tablespoons lemon juice**
**2 tablespoons vinegar**
**1 teaspoon sugar**
**1 teaspoon salt**
**¼ teaspoon freshly ground black pepper**

Place the beans in a bowl. Slice the potatoes and mix lightly with the beans. Sprinkle with the chopped spring onion, olives and parsley. Mix the salad oil, lemon juice and vinegar in a bowl. Add the sugar, salt and freshly ground black pepper. Whisk well and pour over the salad.

# Large salad tray

Preparation time: 10 minutes
Serves: 4–6

**1 small crisp lettuce**
**1 bunch endive or chicory**
**1 teaspoon sugar**
**3 hard-boiled eggs**
**6 tablespoons thick mayonnaise**
**¼ teaspoon rose paprika or paprika pepper**
**3 stalks celery**
**6 small tomatoes**
**1 cucumber**
**1 medium-sized can green or white asparagus**
**1 small avocado**
**1 tablespoon lemon juice**
**12 large green olives**
**125 ml./¼ pint vinegar**
**125 ml./¼ pint salad oil**
**2 teaspoons sugar**
**1 teaspoon salt**
**¼ teaspoon freshly ground black pepper**

Wash the lettuce and endive and shake to dry. Cut into wedges. Place on a tray and sprinkle with sugar. Shell the hard-boiled eggs, quarter and place neatly in a row next to the lettuce. Cover with mayonnaise and sprinkle with rose paprika. Place the celery stalks at an angle over the lettuce. Slice the tomatoes, layer in a row next to the eggs. Wash and slice the unpeeled cucumber. Place in a row next to the tomatoes. Drain the asparagus, arrange in groups of four in a row next to the cucumbers. Peel the avocado and slice in crescents following the curve of the fruit. Arrange in a corner of the tray. Sprinkle with lemon juice, to prevent discolouration, and a little freshly ground black pepper. Place the olives amongst the avocado slices. Blend the vinegar, oil, sugar, salt and freshly ground black pepper in a bowl. Just before serving whisk until creamy. Pour over the lettuce, tomato and cucumber.
**Note** If you prepare this salad tray in advance cover it with wax paper or foil and refrigerate to crisp. Pour over dressing just before serving.

*Basic mayonnaise, curry mayonnaise, pink seafood mayonnaise* *(see page 150)*

*Brandy butter, spiced cranberry sauce, bread sauce (see pages 155, 154, 152)*

# Duck and orange salad

*Illustrated on page 97*
Preparation time: 10 minutes
Serves: 4–6

**1 roasted duck**
**6 oranges**
**4 stalks celery**
**250 ml./$\frac{1}{2}$ pint orange juice**
**2 tablespoons lemon juice**
**2$\frac{1}{2}$ teaspoons sugar**
**3 tablespoons olive or salad oil**
**2 teaspoons salt**
**1 teaspoon freshly ground black pepper**
**about 2 teaspoons capers**
**2 tablespoons chopped parsley**
**12 black olives, stoned**
**2 tablespoons chopped spring onion**

Slice the duck. Peel the oranges, removing all the pith, and slice into thin rounds. Cube or curl the celery. Mix together the orange juice, lemon juice, sugar and oil; add the salt, pepper, capers and parsley. Arrange the orange slices around the edge of a serving dish. Place the duck slices in the dish and arrange stoned olives and celery curls in the centre. Sprinkle over the chopped spring onion. Just before serving pour the orange juice mixture over the duck.

# Tongue and pasta salad

*Illustrated on page 93*
Preparation time: 10 minutes
Serves: 4–6

**2 thick smoked sausages**
**500 g./1 lb. cooked pickled tongue**
**500 g./1 lb. cooked pasta shells**
**4 tomatoes**
**2 small cucumbers**
**12 green olives**
**2 tablespoons chopped spring onion**
**2 tablespoons chopped parsley**
**250 ml./$\frac{1}{2}$ pint thick mayonnaise**
**1 tablespoon lemon juice**
**2 teaspoons salt**
**1 teaspoon freshly ground black pepper**

Boil the sausages, cool and slice finely. Cut the tongue into strips and place with sausage slices and pasta in a bowl. Quarter the tomatoes. Wash (do not peel) the cucumbers and cube. Add the tomato and cucumber to the bowl together with the olives, spring onion and parsley. Mix the mayonnaise with the lemon juice, salt and pepper, pour over the salad, and toss lightly but thoroughly.

**Note** If preferred, this salad may be tossed in a dressing instead of mayonnaise, or the mayonnaise or dressing served separately.

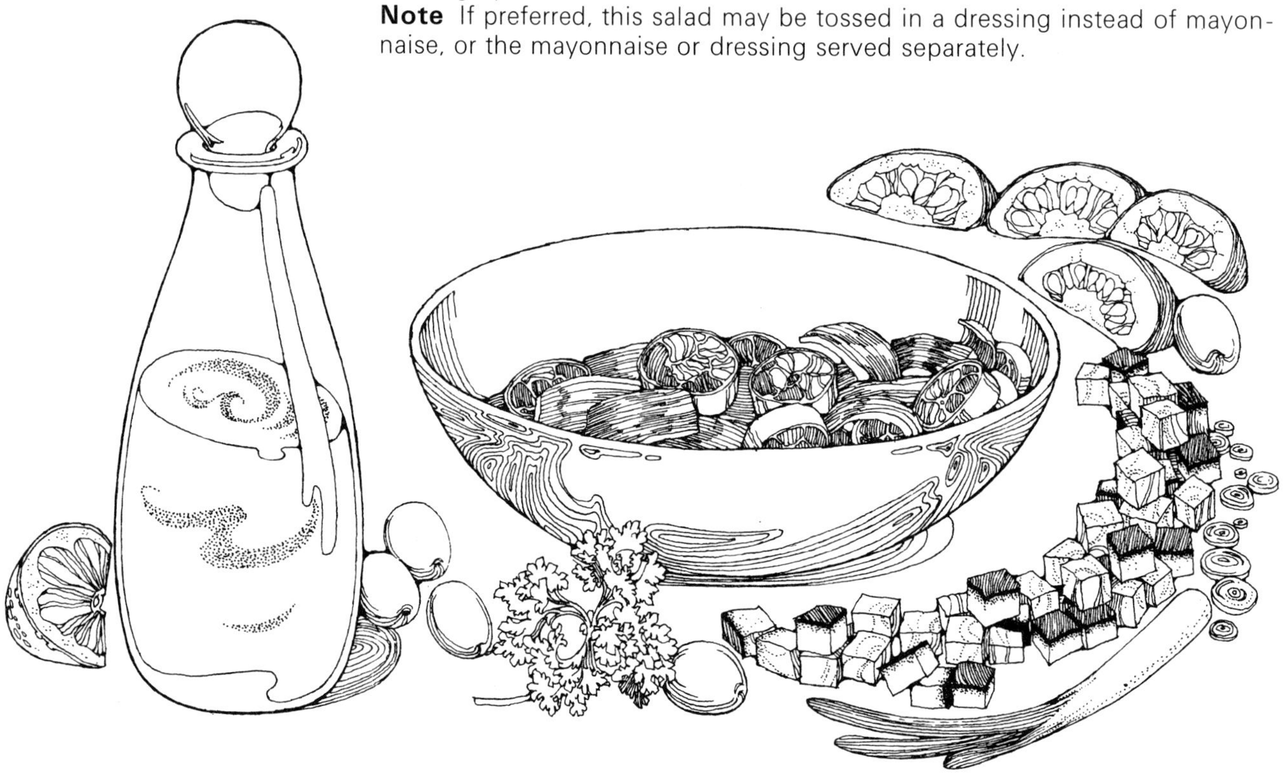

# Desserts and puddings

The ultimate triumph is the sweet surprise that crowns the menu. It can, with its final flourish, help redeem a mediocre dinner, or if dull almost spoil a good beginning. Puddings need not be elaborate to please. Crisp bread or rice pudding, fluffy sago, baked noodles, are all basic and good. Perfectly poached or fresh fruit are amongst the nicest. To achieve an excellent sweet at a moment's notice, keep a selection of light crisp meringues in an airtight container and the ever useful crêpes in the freezer between layers of foil, bags of choux pastry puffs, simple to fill with custard or whipped cream and dust with icing sugar, and ices, both cream and sherbet. Pastry and sponge cases can be stacked and frozen. Fillings are quick to make if you keep a small store of canned fruits in your cupboard, such as black and red cherries, sour and sweet plums, peaches. Other useful ingredients are blocks of cooking chocolate, preserves, watermelon konfyt and figs, ginger in syrup, a good orange liqueur and a bottle of rum; spices such as fresh nutmeg and cinnamon. There are many other tempting ingredients you can add to your store but with the ones listed you should be able to ring the changes.

Good-looking dishes to have: large clear glass bowls for fruit; small individual glass bowls; soufflé dish; brown ovenproof pottery dishes for rice and bread puddings; small individual ovenproof pots, with lids if possible, for custards, creams and soufflés.

## Caramel delight

Preparation time: about 20 minutes, plus chilling time
Serves: 4

**500 g./1 lb. strawberries**
**375 g./9 oz. granulated sugar**
**8 tablespoons water**
**125 g./4 oz. ground almonds**
**125 g./4 oz. castor sugar**
**¼ teaspoon almond essence**
**¼ teaspoon grated orange rind**
**2 egg yolks**
**125 ml./¼ pint double cream**

Wash, hull and drain the strawberries. Cook granulated sugar and water in a saucepan until the soft crack stage is reached. (A confectioner's thermometer will register 141°C., 186°F.) To test, drop a little syrup into a cup of water. It should form a ball when rolled between the fingers. Remove from heat and pour the syrup into the top of a double boiler, or a bowl placed over a pan of hot water. Dip the strawberries into the caramel, using a sharp-pronged fork; cool the coated strawberries on oiled foil. Meanwhile mix together the almonds, sugar, almond essence and orange rind. Add the egg yolks to the cream and mix thoroughly. Put all together in a saucepan and whisk over a low heat until frothy and thick. Do not allow to boil. Remove from the heat and chill well. Place the caramelised strawberries in bowls and serve with the almond cream.

# Strawberry fool

Preparation time: 10 minutes
Serves: 4–6

**1 kg./2 lb. fully ripe strawberries**
**250 ml./$\frac{1}{2}$ pint double cream**
**8 tablespoons icing sugar**
**2 tablespoons strawberry cordial**

Hull all but a few choice strawberries for decoration. Wash well and dry. Whip the cream in a bowl with 2 tablespoons of the icing sugar. Place half the strawberries in a glass bowl. Sprinkle with 2 tablespoons icing sugar. Place the remaining strawberries and 4 tablespoons sugar in a blender, or purée with a hand mixer, or press through a sieve. Blend the strawberry pulp with the strawberry cordial. Fold in the cream using a spatula. Blend with the whole strawberries. Place the remaining unhulled strawberries on the top and serve with sponge fingers.

# Three ways to freeze peaches

## 1 Poached peaches

Preparation time: 15 minutes
Serves: 4–6

**1 litre/1$\frac{3}{4}$ pints water**
**500 g./1 lb. sugar**
**8 ripe pink Early Dawn peaches**
**3 drops red food colouring**

Bring the water and sugar to the boil in a saucepan. Wash the peaches well under cold running water. Add to pan and simmer for 5–6 minutes, then plunge the peaches into cold water and peel off the skins. Add the red colouring to the syrup, then pour the boiling syrup over the peaches in a bowl. When lukewarm transfer to a polythene, airtight container, allowing a 2$\frac{1}{2}$-cm. (1-inch) headspace. Cool for 15 minutes, then cover and seal. Pack into the freezer. Defrost the morning of the day peaches are to be served. No cream or sauces are necessary as the fruit will have a fresh sweet flavour.

## 2 Peaches in syrup

Preparation time: 15 minutes
Serves: 4–6

**1 litre/1$\frac{3}{4}$ pints water**
**750 g./1$\frac{1}{2}$ lb. sugar**
**8 ripe Early Dawn peaches**
**2 tablespoons lemon juice**

Bring the water and sugar slowly to the boil, then cook for 5–8 minutes, uncovered. Remove and allow to stand until cold. Peel the peaches by plunging them into boiling water for 1 minute which will loosen the skins and set the colour. Mix 500 ml. (1 pint) cold water with the lemon juice and slice the peaches straight into this solution. Remove and pack into a polythene container. Pour over the cold syrup, leaving about a 2$\frac{1}{2}$-cm. (1-inch) headspace. Cover, seal and freeze. About 5–6 hours before serving, remove from the freezer and place in refrigerator until ready to serve.

## 3 Sugared peaches

Preparation time: 5 minutes
Serves: 4–6

**8 yellow cling peaches**
**6 tablespoons lemon juice**
**500 g./1 lb. sugar**

Peel the peaches and slice thinly following the curve of the peach. Sprinkle the slices with lemon juice. Layer into a polythene container. Liberally sprinkle each layer with sugar. Shake the container when full to make quite sure the fruit is coated. Seal, label and freeze. To serve, thaw slowly in the refrigerator to prevent discolouration.

*Orange baskets (see page 115)*

# Tipsy meringue peaches

*Illustrated on page 81*
Preparation time: 20 minutes
Cooking time: 20 minutes
Oven temperature: cool (300°F., 150°C., Gas Mark 3)
Serves: 8

**4 large yellow peaches**
**250 ml./$\frac{1}{2}$ pint white wine**
**8 teaspoons orange liqueur or lemon juice**
**125 g./4 oz. walnuts or almonds, chopped (optional)**
**2 egg whites**
**125 g./4 oz. icing or castor sugar**

Peel, halve and stone the peaches. Bring the wine to the boil. Add the peaches and poach until just soft, 10–12 minutes. Arrange the peaches, cut side up, in an ovenproof dish. Pour a teaspoon of orange liqueur or lemon juice into each hollow and pour cooled wine around the fruit. Sprinkle the chopped nuts (if used) around the fruit. Beat the egg whites and sugar together until stiff. Pipe a topping of meringue over each peach half and bake in a cool oven until golden brown. Serve immediately.

# Peaches in white wine

Preparation time: 5 minutes, plus chilling time
Serves: 4–6

**8 ripe pink Early Dawn peaches**
**500 ml./1 pint semi-sweet white wine**
**4 tablespoons sugar**
**1 sprig mint**

Plunge the peaches into a saucepan of boiling water for 1 minute, then remove and peel off the skins. (The lovely pink blush will remain behind on the peach.) Slice into segments, following the line of the peach, and place in a shallow glass bowl. Cover with the white wine and sugar. Place a mint sprig in the centre and chill thoroughly before serving.

# Peach grape shortbread

Preparation time: 30 minutes
Cooking time: about 50 minutes
Oven temperature: moderate (350°F., 180°C., Gas Mark 4), reducing to cool (300°F., 150°C., Gas Mark 2)
Serves: 6

*shortbread*
**125 g./4 oz. butter**
**4 tablespoons castor sugar**
**1 large egg yolk**
**6 tablespoons cornflour**
**6 tablespoons flour**
*meringue*
**1 large egg white**
**4 tablespoons castor sugar**
*filling*
**220 g./8 oz. green grapes**
**1 medium-sized can peach slices**
**2 tablespoons liqueur or brandy**
**250 ml./$\frac{1}{2}$ pint double cream**

Cream the butter and sugar with a wooden spoon until soft; beat in the egg yolk and work in the cornflour and flour to form a smooth dough. Roll out to about $1\frac{1}{4}$ cm. ($\frac{3}{4}$ inch) thick and press into a 20-cm. (8-inch) fluted flan ring on a baking sheet. Prick thoroughly and bake in a moderate oven for 20 minutes. Lower the oven temperature to cool.

Whisk the egg white until stiff and dry, add the sugar and continue whisking until stiff. Pipe rosettes of meringue around the edge of the shortbread and return to a cool oven for 30 minutes, until the meringue is crisp and pale golden. Remove and cool on the baking sheet for 10 minutes, then lift onto a wire cooling rack.

Halve the grapes and remove the pips. Drain the peach slices and, reserving a little of each fruit for decoration, pour the liqueur over the rest. Whisk cream until just stiff, fold in the fruit and liqueur and spoon into the centre of the meringue and shortbread case. Decorate with remaining grapes and peach slices.

# Yellow peach brûlée

Preparation time: 15 minutes, plus chilling time
Serves: 4

**2 yellow cling peaches**
**3 egg yolks**
**4 tablespoons sugar**
**250 ml./$\frac{1}{2}$ pint double cream**
**1 teaspoon vanilla essence**
**4 tablespoons soft brown sugar**

Peel and slice the peaches into thin segments. Place in four individual ovenproof dishes. Whisk the yolks together with the sugar until thick and creamy. Scald the cream. Blend the egg mixture and cream together in a heavy saucepan. Cook over a low heat, stirring with a wooden spoon, until the mixture thickens. Add the vanilla essence, then pour over peaches. Chill for 2–3 hours. Sieve the brown sugar over the custard before serving and place under preheated grill until the sugar melts and browns. Remove, chill for 30 minutes then serve.

# Gingered peach cream

Preparation time: 20 minutes, plus chilling time
Serves: 4–6

**1 tablespoon gelatine**
**4 tablespoons hot water**
**250 ml./$\frac{1}{2}$ pint double cream**
**pinch nutmeg**
**125 g./4 oz. castor sugar**
**1 tablespoon ginger syrup**
**2 egg whites**
**3 large yellow cling peaches, thinly sliced**
**1 tablespoon icing sugar**
**1 tablespoon preserved ginger slivers**

Pour the gelatine into the hot water and stir to dissolve. Whisk the cream and fold in the nutmeg, castor sugar and ginger syrup. Fold in the dissolved gelatine. Whisk the egg whites and fold in. Refrigerate for 5–10 minutes, until the mixture just begins to slightly firm. Using a spatula gently fold in half the fruit. Pour into a wet mould and chill for 5–6 hours. Unmould onto a chilled dish and arrange the remaining peach slices in overlapping circles. Sprinkle with the icing sugar and ginger slivers.
**Note** In recipes where gelatine is used as a setting agent, it is advisable to add gelatine to the hot water rather than to pour the water over the gelatine which may lead to incomplete dissolving of the granules.

# Orange sabayon

Preparation time: 30 minutes, plus chilling time
Serves: 6

**3 large oranges**
**1 tablespoon castor sugar**
**125 g./4 oz. granulated sugar**
**3 large egg yolks**
**3 teaspoons orange-flavoured liqueur**
**125 ml./$\frac{1}{4}$ pint double cream**

Pare the rind from one of the oranges, cut into thin strips and cook in a little water until soft. Drain and set aside. Peel the rind and pith from the remaining oranges and slice the flesh of all three thinly. Discard the pips. Place the orange slices in a shallow dish and sprinkle with castor sugar. Leave for 30 minutes. Strain off the juice, add enough water to make 6 tablespoons of liquid. Divide the slices between six glasses and chill. Put the granulated sugar into a heavy saucepan. Add the orange liquid. Heat gently until dissolved, brushing round the sides with a spoon handle that has been wrapped with a cloth and dipped in cold water. Bring to the boil and cook briskly for 4–5 minutes, until the syrup forms a thread when a drop is taken from the spoon and pulled between the thumb and forefinger. Remove from the heat. Beat the yolks with a whisk until light coloured and slightly thick. Pour in the cooled syrup steadily, whisking constantly. Stand the bowl in iced water and whisk until the mixture is stiff and thick. Remove the bowl from the water and stir in the liqueur. Fold in cream, whipped until thick but not stiff. Divide between the dessert glasses and chill for 1 hour. Decorate with the strips of orange peel.

# Orange fluff

Preparation time: 20 minutes, plus chilling time
Serves: 4

**4 eggs, separated**
**6 tablespoons sugar**
**3 tablespoons frozen orange concentrate**
**1 teaspoon finely grated orange rind**
**250 ml./$\frac{1}{2}$ pint double cream**

Whisk the egg yolks until thick and pale. Gradually blend in the sugar, using a whisk or an electric mixer. Gradually add the orange concentrate and rind. Pour into a double boiler. Cook over hot water, stirring constantly with a wooden spoon until the mixture thickens. Cool. Whisk the egg whites and fold in using a metal spoon. Whisk the cream and blend into the mixture using a spatula. Spoon into individual glasses and chill thoroughly before serving.

# Baked lemon cream

Preparation time: 10 minutes
Cooking time: about 35 minutes
Oven temperature: moderate (325°F., 170°C., Gas Mark 3)
Serves: 6

**5 large egg yolks**
**5 tablespoons sugar**
**finely grated rind of 1 large lemon**
**500 ml./1 pint milk**
**2 teaspoons vanilla essence**
**$\frac{1}{4}$ teaspoon freshly grated nutmeg**

Combine the egg yolks, sugar and lemon rind in a bowl. Whisk for 1 minute. Heat the milk in a saucepan to nearly boiling point. Very gradually add the milk into the egg mixture whisking constantly. Add the vanilla essence. When well blended pour into an ovenproof dish. Place the dish in a pan of hot water and bake in a moderate oven for 30–35 minutes. (Do not let the water in the pan come to the boil – add cold water, if necessary, to keep the temperature down.) Serve the custard well chilled and sprinkled with a little nutmeg.

# Pears in apple juice

Preparation time: about 25 minutes, plus chilling time
Serves: 8

**8 large pears**
**1 tablespoon lemon juice**
**1 litre/1$\frac{3}{4}$ pints unsweetened apple juice**
**about 375 g./12 oz. granulated sugar**
**2 sticks cinnamon**
**2 cloves**
**1 twist lemon peel**

Carefully peel the whole pears using a vegetable parer. To make them look more attractive, leave the stems on. As you finish peeling each pear place it in a bowl of water with lemon juice. Bring the apple juice, sugar, cinnamon sticks, cloves and lemon peel to the boil. Add the pears and cook, covered, over a medium heat for 15–20 minutes. (The timing will depend on just how ripe the pears are.) Test by lightly pricking one with a skewer. They should be firm in shape but yielding in texture when removed from the syrup. Bring the syrup to the boil and slightly reduce by boiling rapidly for 10 minutes before pouring over the pears. Chill lightly before serving with a jug of thick cream.

# Gooseberries in liqueur

*Illustrated opposite*
Preparation time: about 15 minutes, plus chilling time
Serves: 2–4

**500 g./1 lb. gooseberries**
**250 ml./$\frac{1}{2}$ pint water**
**125 g./4 oz. sugar**
**5 twists lemon peel**
**2 tablespoons orange liqueur**

Wash the gooseberries. Bring the water and sugar to the boil in a saucepan. Add the gooseberries and one of the lemon twists. Simmer for 8–10 minutes, until just soft. Chill, then spoon into individual glasses and top each with a lemon twist. Just before serving, trickle a little liqueur into each glass.
**Note** The flavour of gooseberries is delicate; adding just a little liqueur before serving enhances the flavour without masking it.

*Gooseberries in liqueur (see opposite)*

# Old-fashioned trifle

Preparation time: 15 minutes
Serves: 4–6

**1 large can pears**
**1 23-cm./9-inch sponge cake**
**4 tablespoons strawberry jam**
**1 tablespoon maraschino juice**
**5 tablespoons sherry**
**12 maraschino cherries, chopped**
**2 egg yolks**
**2 tablespoons castor sugar**
**250 ml./$\frac{1}{2}$ pint milk**
**250 ml./$\frac{1}{2}$ pint double cream**
**12 slices watermelon konfyt**
**2 tablespoons blanched, split almonds**

Drain and dice the pears, reserving the juice. Split the sponge cake in half and sandwich together with jam. Arrange in a shallow serving dish, mix the pear juice, maraschino juice and sherry and sprinkle over the cake. Top with the diced pears and cherries. Mix the egg yolks and sugar. Warm the milk and pour onto the yolks. Return to the pan and cook over low heat, stirring with a wooden spoon until thick – do not allow to boil. Strain into the dish and leave to cool and set. Whisk the cream and spread half over the top. Pipe or spoon on the remaining cream. Top with the watermelon konfyt and spike with almonds.
**Note** If watermelon konfyt is not available substitute glacé cherries and angelica, or crystallised violets and mimosa balls.

# Winter fruit medley

Preparation time: 10 minutes, plus overnight soaking, and chilling time
Serves: 10

**250 g./8 oz. dried apricots**
**250 g./8 oz. dried prunes**
**2 lemon twists**
**2 sticks cinnamon**
**$\frac{1}{2}$ teaspoon freshly grated nutmeg**
**5 oranges**
**5 bananas**
**2 tablespoons lemon juice**
**1 large can pineapple pieces**
**5 green apples**
**1 large can grapes**
**2 tablespoons orange liqueur**

Wash and soak the apricots and prunes separately overnight, covered. Place in separate saucepans with the water (to cover) in which they soaked and a twist of lemon, a cinnamon stick and $\frac{1}{4}$ teaspoon nutmeg to each pan. Bring to boil and cook for 5 minutes. Remove and cool. Peel and slice the oranges thinly. Peel and slice the bananas. Sprinkle with the lemon juice. Drain the pineapple pieces, reserving the juice. Slice the unpeeled apples thinly. Drain the grapes. Layer all the fruit into a glass bowl beginning with prunes and apricots and ending with grapes. Pour over 4 tablespoons of pineapple juice and the orange liqueur. Chill thoroughly before serving with vanilla cream (see below).
**Note** The apricots and prunes can be prepared in advance and stored in an airtight container in the refrigerator.

# Plums in liqueur

Preparation time: about 15 minutes, plus chilling time
Serves: 4–6

**12 large red sweet plums**
**500 ml./1 pint water**
**500 g./1 lb. sugar**
**2 tablespoons Kirsch**

*vanilla cream*
**250 ml./$\frac{1}{2}$ pint double cream**
**2 tablespoons icing sugar**
**1 teaspoon vanilla essence**

Wash the plums and place in a saucepan of boiling water for 1–2 minutes. Remove and peel off the skins. Bring the water and sugar to the boil in a saucepan. Add the plums and cook for 2–4 minutes, until just soft. Remove, and place in a bowl. Continue boiling the syrup until it has reduced by half then blend in the Kirsch. Pour over the plums and leave to chill.

Meanwhile make the vanilla cream. Whisk the cream in a bowl with the icing sugar. Fold in the vanilla essence. (Try to use a balloon whisk rather than a mixer or beater for whipping cream as it makes a far lighter whipped cream.)

# Liqueur custard

Preparation time: 20 minutes, plus chilling time
Serves: 4–6

**4 egg yolks**
**6 tablespoons sugar**
**3 tablespoons flour**
**500 ml./1 pint milk**
**1½ tablespoons orange-flavoured liqueur**
**1 teaspoon grated lemon rind**
**125 ml./¼ pint double cream**
**1 tablespoon icing sugar**
**1 tablespoon thin chocolate-coated orange peel strips (see page 158) or blanched almonds**

Whisk the egg yolks in a bowl with the sugar and flour until thick and pale. Heat the milk in a saucepan; when warm, whisk very slowly into the egg mixture. Return the blended custard to the pan and cook over low heat until it thickens and nearly reaches boiling point, stirring constantly using a wooden spoon. Remove from the heat and add 1 tablespoon orange liqueur and the lemon rind. Leave to cool, stirring from time to time, then pour into a glass serving bowl. Whisk the cream in a bowl with icing sugar. When it forms soft peaks, fold in the remaining orange liqueur. Fill an icing bag and edge the bowl with orange cream rosettes and place the chocolate-coated orange peel strips or almonds on the cream rosettes.

# Rosy pears with vanilla cream

Preparation time: 15 minutes, plus chilling time
Cooking time: about 3 hours
Oven temperature: cool (300°F., 150°C., Gas Mark 2)
Serves: 4–6

**6 firm pears**
**250 ml./½ pint water**
**250 g./8 oz. brown or white sugar**
**2 sticks cinnamon**
**3 cloves**
**1 twist lemon peel**
**250 ml./½ pint heavy red wine**

Peel the pears leaving on the stems. Combine the water, sugar, cinnamon sticks, cloves and lemon peel in a saucepan. Bring to the boil and simmer for 5–8 minutes, then add the wine. Place the pears in a small deep ovenproof dish and pour over the sugar and wine syrup. Cover with a lid or foil and bake in a cool oven for 2–3 hours, until pears are transparent and tender and the wine a rich colour. Serve lightly chilled in a china bowl with a fresh spiral of lemon peel on the top. Whipped vanilla cream (see page 110) goes particularly well with these pears.
**Note** Brown sugar gives a rich, deep-crimson colour; white sugar gives a pinky-red translucent look. The pears may be divided into two portions using one kind of sugar for each. Blend the pears together in the bowl before serving.

# Fresh pineapple in vanilla syrup

Preparation time: 15 minutes, plus chilling time
Serves: 4

**1 fresh pineapple**
**125 g./4 oz. vanilla sugar**
**2 tablespoons water**

Cut away the skin of the pineapple and slice the fruit into thick half-moon wedges. Place the vanilla sugar in a saucepan with the water. Allow to boil until it reaches firm ball stage (118°C., 213°F.); when a drop of the sugar syrup is poured into a glass of cold water it will form a ball instantly between your fingers. Spoon over the pineapple slices. Chill well before serving.
**Note** This would be ideal to take on a picnic. Pack the chilled fruit and syrup in an insulated container.

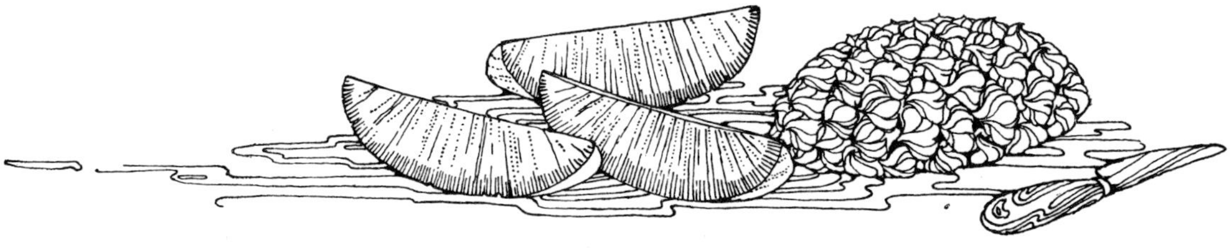

*Fair Lady pashka (see page 118)*

*Oranges and litchis (see page 115)*

# Ice-creams

## Youngberry ice

Preparation time: 20 minutes, plus freezing time
Serves: 4–6

**250 g./8 oz. sugar**
**500 ml./1 pint water**
**500 g./1 lb. fresh youngberries, loganberries or raspberries**
**2 tablespoons bottled youngberry or raspberry syrup**
**6 lemons**
**double cream to decorate**

Combine the sugar and water in a saucepan. Boil for 5 minutes. Add the well washed youngberries and youngberry syrup and simmer for 10–15 minutes. Remove and strain the syrup into a bowl, pressing through all the juices from the berries. Squeeze the lemons and strain the juice. Combine with the youngberry syrup. Pour into refrigerator trays. Cover with aluminium foil and freeze until it forms a granular mass. To serve, spoon into glasses and pipe whipped cream around the edges.

## Coffee ice-cream

Preparation time: 10 minutes, plus freezing time
Serves: 4

**2 eggs, separated**
**4 tablespoons icing sugar, sieved**
**2 tablespoons coffee essence**
**125 ml./$\frac{1}{4}$ pint double cream**

Beat the egg whites until very stiff, then gradually fold in the icing sugar. Whisk the yolks and coffee essence together and add to the whites, a little at a time, beating gently. Whip the cream lightly and fold into the mixture. Place in ice trays and freeze until thick. (This ice-cream does not need any further beating.) To serve, spoon into a bowl. Sprinkle with cocoa powder and pour a little single cream over the top.

## Honey-orange ice-cream

Preparation time: 5 minutes, plus freezing time
Serves: 4–6

**500 ml./1 pint double cream**
**5 tablespoons honey**
**1 teaspoon grated orange rind**
**pinch salt**
**$\frac{1}{2}$ teaspoon almond essence**
**5 tablespoons toasted almonds**

Beat the cream until slightly thickened. Gradually fold in the honey and beat until well blended. Add the grated rind, salt and almond essence. Spoon into a refrigerator tray, cover with wax or greaseproof paper and freeze for 1 hour. Remove and beat with a wooden spoon for 1–2 minutes. Mix in the almonds, return to the tray and re-cover with the paper. Freeze until solid. Using an ice-cream scoop, scoop out small balls and serve in hollowed-out melon shells.

## Ice-cream bombe praline

*Illustrated on page 144*
Preparation time: 10 minutes, plus freezing time
Serves: 4–6

**500 ml./1 pint double cream**
**250 g./ 8 oz. sugar**
**500 ml./ 1 pint milk**
**praline (see page 115)**
**whipped cream to decorate (optional)**

Whisk the cream and sugar together in a bowl until thick and creamy. Add the milk. Pour into a round airtight mould. Freeze, covered, until the mixture is half solid. Fold in three-quarters of the praline; beat the mixture for 5 minutes with a wooden spoon. Cover and freeze until solid. Before serving, turn out onto a dish a little larger than the mould. Pipe with rosettes of whipped cream, if liked, and sprinkle with remaining praline.

**Note** When serving ice-cream or any other frozen sweet, it is quite a good idea to unmould it onto the serving dish ahead of time. Cover completely with foil and replace in the freezer until needed.

# French chocolate ice-cream (made in a blender)

Preparation time: 10 minutes, plus freezing time
Makes: 1 litre ($1\frac{3}{4}$ pints)

**4 tablespoons sugar**
**8 tablespoons water**
**250 g./8 oz. bitter chocolate**
**3 egg yolks**
**375 ml./ generous $\frac{1}{2}$ pint double cream**
**4 tablespoons chopped walnuts**
**8 crystallised violets**

Mix the sugar and water in a saucepan. Bring to the boil and cook rapidly for 3 minutes. Place the chocolate, broken up, and the slightly cooled syrup into the blender. Cover and blend at high speed for 6 seconds, or until the chocolate mixture is smooth. Add the egg yolks and blend at high speed for 5 seconds, or until well blended. Whisk the cream in a bowl until thick. Fold into the chocolate mixture. Spoon the mixture into a round airtight container. Cover and freeze for 3–4 hours. To serve, turn onto a chilled plate well in advance. Cover with foil and return to the freezer until needed. Decorate with walnuts and crystallised violets.

# Orange baskets

*Illustrated on page 105*
Preparation time: 15 minutes, plus chilling time
Serves: 4

**4 oranges**
**2 egg yolks**
**about 2 teaspoons sugar**
**2 tablespoons frozen orange concentrate**
**125 ml./$\frac{1}{4}$ pint double cream or cream substitute**
**1 teaspoon grated orange rind**

Slice the tops off the oranges, hollow out carefully using a sharp knife. Reserve the flesh for a fruit salad. Whisk the egg yolks and sugar until thick and pale. Whisk in the frozen orange concentrate. Whisk the cream until thick. Blend into the egg mixture. Spoon or pipe into the orange cases. Sprinkle tops with orange rind and chill for 2 hours before serving. Serve with meringue fingers or sponge finger biscuits.

# Oranges and litchis

*Illustrated on page 113*
Preparation time: 5 minutes, plus chilling time
Serves: 4

**4 oranges**
**4 pieces preserved ginger**
**1 medium-sized can litchis**
**1 small can granadilla or passion fruit pulp**

Peel the oranges and remove all pith. Slice the ginger thinly. Place the oranges in a glass bowl and sprinkle with the ginger. Add the litchis and syrup. Spoon over the granadilla or passion fruit pulp. Top with mint, if liked, and chill for 1–2 hours before serving.

# Praline

Preparation time: about 15 minutes
Cooking time: about 5 minutes
Oven temperature: moderate (350°F., 180°C., Gas Mark 4)

**110 g./4 oz. almonds**
**110 g./4 oz. sugar**
**3 tablespoons water**

Arrange the almonds in a shallow ovenproof dish. Bake in a moderate oven until browned and crisp. Cool and chop finely. Place the sugar and water in a saucepan. Swirl the pan over a moderately high heat until the sugar has dissolved completely. Then allow mixture to boil, without stirring, until the syrup turns a light golden brown, 3–4 minutes. Stir in the chopped almonds and pour onto an oiled baking sheet. Leave to cool and set. Chop in a liquidiser, or use a mallet. This mixture may be made in larger quantities and kept in an airtight container for use on cakes, puddings or ice-cream.

*Crêpes with cherries, blintzes (see pages 122, 123)*

*Puffy pancakes with assorted fillings (see page 123)*

# Fair Lady pashka

*Illustrated on page 112*
Preparation time: 15 minutes, plus overnight standing
Serves: 6–8

**3 egg yolks**
**250 g./8 oz. sugar**
**125 ml./$\frac{1}{4}$ pint milk**
**$\frac{1}{2}$ teaspoon vanilla essence**
**125 g./ 4 oz. butter**
**750 g./1$\frac{1}{2}$ lb. cottage cheese**
**1 tablespoon currants**
**1 teaspoon grated lemon rind**
**2 tablespoons finely chopped almonds**
**125 ml./$\frac{1}{4}$ pint double cream**

Beat the egg yolks with half the sugar until white and fluffy. Add the milk and vanilla essence. Cook in a double boiler until the mixture thickens. Remove from the heat, add the butter in very small pieces and allow it to melt. Cool. Sieve the cheese into a large bowl. Mix in the cooled custard and the remainder of the sugar. Add the currants, lemon rind and almonds. Whip the cream and add, mixing well. Line a large clean flower pot with a hole in the base with a double layer of wet muslin. (Alternatively, use a shaped foil container with a hole made in the base.) Spoon in the pashka, packing it in firmly, and fold the muslin over the top. Stand the flower pot over a dish to catch the liquid that drains away and place a plate with a small weight on top of the muslin. Leave in a cool place to drain overnight. On the following day, turn the pashka out onto a large dish and decorate with almonds, currants, angelica and sultanas.

# Cherry custard flan

Preparation time: 20 minutes
Cooking time: about 12 minutes
Oven temperature: moderately hot (375°F., 190°C., Gas Mark 5)
Serves: 6–8

**8 tablespoons flour**
**pinch salt**
**1 teaspoon baking powder**
**4 tablespoons milk**
**1 tablespoon/$\frac{1}{2}$ oz. butter**
**1 large egg**
**6 tablespoons castor sugar**
**$\frac{1}{4}$ teaspoon vanilla essence**
*custard cream base*
**2 large egg yolks**
**2 tablespoons sugar**
**2 tablespoons flour**
**250 ml./$\frac{1}{2}$ pint milk**
**1 teaspoon vanilla essence**
*cherry filling*
**2 large cans stoned cherries**
**1 dessertspoon custard powder**
**1 tablespoon water**
**2 tablespoons cherry cordial**

Sift the flour, salt and baking powder together twice. Bring the milk and butter to the boil in a saucepan. Whisk the egg and castor sugar together in a bowl until thick and fluffy. Fold the dry ingredients into the whisked egg mixture using a spatula. Add the boiling milk and butter together with the vanilla essence. Fold in thoroughly. Pour into a 26-cm. (10-inch) flan tin and bake in a moderately hot oven for 10–12 minutes. Remove, cool and turn out onto a wire rack.

Whisk the egg yolks and sugar together in a bowl for 1 minute. Add the flour, blend and pour in the milk and vanilla essence. Pour into a double boiler. Place over a moderate heat and stir continuously until the cream thickens. Remove and beat for 2–3 minutes. Chill for 12–15 minutes. Using a spatula, smooth into the sponge flan case.

Drain the cherries, reserving the liquid from one of the cans. Arrange on the custard cream. Mix the custard powder in a cup with water until smooth. Pour the cherry liquid into a saucepan. Add the custard powder and cherry cordial (or use extra liquid from the canned cherries). Bring to the boil stirring constantly. Spoon over the cherries while hot and chill lightly before serving.

# Hot puddings

## Golden cobbler

Preparation time: 20 minutes
Cooking time: about 40 minutes
Oven temperature: moderately hot (400°F., 200°C., Gas Mark 6) reducing to 375°F., 190°C., Gas Mark 5
Serves: 4–6

**125 g./4 oz. butter**
**125 g./4 oz. cake or plain flour**
**1 teaspoon baking powder**
**$\frac{1}{2}$ teaspoon salt**
**1 tablespoon sugar**
**2 egg yolks**
**$2\frac{1}{2}$ tablespoons rich milk**
**6 yellow peaches**
*topping*
**125 g./4 oz. sugar**
**8 tablespoons flour**
**pinch cinnamon**
**3 tablespoons/$1\frac{1}{2}$ oz. butter**

Cream the 125 g. (4 oz.) butter until light and fluffy. Combine the flour, baking powder, salt and 1 tablespoon sugar. Sift twice then add to the creamed butter using a wooden spoon. Whisk the egg yolks together with the milk and stir into flour mixture. Spread into a buttered 23-cm. (9-inch) cake tin. Peel and slice the peaches into crescents. Layer over the cake mixture. Mix together the sugar, flour and cinnamon. Rub in the butter until the mixture is like coarse crumbs. Sprinkle over the top of the peaches. Bake in a moderately hot oven for about 40 minutes (reducing the temperature after 30 minutes), until the topping is golden brown.

## Brandied apples

Preparation time: 5 minutes
Cooking time: 40 minutes
Oven temperature: moderate (350°F., 180°C., Gas Mark 4)
Serves: 6

**6 large cooking apples**
**3 tablespoons raisins**
**2 tablespoons sultanas**
**4 tablespoons brown sugar**
**250 ml./$\frac{1}{2}$ pint white wine**
**2 tablespoons water**
**3 teaspoons sugar**
**3 tablespoons brandy**
**1 lump sugar**

Peel and core the apples and place in a buttered ovenproof dish. Fill the centres with a mixture of raisins and sultanas. Sprinkle with brown sugar. Pour over the white wine and water. Bake in a moderate oven for 40 minutes, or until apples are tender. Place on a hot serving dish with any cooking liquid. Sprinkle each apple with $\frac{1}{2}$ teaspoon white sugar and $\frac{1}{2}$ teaspoon brandy. Place the lump of sugar in a heated ladle. Add the remaining brandy, ignite and pour the flaming brandy over the apples. Serve with custard.

## Apples in 'kerchiefs

*Illustrated on page 80*
Preparation time: 15 minutes
Cooking time: about 30 minutes
Oven temperature: moderately hot (400°F., 200°C., Gas Mark 6)
Serves: 4

**4 medium-sized cooking apples**
**4 teaspoons brown sugar**
**4 teaspoons honey**
**2 teaspoons sultanas**
**2 teaspoons lemon juice**
**pinch nutmeg**
**$\frac{1}{4}$ teaspoon cinnamon**
**375 g./12 oz. ready-made flaky pastry**
**1 egg yolk**

Peel and core the apples. Place a teaspoon of the sugar in each cavity and trickle over the honey and add the sultanas. Sprinkle with lemon juice, nutmeg and cinnamon. Roll out the pastry 6 mm. ($\frac{1}{4}$ inch) thick on a lightly floured board. Cut into four squares, each large enough to completely enclose an apple. Place an apple in the centre of each square and using a sharp knife, round the pastry on each of the corners. Dampen the edges and bring them up to enclose the apple. Secure the top with twine. Make pastry decorations from the trimmings and place on the top, securing with a little beaten egg yolk. Place on a baking sheet and brush with beaten egg yolk. Bake in a moderately hot oven for 30 minutes, until the pastry is cooked Serve with thick unsweetened cream.

# Rum bananas

Preparation time: 5 minutes
Cooking time: about 15 minutes
Oven temperature: moderate (350°F., 180°C., Gas Mark 4)
Serves: 4–6

**6 medium-sized bananas**
**juice of 2 oranges**
**4 tablespoons brown sugar**
**½ teaspoon cinnamon**
**pinch nutmeg**
**6 tablespoons rum**
**2 tablespoons/1 oz. butter**

Peel the bananas and split them in half lengthways. Place in a buttered ovenproof dish and pour over the orange juice mixed with the sugar, cinnamon, nutmeg and 2 tablespoons of the rum. Dot with a few small pieces of butter and bake in a moderate oven for 10–15 minutes, until the bananas are tender, basting once or twice during cooking. Remove from the oven, sprinkle with the remaining rum, warmed. Serve with ice-cream or cream.

# Christmas pudding

*Illustrated opposite*
Preparation time: 30 minutes, plus overnight standing
Cooking time: 8 hours, plus 2 hours before serving
Makes: 2 puddings

**125 g./4 oz. currants**
**125 g./4 oz. seedless raisins**
**125 g./4 oz. sultanas**
**4 green figs, finely chopped**
**2 large pieces watermelon konfyt, finely chopped (optional)**
**125 g./4 oz. mixed candied fruit**
**128 g./4 oz. glacé cherries**
**125 g./4 oz. blanched almonds, slivered**
**1 tart apple, coarsely chopped**
**½ carrot, grated**
**2 teaspoons finely grated orange rind**
**1 teaspoon finely grated lemon rind**
**125 g./ 4 oz. finely chopped or shredded beef suet**
**125 g./4 oz. cake or plain flour**
**30 g./1 oz. fresh white breadcrumbs**
**125 g./4 oz. soft brown sugar**
**1 teaspoon mixed spice**
**½ teaspoon freshly grated nutmeg**
**½ teaspoon cinnamon**
**3 standard eggs**
**1 tablespoon orange marmalade**
**4 tablespoons stout**
**8 tablespoons brandy**
**2 tablespoons fresh orange juice**
**1 tablespoon lemon juice**

Place the currants, raisins, sultanas, chopped figs, watermelon konfyt (if used), candied fruit, cherries, almonds, apple, carrot, orange and lemon rinds and beef suet into a large bowl. Blend well. Stir in the flour, breadcrumbs, brown sugar and spices. Whisk the eggs in a separate bowl until frothy then stir in the marmalade, stout, 2 tablespoons of the brandy, the orange and lemon juice. Pour the mixture over the fruit. Mix well with the hands then beat with a wooden spoon until well blended. The longer the mixture is stirred the better. Cover the bowl with a damp cloth and leave overnight. The next morning, stir the mixture again before spooning into two well buttered basins. Fill each one three-quarters full, pressing the mixture down well to prevent air holes. Butter three thicknesses of wax or greaseproof paper and place, buttered side down, over the pudding basins to cover completely. Tie down tightly with string under the rim. Trim off the edges of the paper. Over the paper covers tie a double thickness of foil. Steam in a large heavy saucepan filled with fast boiling water, enough to reach halfway up the sides of the pudding basins, which must be placed side by side in one pan, or steamed in separate pans. Cover the pan with a well fitting lid. Keep the water gently but steadily boiling for the whole of the cooking time, adding more *boiling* water when necessary. Steam for 8 hours. Lift the basins out of the water and leave to cool. Remove the wrappings and re-cover with fresh foil. Store for at least 3 weeks before serving. To reheat, place the basins in a pan. Pour in enough boiling water to reach three-quarters of the way up the sides of each. Bring to the boil and cover. Reduce the heat to low and steam for 2 hours. Remove the basins from the water. Remove the foil. Loosen the puddings around the edges with a thin bladed knife. Hold a warm serving dish on top of the pudding basin and holding the two firmly, turn over. Top with a sprig of holly. To flame, pour the remaining brandy into a heated silver ladle and ignite with a match. Pour it flaming over the pudding.

*Christmas pudding (see opposite)*

# Basic pancake batter

Preparation time: 5 minutes
Cooking time: few minutes for each pancake
Makes: about 12 pancakes

**125 g./4 oz. flour**
**pinch salt**
**1 extra large egg**
**375 ml./generous $\frac{1}{2}$ pint milk**
**2 tablespoons/1 oz. butter or salad oil**
**oil for frying**

Sieve the flour and salt into a basin. Make a well in the centre, add the egg and gradually stir in the milk. Using an egg beater, mixer or wooden spoon, beat well until the mixture is smooth. Fold in the melted butter or oil. Using a 12-, 15-, or 17-cm. (5-, 6- or 7-inch) heavy-based frying pan (depending on the size of pancakes required), just cover the base with oil, pouring off the surplus into a jug to keep for further greasing. When the oil begins to smoke, remove the pan from the heat and allow the oil to cool slightly before pouring in the mixture. Pancakes must be paper-thin, so add only about a tablespoon of batter at a time, tilting the pan quickly for even spreading. Cook for 1–2 minutes, until slightly bubbling; loosen the edges of the pancake gently with a metal spatula and flip over to brown the other side.

# Banana and Curaçao crêpes

Preparation time: 20 minutes
Cooking time: 10 minutes
Oven temperature: moderate (350°F., 180°C., Gas Mark 4)
Serves: 4–6

**1 large or 2 small bananas per crêpe**
**125 g./4 oz. butter**
**125 g./4 oz. castor sugar**
**basic pancake batter (see above)**
**4 tablespoons Curaçao**
**chopped walnuts to decorate**

Peel and slice the bananas and sauté in a pan with the butter. Add the sugar and blend together well. When the bananas are soft, rub them through a coarse sieve. Make paper-thin pancakes with the batter (see above). Spread out the pancakes and sprinkle with Curaçao. Place 3 tablespoons of filling down the centre of each pancake and fold to form a roll. Place in an ovenproof dish and heat in a moderate oven for 10 minutes. Sprinkle with chopped walnuts and serve with vanilla ice-cream.

# Crêpes with cherries

*Illustrated on page 116*
Preparation time: 15 minutes
Cooking time: 8 minutes
Oven temperature: moderate (350°F., 180°C., Gas Mark 4)
Serves: 6–7

**14 crêpes (made from basic pancake batter, see above)**
*filling*
**1 450-g./1-lb. can stoned black or red cherries**
**4 tablespoons/2 oz. butter**
**4 tablespoons lemon juice**
**1 teaspoon cinnamon**
**$\frac{1}{4}$ teaspoon nutmeg**
**2 tablespoons brandy**
**250 ml./$\frac{1}{2}$ pint cherry juice**
**2 teaspoons cornflour**
**3 tablespoons sugar**
*ice-cream sauce*
**1 small block vanilla ice-cream**
**125 ml./$\frac{1}{4}$ pint double cream, whipped**
**1 teaspoon vanilla essence**

Drain the cherries. Place the butter in a frying pan and when moderately hot add the cherries, lemon juice, cinnamon, nutmeg, brandy and most of the cherry juice. Mix the cornflour with the reserved cherry juice and add to the pan, stirring gently until the mixture thickens slightly. Cool. Put 3 tablespoons filling on each crêpe. Fold over the ends to cover, and form a roll. Place in an ovenproof dish, sprinkle with sugar and bake in a moderate oven for 8 minutes. When piping hot, grill to lightly crisp the tops of the crêpes. If liked, serve topped with a little ice-cream sauce made by blending the ingredients together.

For an alternative way of serving the crêpes, fold the cooked hot crêpes into triangles and place on a serving dish. Spoon the cherry filling into the centre of the dish.

**Note** If stoned cherries are not available remove each stone by inserting the round end of a hairpin into the cherry and twisting stone out.

# Blintzes

*Illustrated on page 116*
Preparation time: 10 minutes
Cooking time: about 12 minutes
Oven temperature: moderate (350°F., 180°C., Gas Mark 4)
Makes: 8–10 blintzes

**basic pancake batter (see page 122)**
**375 g./12 oz. cottage cheese**
**2 eggs**
**125 ml./$\frac{1}{4}$ pint cream**
**2 tablespoons sugar**
**pinch salt**
**1 teaspoon vanilla essence**
**1 tablespoon raisins**
**4 tablespoons/2 oz. butter**
**1 teaspoon cinnamon or 2 sticks cinnamon**
**2 tablespoons sugar**

Make the pancakes, cooking on one side only, and stack brown side up. Mix the cottage cheese, eggs, cream, sugar, salt, vanilla essence and raisins together and blend well. Place a tablespoon of the filling on the cooked side of each pancake and fold both sides of the crêpes over the filling to the centre to look like small envelopes. Heat the butter in the pan and fry blintzes until golden brown. Arrange on a heated serving dish; dust with cinnamon (or decorate with cinnamon sticks) and sprinkle with sugar. Serve with sour cream.

For a richer version (as shown in the picture), place the filled (unfried) pancakes in a buttered ovenproof dish, pour over 280 ml. ($\frac{1}{2}$ pint) cream mixed with sugar, a little cottage cheese and cinnamon. Bake in a moderate oven for 10–12 minutes.

# Puffy pancakes with assorted fillings

*Illustrated on page 117*
Preparation time: 5 minutes
Cooking time: few minutes for each pancake
Makes: 30 35 pancakes

For a party sweet, let guests choose their own pancake filling. Have little dishes and pots filled with chopped walnuts, honey, whipped cream, fried bananas, chocolate and caramel sauce plus hot cherries.

**3 egg yolks**
**$\frac{1}{2}$ teaspoon salt**
**$\frac{1}{2}$ teaspoon finely grated orange rind**
**250 g./8 oz. flour**
**pinch salt**
**500 ml./1 pint milk**
**3 egg whites**
**butter**

Beat the yolks, $\frac{1}{2}$ teaspoon salt and orange rind together. Sift the flour with a pinch of salt; gradually add the milk, beating until smooth, to form a mixture the consistency of thick cream. Beat in the egg yolk mixture, then strain the mixture through a fine sieve. Beat the egg whites stiffly and fold in. Heat a 15-cm. (6-inch) light frying pan, remove from the heat, brush with butter, and pour in enough batter to spread and cover the surface of the pan. Cook on high heat until the edges of the pancake curl slightly. Lower the heat and cook very gently until lightly browned and puffed. Turn and cook for 1 minute on the other side. Serve at once with a selection of the suggested fillings.

# Baking

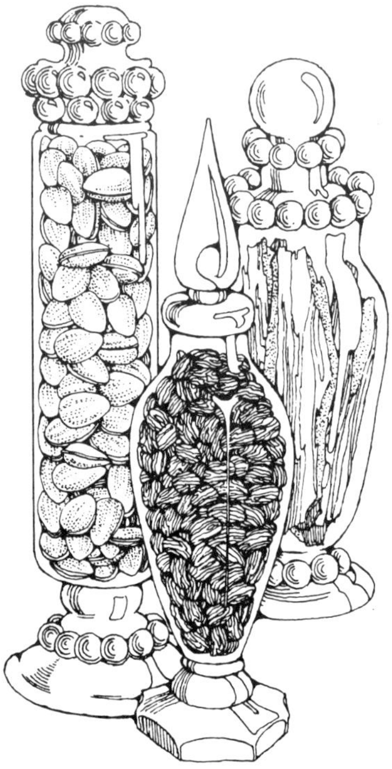

There is a never-ending glow of satisfaction at the sight of a perfect cake or a golden crusty loaf, and what is nicer than a cosy kitchen and enticing aromas for the family to come home to.

Have a baking day and fill up your biscuit jars, cake tins and freezer. Scones, milk breads, biscuits, sponge cakes all freeze outstandingly well and are ready in a trice. Pastry cases and sponge flans can be stacked waiting for fruit fillings – apple with lemon curd, plums and cherries with custard cream. Pound cakes, chocolate and vanilla are the basic beginnings for luscious flavourings and toppings – lemon frosting, rum cream or chocolate. On rainy days prepare and store spiced nuts, vanilla and citrus sugars, glacé fruits and praline in large glass jars – just to add that final touch.

Good-looking dishes to have: a large round flat dish, suitable for tarts and flans; wicker baskets for scones; an old-fashioned cake stand; jars, glass or pottery, for biscuits.

## Raisin tea cake

*Illustrated on opposite page*
Preparation time: 10 minutes
Cooking time: about 1 hour
Oven temperature: moderate (325°F., 170°C., Gas Mark 3)

**250 g./8 oz. flour**
**1 teaspoon baking powder**
**$\frac{1}{4}$ teaspoon bicarbonate of soda**
**$\frac{1}{2}$ teaspoon salt**
**170 g./6 oz. butter or vegetable fat**
**250 g./8 oz. light brown sugar**
**4 eggs**
**125 g./4 oz. walnuts, finely chopped**
**125 g./4 oz. raisins**
**1 teaspoon vanilla essence**

Sift the flour, baking powder, soda and salt together. Cream the butter or fat until light and fluffy. Gradually beat in the sugar. Whisk in the eggs, one at a time, beating well after each addition and adding a little of the sifted flour mixture. Fold in the remaining flour mixture. Add the nuts, raisins and essence and blend thoroughly. Spoon into a lined 20-cm. (8-inch) round cake tin, or a ring tin and bake in a moderate oven for about 1 hour, until the cake is firm and golden. Cool on a wire rack and dust with icing sugar before serving.

*Raisin tea cake (see opposite)*

# Granny's gingerbread

Preparation time: 10 minutes
Cooking time: about 50 minutes
Oven temperature: moderate (325°F., 170°C., Gas Mark 3)

**250 g./8 oz. cake or plain flour**
**2 teaspoons baking powder**
**$\frac{1}{4}$ teaspoon bicarbonate of soda**
**$\frac{1}{2}$ teaspoon salt**
**$1\frac{1}{2}$ teaspoons ginger**
**1 teaspoon cinnamon**
**5 tablespoons/$2\frac{1}{2}$ oz. butter**
**125 g./4 oz. castor sugar**
**1 egg**
**10 tablespoons light molasses or golden syrup**
**12 tablespoons sour milk or buttermilk**

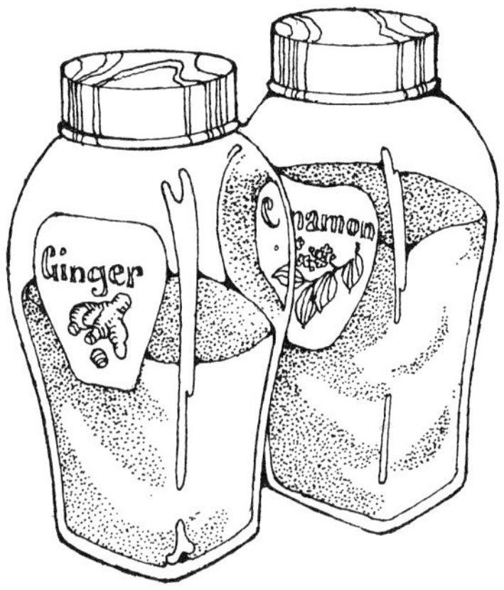


Sift the flour, baking powder, soda, salt and spices twice. Cream the butter and sugar until light and fluffy. Add the dry ingredients, blending well. Beat the egg thoroughly and add the molasses or golden syrup. Pour into the dry ingredients alternating with the sour milk or buttermilk. After each addition, stir just enough to blend thoroughly. Pour into a greased oblong tin, 20 cm. by 5 cm. (or use an 8-inch square tin). Bake in a moderate oven for about 50 minutes, until firm. Remove and cool on a wire rack. Store in an airtight polythene container.

# Lemon-frosted pound cake

*Illustrated on page 128*
Preparation time: 20 minutes
Cooking time: about $1\frac{3}{4}$ hours
Oven temperature: cool (300°F., 150°C., Gas Mark 3)

**250 g./8 oz. butter or vegetable fat**
**250 g./8 oz. castor sugar**
**1 teaspoon grated lemon rind**
**4 large eggs**
**375 g./12 oz. flour**
**2 teaspoons baking powder**
**$\frac{1}{2}$ teaspoon salt**
**250 ml./$\frac{1}{2}$ pint milk**
*frosting*
**juice of 1 large lemon**
**125 g./4 oz. icing sugar, sieved**
*decoration*
**strips lemon rind**

Cream the butter or fat until soft and fluffy. Gradually add the sugar and beat together until light and creamy. Mix in the lemon rind. Add the eggs, one at a time, beating for 1 minute after each addition. Sift together the flour, baking powder and salt. Add the milk, alternating with the flour mixture, to the butter mixture, beginning and ending with the dry ingredients. Pour into a well buttered and floured 25-cm. (10-inch) cake tin, either round or square, or a ring tin. Bake in a cool oven for about $1\frac{3}{4}$ hours. When firm and golden remove from the oven. Blend the lemon juice and sugar together. Turn the cake onto a wire rack and pour the frosting over the hot cake. Decorate with strips of lemon rind.

**Variations**
This cake is also very good with a glistening chocolate frosting. Use orange rind and juice in place of the lemon rind and juice, which complements the chocolate flavour, or substitute 1 teaspoon vanilla essence. If using the orange-chocolate flavour, add 1 teaspoon grated orange rind to the chocolate frosting to heighten the flavour.
**Chocolate frosting** Place 4 tablespoons (2 oz.) butter or vegetable fat in a saucepan. Sift together 250 g. (8 oz.) icing sugar and 2 tablespoons cocoa powder. Add with 1 tablespoon water and 1 tablespoon brandy to the pan. Heat together until dissolved, creamy and glistening. Turn off the heat, but keep the frosting warm while it is being spooned over the cake as it sets very quickly.

To make a chocolate pound cake as illustrated on page 128 use 50 g. (2 oz.) cocoa powder in place of the same amount of flour; omit the lemon rind. Bake the mixture in a fluted ring tin and sprinkle sifted icing sugar over the top of the cooled cake.

# Chocolate pound gâteau with rum cream

*Illustrated on page 129*
Preparation time: 15 minutes
Cooking time: $1\frac{1}{2}$ hours
Oven temperature: moderate (350°F., 180°C., Gas Mark 4)

**125 g./4 oz. cocoa powder or chocolate, melted**
**375 g./12 oz. flour**
**375 g./12 oz. castor sugar**
**3 teaspoons baking powder**
**1 teaspoon salt**
**250 g./8 oz. soft butter or vegetable fat**
**375 ml./generous $\frac{1}{2}$ pint milk**
**3 teaspoons vanilla essence**
**3 large eggs**
**4 tablespoons single cream**

*rum cream*
**250 ml./$\frac{1}{2}$ pint double cream**
**5 teaspoons icing sugar**
**5 teaspoons rum**

*decoration*
**1 slab bitter chocolate**
**few walnuts, chopped**

Blend the cocoa powder with 4 tablespoons hot water and leave to cool. Sift the flour, sugar, baking powder and salt together in the large bowl of an electric mixer. Make a well in the centre. Add the butter, milk and vanilla essence. Beat for 5 minutes. Add the blended cocoa powder or melted chocolate; add the eggs, one at a time, beating well after each addition. Add the cream and beat for 1 minute. Pour into a well oiled 25-cm. (10-inch) square tin, or a tube tin. Bake in a moderate oven for $1\frac{1}{2}$ hours. Test by inserting a thin skewer which should come out clean. Cool the cake completely before removing from the tin.

Pour the cream into a bowl. Sift in the icing sugar and whisk until the mixture forms soft peaks. Fold in the rum.

Melt the chocolate in the top of a double boiler. Pour out onto a flat dish or marble slab to cool. Before the chocolate hardens and is still pliable, draw a knife or vegetable parer across the top, scraping it forward to form the curl.

Pipe or spoon the rum cream over the cake and top with chocolate curls and chopped walnuts.

# Lemon cheese cake in a nut crust

Preparation time: 15 minutes
Cooking time: about 1 hour
Oven temperature: moderate (350°F., 180°C., Gas Mark 4) reducing to 325°F., 170°C., Gas Mark 3
Serves: 6–8

*crust*
**125 g./4 oz. Brazil nuts, chopped**
**3 tablespoons sugar**
**2 tablespoons flour**
**pinch salt**
**3 tablespoons/$1\frac{1}{2}$ oz. butter, melted**

*filling*
**375 g./12 oz. homogenised or crumbly cream cheese**
**$1\frac{1}{2}$ teaspoons vanilla essence**
**pinch salt**
**2 eggs**
**125 g./4 oz. castor sugar**
**2 tablespoons double cream**
**2 tablespoons currants**
**3 teaspoons finely grated lemon rind**

Mix together the Brazil nuts, sugar, flour, salt and melted butter. When well blended, press the mixture over the base of a 20-cm. (8-inch) spring form tin or fluted flan dish. Bake in a moderate oven for 10–12 minutes, until golden. Reduce the oven temperature. Allow to cool.

Beat the cheese in a bowl with the vanilla and salt until smooth. Beat the eggs in a bowl with the sugar until thick and light in colour. Add the egg mixture to the cheese with the cream and blend well. Fold in the currants and lemon rind. Spoon into the spring form tin or flan dish and bake in the oven for about 45 minutes, until the filling has set. Turn off the oven, open the door slightly; leave the cheese cake in the oven for 30 minutes. Cool thoroughly (out of the spring form tin) and serve at room temperature.

*Chocolate pound cake, lemon-frosted pound cake (see page 126)*

*Chocolate pound gâteau with rum cream* *(see page 127)*

# Apricot cream tartlets

*Illustrated on page 132*
Preparation time: 20 minutes, plus chilling time
Cooking time: about 15 minutes
Oven temperature: moderately hot (400°F., 200°C., Gas Mark 6)
Makes: 12 apricot cream tartlets

*tart pastry*
**125 g./4 oz. flour**
**1 egg yolk**
**1 tablespoon castor sugar**
**8 tablespoons/4 oz. soft butter**
**grated rind of 1 lemon**
**pinch salt**
*filling*
**5 tablespoons brown sugar**
**2 tablespoons cornflour**
**250 ml./$\frac{1}{2}$ pint apricot juice**
**2 tablespoons/1 oz. butter**
**250 g./8 oz. cream cheese**
**2 tablespoons rum or 1 tablespoon apricot or orange liqueur**
**1 tablespoon fresh orange juice**
**12 apricot halves, canned or cooked**
**250 ml./$\frac{1}{2}$ pint cream**

Sift the flour into a bowl. Make a well in the centre. Add the egg yolk, sugar, butter, lemon rind and salt. Mix these centre ingredients with one hand into a smooth paste. Quickly work in the flour. Add a few teaspoons ice cold water if needed to moisten the dough just enough to gather it together. Wrap in greaseproof or wax paper and chill for 1–2 hours. Roll out the chilled dough to about 3 mm. ($\frac{1}{8}$ inch) in thickness. Cut into twelve circles, a little larger than tartlet tins. Grease the tins and line each one with a pastry circle. Trim the edges of the pastry circles to about $1\frac{1}{4}$ cm. ($\frac{3}{4}$ inch) beyond the edge of each tin. Moisten the rims of each tin with a little cold water. Fold the overlapping edge back and flute with your fingertips or press with a fork. Prick small holes lightly over the sides and bottom of each tartlet to prevent them rising. Chill for 20–30 minutes before baking in a moderately hot oven for 10–15 minutes, or until lightly browned. Cool on a wire rack.

Combine the sugar and cornflour in a saucepan. Stir in the apricot juice and butter. Bring to the boil. Cook for 5 minutes, stirring constantly, until smooth and thickened. Beat the cream cheese in a bowl with rum or liqueur and orange juice. Place 2 tablespoons in each tart shell. Put an apricot half, rounded side up, on top of cream cheese. Spoon over a tablespoon of the thickened apricot juice. Pipe a border of whipped cream around the edge of each tartlet.

**Note** This pastry is delicious to eat, but very fragile. To make a dough that is easier to handle reduce the butter to 75 g. (3 oz.).

# Rum chocolate puffs

Preparation time: 15 minutes
Cooking time: about 25 minutes
Oven temperature: moderately hot (400°F., 200°C., Gas Mark 6) reducing to 375°F., 190°C., Gas Mark 5
Makes: 24 rum chocolate puffs

**280 ml./$\frac{1}{2}$ pint water**
**110 g./4 oz. butter**
**1 teaspoon sugar**
**$\frac{1}{2}$ teaspoon salt**
**110 g./4 oz. flour**
**4 large eggs**
*rum chocolate cream*
**2 eggs**
**90 g./3 oz. sugar**
**570 ml./1 pint milk**
**110 g./4 oz. bitter chocolate**
**4 teaspoons rum**
**3 tablespoons cornflour**
**4 tablespoons water**
**icing sugar**

Place the water in a saucepan, add the butter, sugar and salt, and bring mixture to the boil. Add the flour all at once and cook over a low heat, beating briskly and constantly with a wooden spoon until the mixture combines thoroughly and forms a ball. Remove the pan from the heat and add 3 eggs, one by one. Mix each smoothly into the paste. Beat the remaining egg with a fork and add it slowly, bit by bit, until the mixture has the consistency of thick cream. Do not allow the paste to become runny or the puffs will not keep their shape. Drop tablespoonfuls of the paste, well apart, onto greased baking sheets, making 24 puffs. Bake in a moderately hot oven for 15–18 minutes. Reduce the temperature and bake for a further 5 minutes, until brown and light. Cool on a wire rack.

To make the cream, place the eggs and sugar in the top of a double boiler and beat until thick and creamy, using a hand mixer. In a separate saucepan, heat the milk and chocolate until the chocolate dissolves, then add the rum. Slowly add to the egg mixture, beating constantly. Mix the cornflour with water and add to the chocolate mixture. Cook, stirring, until the mixture is thick. Remove and cool. Slit the bottom of each puff and fill with the rum chocolate cream. Dust with icing sugar and serve alone or with a slice of vanilla ice-cream.

# Rich fruitcake

Preparation time: 45 minutes, plus soaking time for the fruit
Cooking time: about 2½ hours
Oven temperature: moderate (350°F., 180°C., Gas Mark 4) reducing to very cool (250°F., 130°C., Gas Mark ½)
Makes: eight 1-kg. (2-lb.) cakes

**2 kg./4½ lb. sultanas**
**2.5 kg./5 lb. seedless raisins**
**1 kg./2 lb. currants**
**500 g./1 lb. watermelon konfyt (see note)**
**6 preserved figs**
**1 kg./2 lb. glacé cherries**
**500 g./1 lb. candied orange and lemon peel**
**1 litre/1¾ pints brandy**
**500 g./1 lb. blanched almonds**
**250 g./8 oz. flour**
**750 g./1½ lb. butter**
**1 kg./2 lb. brown sugar**
**12 large eggs**
**125 ml./¼ pint molasses or 4 tablespoons treacle**
**1 kg./2 lb. flour**
**3 teaspoons cinnamon**
**2 teaspoons allspice**
**2 teaspoons freshly ground cloves**
**2 teaspoons nutmeg**
**1¼ teaspoons bicarbonate of soda**
**2 teaspoons baking powder**
**250 ml./½ pint medium sherry**
**4 tablespoons vanilla essence**
**250 ml./½ pint orange juice**
**brandy or medium-sweet sherry for soaking the cloths (optional)**

Two days before baking the cakes, put the sultanas, raisins and currants in a bowl and heat gently in a moderate oven for 30 minutes. Remove and reserve. Meanwhile, chop the konfyt and preserved figs. Halve the cherries. Put in a bowl together with the peel. Add the warmed fruit and pour over the brandy. Cover and leave to stand for 2 days. Stir in the almonds. Blend all the fruit together with the 250 g. (8 oz.) flour. Cream the butter and sugar together until light and fluffy using a mixer. Transfer into a large basin. Drop in the eggs, two at a time. Beat until smooth after each addition. Add the molasses or treacle. Sift the flour together with the cinnamon, allspice, cloves, nutmeg, bicarbonate of soda and baking powder. Stir in the dry ingredients alternately with the liquid. Finally fold in the floured fruit and nuts. Mix well using a wooden spoon or your hands. Grease and line eight 1-kg. (2-lb.) loaf tins with heavy brown paper, then grease the paper well. (Alternatively, line the tins with greaseproof paper, brush with oil and tie brown paper around the outsides of the tins.) Spoon in the mixture and let it stand for 2 hours before baking. To bake, place the tins in a casserole dish or large pan. Cover with double layers of foil or buttered brown paper. If the dish has a lid, cover the casserole as well. Bake in a very cool oven for 2–2½ hours. Test the cakes by inserting a skewer which should come out clean. Cool on a wire rack.

**Note** To store the cakes, wrap them in clean cloths that have been well soaked in brandy or sherry, then put in double polythene bags and seal each one separately. If the cakes are to be stored for a few months, re-soak the cloths from time to time. The longer the cakes are left to mature the more moist they become.

If watermelon konfyt is not available substitute an extra 250 g. (8 oz.) currants and 250 g. (8 oz.) chopped dates.

If liked, these quantities may be quartered and baked in a 20-cm. (8-inch) round cake tin for about 2½ hours.

*Apricot cream tartlets* *(see page 130)*

*Hazel nut and plain meringues (see page 138)*

# Mango turnovers

Preparation time: 30 minutes, plus chilling time
Cooking time: about 20 minutes
Oven temperature: hot (425°F., 220°C., Gas Mark 7)
Makes: 8 mango turnovers

*flaky pastry*
**250 g./8 oz. flour**
**1 teaspoon salt**
**12 tablespoons/5 oz. butter or vegetable fat**
**4–5 tablespoons water**
**3 tablespoons/1½ oz. hard butter shavings**
*filling*
**1 medium-sized can mangoes or 2 fresh mangoes**
**about 2 teaspoons lemon juice**
**¼ teaspoon cinnamon**
**pinch ground nutmeg**
*topping*
**1 egg white**
**2 teaspoons apricot jam, melted**
**2 tablespoons slivered almonds**

For turnovers, flaky pastry is especially delightful, but puff pastry trimmings or a rich tart pastry may also be used. A vegetable fat may be substituted for butter; although butter gives the finest flavour, vegetable fat is less rich, and where you are using a spicy fruit filling and serving it hot, vegetable fat does very well.

Sift the flour and salt in a bowl. Cut in the butter using a pastry blender or two knives until the mixture looks like breadcrumbs. Sprinkle the water over, 1 tablespoon at a time, mixing lightly with a fork until all the flour is moistened. Gather the dough into a ball, wrap in greased paper and chill for 2–3 hours. Roll out lengthwise 8 mm. (good ¼ inch) thick. Spread the surface with the thin shavings of hard butter. Fold the upper third of the dough over the centre. Fold the lower third over the upper flap, making three layers. Roll out again and fold once again. Chill for 5–6 hours or overnight.

Drain the mangoes very well, or slice and quarter the fresh fruit. Sprinkle with the lemon juice, cinnamon and nutmeg. Roll out the dough 6 mm. (¼ inch) thick and cut into eight 10-cm. (4-inch) rounds. Place 1 dessertspoon of the mango filling just off the centre of each round of pastry. Moisten edges with water. Fold pastry over to form a semi-circle. Seal firmly by pressing edges together with the prongs of a fork. Lightly whisk the egg white and brush over the tops. Place on a greased baking sheet and bake in a hot oven for 12–15 minutes. Remove. Brush each turnover with apricot jam and sprinkle with almonds and replace in the oven for 5 minutes.
**Note** If mangoes are not available use peaches.

# Meringues

## Baking

A delicate light-coloured meringue should be dried rather than baked. It should be crisp and snowy – pale-brown chewy ones are not perfect although they are good to eat! For best results set the oven to very cool (225°F., 110°C., Gas Mark ¼) before beating egg whites into peaks. As soon as the mixture is on the oiled or silicone paper-lined baking sheet, place in the oven, and leave to dry out for 4–5 hours. (If the meringues start to colour, turn off the oven heat after about 2 hours.) If possible, leave in the oven overnight; if time is short bake the meringues in a very cool oven (250°F., 130°C., Gas Mark ½) for about 40 minutes; small meringues for 30 minutes.

## Mixing

Meringues consist of the correct proportions of fine granulated or castor sugar to egg white. Use a spotlessly clean, dry mixing bowl – preferably an unlined copper bowl which will help the whites to expand fully. Take care to separate whites from egg yolks without getting a speck of yolk in the bowl and use eggs that have been standing at room temperature.

## Whisking

Use a balloon whisk to incorporate as much air as possible (this makes the meringue light). An electric hand-beater set at medium speed is also excellent because it can be moved evenly around the bowl.

### Colouring

Colouring or flavouring should be included just before whisking is finished. For example, tint meringues pink with a couple of drops of cochineal or pale yellow with saffron.

### Storing

Thoroughly dry meringues may be kept in a dry airy place for several weeks. A paper-lined kitchen drawer is suitable. If the meringues are chewy, use an airtight container.

# Basic meringue

Preparation time: 5 minutes
Cooking time: see page 134
Oven temperature: see page 134
Makes: 48 small meringues

**4 egg whites**
**pinch salt**
**$\frac{1}{4}$ teaspoon cream of tartar**
**250 g./8 oz. castor sugar**
**1 teaspoon vanilla essence**

Whisk the egg whites until frothy. Sprinkle with salt and cream of tartar and continue whisking until stiff but not dry. Add the sugar, 1 tablespoon at a time, whisking constantly until three-quarters of the sugar has been added. The meringue should be stiff, thick and smooth – not a grain of sugar should be felt when a little of the mixture is rubbed between the fingers. Fold in the remaining sugar and the flavouring with a teaspoon. Shape in high tufted moulds on a lightly greased baking sheet. Bake according to methods described. Remove when dry, cool and sandwich together with whipped cream.

**Variations**
**Nut kisses** Fold in 165 g. (6 oz.) finely chopped almonds just before shaping.
**Coconut kisses** Fold in 120 g. (4 oz.) desiccated coconut just before shaping.
**Butter-crunch kisses** Fold in 125 g. (4 oz.) butter-crunch or any nut brittle just before shaping.

# Meringue circles

Preparation time: 10 minutes
Cooking time: about 2 hours
Oven temperature: very cool (250°F., 130°C., Gas Mark $\frac{1}{2}$)
Serves: 6

**basic meringue (see above)**
*peach filling*
**250 ml./$\frac{1}{2}$ pint double cream**
**2 tablespoons castor sugar**
**250 g./8 oz. fresh or canned peach slices**
**4 tablespoons sliced watermelon konfyt (optional)**

Line two baking sheets with ungreased paper. Trace two circles on each, 20 cm. (8 inches) in diameter and at least $2\frac{1}{2}$ cm. (1 inch) apart. Using a spatula, spread the meringue thinly in the circles. Bake in a very cool oven for about 2 hours. (Watch to see they do not brown.) Remove from the oven and loosen the circles with a spatula while they are still pliable. Leave on a wire rack to crisp and cool.

To make the filling, whisk the cream and castor sugar until thickened. Reserve a quarter for top and fold the peaches and konfyt (if used) into the remainder. Spread thickly over one meringue layer and top with the second layer. Pipe swirls of remaining cream on the top in a lattice pattern. Serve well chilled.

**Note** If watermelon konfyt is not available use extra peaches or any sliced fresh fruit.

# Lemon chiffon ring

Preparation time: 10 minutes
Cooking time: about 2 hours
Oven temperature: very cool (250°F., 130°C., Gas Mark ½)
Serves: 4–6

**basic meringue (see page 135)**
*lemon chiffon filling*
**1 tablespoon gelatine**
**4 tablespoons cold water**
**8 tablespoons lemon juice**
**pinch salt**
**250 g./8 oz. castor sugar**
**4 eggs, separated**
**1 teaspoon grated lemon rind**

Place the meringue in an icing bag and pipe a 1¼-cm. (¾-inch) layer in a 23-cm. (9-inch) round on an oiled baking sheet. Build up the sides, by coiling the meringue or piping rosettes, to a depth of about 5 cm. (2 inches). Bake in a very cool oven for about 2 hours. Loosen with a spatula and leave to cool.

To make the filling, soak the gelatine in cold water for 5 minutes. Combine the lemon juice, salt and half the sugar in the top of a double boiler. Beat the egg yolks lightly and add. Cook, stirring, over the boiling water until the mixture coats the spoon. Stir in the dissolved gelatine and grated lemon rind and leave to cool. Whisk the egg whites until stiff and fold in the remaining sugar. Beat the mixture until it is glossy and stiff and fold into the cooled custard. Place the meringue ring on a serving plate and fill with the chiffon filling. Chill in the refrigerator for several hours and serve topped with whipped cream.

**Variations**

**Apricot filling** Soak 500 g. (1 lb.) dried apricots with water to cover overnight. Drain and place in a pan with 500 ml. (1 pint) water. Bring to the boil, cover and simmer for 15 minutes, until tender. Stir in 125 g. (4 oz.) sugar and 2 tablespoons lemon juice. Press through a sieve or purée in a blender. (If the purée is too thin return to the heat and cook until the excess liquid has evaporated.) Cool. Whisk 125 ml. (¼ pint) double cream until thick and blend into the purée. Spoon into the ring. Arrange 12 drained canned apricot halves on top, rounded sides up. Sprinkle with Brazil nut slivers.

**Rum chocolate filling** Soften 2 tablespoons gelatine in 4 tablespoons cold water. Blend 2 whole eggs, 2 egg yolks and 6 tablespoons sugar in a bowl. Whisk until light and thick. Break up 750 g. (1½ lb.) semi-sweet chocolate into small pieces; place in a double boiler with 10 tablespoons strong black coffee and stir over a low heat until the mixture is smooth. Gradually stir in 375 ml. (generous ½ pint) hot milk. Allow to cool slightly, then blend the chocolate mixture into the egg mixture. Cook, stirring over a low heat until the mixture thickens (do not allow to boil). Cool. Dissolve the gelatine over a low heat, cool slightly then add, in a steady stream, to the cooled chocolate mixture. Whisk 4 egg whites until stiff and fold into the mixture. Whisk 250 ml. (½ pint) double cream and fold in together with 2 tablespoons rum. Spoon into the meringue case and serve chilled.

*Compote of apple rings and prunes, hot wholewheat porridge with honey (see pages 159, 158)*

# Hazel nut meringues

*Illustrated on page 133*
Preparation time: 5 minutes
Cooking time: see method
Oven temperature: very cool (250°F., 130°C., Gas Mark $\frac{1}{2}$)
Makes: about 48 hazel nut meringues

**4 egg whites**
**pinch salt**
**$\frac{1}{4}$ teaspoon cream of tartar**
**250 g./8 oz. castor sugar**
**125 g./4 oz. hazel nuts, grated or very finely chopped**

*chocolate cream*
**125 g./4 oz. butter**
**4 tablespoons cocoa powder**
**250 g./8 oz. icing sugar**
**1 teaspoon vanilla essence**
**4 tablespoons milk**

Whisk the egg whites with salt and cream of tartar until stiff. Gradually beat in the sugar, 1 tablespoon at a time. Continue to beat until the meringue is stiff and glossy. Fold in the hazel nuts. Grease and lightly flour baking sheets or line with foil. Drop teaspoonfuls of the meringue onto the baking sheets. (Or pipe with a star tube.) Bake in a very cool oven for about 2 hours, then turn off the heat and allow to remain in the oven for 4–5 hours, until thoroughly dry. Remove and peel off the foil (if used).

Using an electric beater, cream the butter until fluffy. Add the cocoa powder, icing sugar, vanilla essence and milk. Beat until well blended and light in texture. To serve, sandwich meringues together with the chocolate cream.

**Variations**
Use an almond-flavoured cream in place of the chocolate cream. Whisk 250 ml. ($\frac{1}{2}$ pint) double cream with 2 tablespoons icing sugar until it forms peaks. Fold in 1 teaspoon vanilla essence, $\frac{1}{4}$ teaspoon almond essence and 2 drops green food colouring.

Make plain meringues by omitting the hazel nuts.

# Scones

## Basic scone mixture

Preparation time: 15 minutes
Cooking time: about 12 minutes
Oven temperature: moderately hot (400°F., 200°C., Gas Mark 6)
Makes: about 24 scones

**500 g./1 lb. flour**
**4 tablespoons castor sugar**
**4 teaspoons baking powder**
**pinch salt**
**125 g./4 oz. butter**
**250 ml./scant $\frac{1}{2}$ pint milk**
**2 large eggs**

Sift the flour, sugar, baking powder and salt into a bowl. Rub in the butter with the fingertips until the mixture resembles fine crumbs. Beat the milk and eggs and add slowly to the dry mixture, folding in with a wooden spoon. (Reserve a little liquid to brush scones with.) When the dough has a soft, moist consistency, turn onto a well floured board and shape and pat gently into squares or cut out rounds with a scone cutter. Brush the tops with the reserved liquid. Place on baking sheets or on oiled foil. Bake in a moderately hot oven for 10–12 minutes, until golden. Remove and sprinkle with sugar if liked.

**Note**
1. Scone dough should be moist – use a little extra flour on the board if the dough is too messy to handle.
2. Handle the dough as lightly as possible. Do not over-mix with the spoon and never knead – pat into shape.
3. Scones freeze well in airtight polythene bags. Reheat in a moderately hot oven for about 8 minutes.

**Variations**
**Cheese** Use the basic mixture; omit the sugar and add 125 g. (4 oz.) grated cheese with the milk.
**Fruit** Use the basic mixture; add 125 g. (4 oz.) seeded raisins to the dry ingredients.

## Walnut orange scones

Preparation time: 15 minutes
Cooking time: about 15 minutes
Oven temperature: moderately hot (400°F. 200°C., Gas Mark 6)
Makes: about 12 walnut orange scones

**250 g./8 oz. flour**
**2 teaspoons baking powder**
**2 tablespoons castor sugar**
**4 tablespoons/2 oz. butter**
**1 large egg**
**125 ml./$\frac{1}{4}$ pint milk**
**1 teaspoon vanilla essence**
**1 egg white**
**4 tablespoons coarsely chopped walnuts**
**1 teaspoon grated orange rind**
**3 teaspoons castor sugar**

Sift the flour and baking powder together into a large bowl. Add the 2 tablespoons sugar. Rub in the butter until the mixture resembles fine bread-crumbs. Whisk the egg, milk and vanilla essence together in a bowl. Make a well in the centre of the dry ingredients and pour in the liquid. Draw in the dry ingredients using a wooden spoon until a soft dough is formed. If necessary, add 1–2 tablespoons extra milk – the dough should be light and soft, not too stiff. Place the dough on a lightly floured board. Lightly roll, keeping the dough at least 2$\frac{1}{2}$ cm. (1 inch) thick. Cut out the scones with a square or round scone cutter and place on greased baking sheets. Whisk the egg white until frothy and brush over the tops of the scones. Sprinkle very thickly with chopped walnuts, grated orange rind and a little sugar. Bake in a moderately hot oven for 12–15 minutes. Serve hot.
**Note** Scones freeze successfully packed in a tightly closed polythene bag. To reheat, unwrap and place, frozen, in a moderately hot oven for about 8 minutes.

## Savoury chive and cheese scones

Preparation time: 15 minutes
Cooking time: about 15 minutes
Oven temperature: moderately hot (400°F., 200°C., Gas Mark 6)
Makes: about 12 savoury chive and cheese scones

**250 g./8 oz. flour**
**2 teaspoons baking powder**
**$\frac{1}{2}$ teaspoon salt**
**4 tablespoons/2 oz. butter**
**4 tablespoons chopped chives**
**12 tablespoons milk**
**little melted butter**
**finely grated cheese**

Sift the flour into a bowl with baking powder and salt. Cut in the butter using a pastry blender or two knives until the mixture looks like fine crumbs. Add the chives. Stir in enough milk to make a soft dough. Turn onto a lightly floured board and roll out 1$\frac{1}{4}$ cm. ($\frac{3}{4}$ inch) thick. Cut into small rounds using a scone cutter and place on greased baking sheets. Brush the tops with a little melted butter and bake in a hot oven for 12–13 minutes. Sprinkle with grated cheese and bake for a further 2–3 minutes. Serve hot at lunch or brunch time.

# Biscuits

## Spiced oatmeal biscuits

Preparation time: 15 minutes
Cooking time: about 20 minutes
Oven temperature: moderate (325°F., 170°C., Gas Mark 3)
Makes: about 30 spiced oatmeal biscuits

**125 g./4 oz. butter or vegetable fat**
**8 tablespoons castor sugar**
**250 g./8 oz. breakfast oats**
**70 g./2$\frac{1}{2}$ oz. desiccated coconut**
**$\frac{1}{4}$ teaspoon ground nutmeg**
**$\frac{1}{4}$ teaspoon cinnamon**
**1 teaspoon vanilla essence**
**1 teaspoon grated lemon rind**
**1 teaspoon grated orange rind**
**$\frac{1}{2}$ teaspoon salt**

Cream the butter and sugar together in a bowl using a wooden spoon or hand mixer, until light and fluffy. Add all remaining ingredients and mix well. Form into a long roll 2$\frac{1}{2}$ cm. (1 inch) in diameter. Wrap in wax paper and chill until completely firm. Cut the roll into 6-mm. ($\frac{1}{4}$-inch) slices. Place on ungreased baking sheets. Bake in a moderate oven for 15–20 minutes, until lightly browned. Cool before removing from the sheets.

# Lacy chocolate biscuits

Preparation time: 10 minutes
Cooking time: about 6 minutes
Oven temperature: moderately hot (375°F., 190°C., Gas Mark 5)
Makes: about 60 lacy chocolate biscuits

**300 g./10 oz. honey**
**125 g./4 oz. butter**
**1 teaspoon grated orange rind**
**½ teaspoon almond essence**
**125 g./4 oz. flour**
**10 tablespoons castor sugar**
**4 tablespoons cocoa powder**
**pinch salt**

Scald the honey in a saucepan. Add the butter, orange rind and almond essence. Stir until the butter has melted. Sift together the flour, sugar, cocoa powder and salt onto a piece of wax or greaseproof paper. Add the mixture to the honey and butter and blend well. Drop teaspoonfuls of the mixture onto well greased and floured baking sheets, allowing room for them to spread. Bake in a moderately hot oven for 5–6 minutes, until firm. Allow the biscuits to cool on the baking sheets for 1 minute, then remove to a wire rack to cool completely.

# Rum orange drops

Preparation time: 10 minutes
Cooking time: about 10 minutes
Oven temperature: moderate (350°F., 180°C., Gas Mark 4)
Makes: about 42 rum orange drops

**4½ tablespoons/generous 2 oz. butter**
**5 tablespoons castor sugar**
**1 egg**
**10 tablespoons/2½ oz. flour**
**1 teaspoon rum**
**5½ tablespoons ground almonds**
**1 teaspoon grated orange rind**

Cream the butter in a bowl using an electric mixer. Add the sugar and beat until fluffy. Add the egg and beat until well blended. Sift the flour onto wax or greaseproof paper. Fold into the butter mixture. Add the rum, almonds and orange rind. Drop half teaspoonfuls of the dough onto lightly greased baking sheets. (The dough should hold a rounded shape. If necessary, a little more flour may be added.) Flatten the mounds using a fork dipped in rum. Bake in a moderate oven for 8–10 minutes, until the edges are light brown. Cool.

# Crunchy coconut macaroons

Preparation time: 10 minutes
Cooking time: about 20 minutes
Oven temperature: moderate (350°F., 180°C., Gas Mark 4)
Makes: 12 crunchy coconut macaroons

**2 large egg whites**
**125 g./4 oz. castor sugar**
**150 g./5 oz. desiccated coconut**
**6 glacé cherries**

Whisk egg whites lightly until frothy but not stiff. Add the sugar and gradually stir in coconut. Place small teaspoonfuls on greased baking sheets, allowing room for the macaroons to flatten out during cooking. Halve the cherries and press one on the top of each macaroon. Bake in the centre of a moderate oven for 18–20 minutes, until golden brown. Cool on the baking sheets.

**Variation**
**Oat macaroons** Substitute rolled oats for coconut and top with almonds.

# Spice cookies

Preparation time: 10 minutes
Cooking time: about 20 minutes
Oven temperature: moderate (350°F., 180°C., Gas Mark 4)
Makes: about 40 spice cookies

**250 g./8 oz. flour**
**1 teaspoon baking powder**
**½ teaspoon salt**
**¼ teaspoon bicarbonate of soda**
**½ teaspoon nutmeg**
**½ teaspoon cinnamon**
**125 g./4 oz. butter**
**250 g./8 oz. castor sugar**
**1 egg, well beaten**
**½ teaspoon lemon essence**
**125 ml./¼ pint sour cream**
**3 tablespoons milk**

Sift the flour, baking powder, salt, bicarbonate of soda and spices twice. Cream the butter, add the sugar gradually and beat until light. Add the egg and lemon essence. Add the sour cream and milk alternately with dry ingredients. Blend well. The mixture should be fairly stiff but moist. Drop teaspoonfuls 5 cm. (2 inches) apart onto well greased baking sheets. Bake in a moderate oven for 15–20 minutes. Cool on a wire rack.

A selection of breads (see pages 142, 143)

# Yeast breads and tea breads

## Milk rolls with caraway seeds

*Illustrated on page 141*
Preparation time: 15 minutes, plus rising times
Cooking time: about 15 minutes
Oven temperature: moderately hot (400°F. 200°C., Gas Mark 6)
Makes: 24 medium-sized rolls

**12 tablespoons milk**
**2 tablespoons castor sugar**
**1 teaspoon salt**
**4½ tablespoons/generous 2 oz. butter**
**2 cakes/1½ oz. fresh yeast**
**12 tablespoons lukewarm water**
**500 g./1 lb. flour**
**1 egg yolk**
**1 teaspoon milk**
**6 teaspoons caraway seeds**

Scald the milk in a saucepan. Stir in the sugar, salt and butter; cool to lukewarm. Soften the yeast in a mixing bowl with the lukewarm water. Add the milk mixture. Mix thoroughly with a wooden spoon. Stir in half the flour. Beat until smooth. Stir in the remaining flour to make a rough sticky dough, adding a little extra flour if necessary. Turn onto a lightly floured board and knead until the dough is smooth and satiny. Put into a buttered bowl and cover with a polythene bag. Leave in a warm place to rise until double in bulk, about 50 minutes. Punch down and divide in half. Roll out each half 6 mm. (¼ inch) thick, cut into 1¼-cm. (¾-inch) wide strips. Braid the three strips together. Cut each long braid into 8-cm. (3½-inch) lengths and press the ends together tightly. Place on buttered baking sheets, cover with a cloth and allow to rise in a warm place until double in bulk. Mix the egg yolk with the 1 teaspoon milk in a bowl. Brush over each roll. Sprinkle lightly with caraway seeds and bake in a moderately hot oven for 12–15 minutes. Cool on a wire rack.
**Note** If fresh yeast is not available, half the quantity of dried yeast may be substituted. Use it according to the directions on the packet.

## Cinnamon milk ring

*Illustrated on page 141*
Preparation time: 15 minutes, plus rising times
Cooking time: about 25 minutes
Oven temperature: moderate (350°F., 180°C., Gas Mark 4)
Makes: 2 rings

**2 cakes/1½ oz. fresh yeast**
**4 tablespoons lukewarm water**
**250 ml./½ pint milk**
**4 tablespoons/2 oz. butter**
**125 g./4 oz. castor sugar**
**½ teaspoon salt**
**about 500 g./1 lb. flour**
**2 eggs**
**3 tablespoons/1½ oz. butter, melted**
*filling*
**5 tablespoons sugar**
**3 teaspoons cinnamon**
**1 egg yolk**

Soften the yeast in a cup with the lukewarm water. Scald the milk in a saucepan. Add the butter, sugar and salt. Cool to lukewarm, then pour into a large mixing bowl. Add 4–6 tablespoons of flour, enough to make a thick batter but not a dough. Lightly beat the eggs in a bowl. Stir the yeast mixture, alternately with the eggs, into the batter. Add the remaining flour to make a soft light dough. (Up to an extra 125 g. (4 oz.) flour may be used if necessary.) Turn onto a lightly floured board and knead until the dough becomes smooth and satiny. Place in a greased bowl. Cover with a large polythene bag. Leave in a warm place to rise until double in bulk, 1–2 hours. Punch down, divide into two and roll each half into a rectangle, 1¼ cm. (¾ inch) thick and about 30 cm. (12 inches) by 15 cm. (6 inches). Brush with melted butter, sprinkle lightly with 4 tablespoons of the sugar and 2 teaspoons of the cinnamon. Roll up, from the longer side, to resemble a Swiss roll and shape into a ring. Place on oiled baking sheets. Cut almost through to the bottom at 1¼-cm. (¾-inch) intervals. Cover with a cloth and allow to rise in a warm place until double in bulk. Lightly beat the egg yolk and brush over top of the rings. Sprinkle with the remaining sugar and cinnamon. Bake in a moderate oven for 20–25 minutes.
**Note** To freeze, allow to cool then pack in a polythene bag and close tightly. To serve, reheat in a moderate oven for 12–15 minutes.

# Crusty poppyseed bread

*Illustrated on page 141*
Preparation time: 15 minutes, plus rising times
Cooking time: about 45 minutes
Oven temperature: moderate (350°F., 180°C., Gas Mark 4)
Makes: 3 medium-sized loaves

**2 cakes/1½ oz. fresh yeast**
**2 tablespoons salt**
**1 tablespoon castor sugar**
**500 ml./1 pint warm water**
**about 1 kg./2¼ lb. flour**
**1 egg white**
**3 tablespoons poppyseeds**

Cream the yeast with the salt and sugar in a large bowl. Add the warm water. Stir in enough flour to make a stiff dough, adding a little extra flour if necessary. Turn out onto a lightly floured board and knead the dough well until it becomes smooth and elastic. Place the dough in a large greased bowl and cover with a large polythene bag. Leave to rise in a warm place until double in bulk, 40–50 minutes. Punch down the dough and divide it into three pieces. Shape each piece into a long sausage about 4 cm. (1½ inches) in diameter. Place the loaves well apart on a greased baking sheet or foil. If liked, slash each loaf diagonally across the top three times. Lightly whisk the egg white and use to brush over the tops of the loaves. Sprinkle with poppyseeds. Allow to rise in a warm place until double in bulk, 15–20 minutes. Bake in a moderate oven for 40–45 minutes, until deep golden brown. Cool on a wire rack.

**Note** For a crustier loaf place a pan filled with boiling water on the shelf below the loaves during baking.

These loaves, like most yeast products, freeze well. To freeze, cool and place in a polythene bag and close tightly. To reheat, place in a moderate oven for 12–15 minutes.

**Variation**
Alternatively, this dough can be shaped into any of the loaves, or rolls shown in the picture on page 141.

# Milk cloud bread

Preparation time: 15 minutes, plus rising times
Cooking time: about 40 minutes
Oven temperature: moderate (350°F., 180°C., Gas Mark 4)

**125 g./4 oz. butter**
**125 ml./¼ pint warm milk**
**1 cake/¾ oz. fresh yeast**
**3 tablespoons warm milk**
**8 tablespoons castor sugar**
**1 teaspoon salt**
**4 egg yolks**
**500 g./1 lb. cake or plain flour**
**125 ml./¼ pint milk**
**1 teaspoon cinnamon**

Place the butter and 125 ml. (¼ pint) warm milk in a saucepan. Allow the butter to melt. Dissolve the yeast in the 3 tablespoons warm milk and add to the lukewarm butter and milk mixture. Pour the mixture into a bowl, add 3 tablespoons sugar, the salt and beat in the egg yolks. Whisk until the sugar has dissolved; add the flour and stir until the dough is smooth. Shape into a long roll on a lightly floured board. Using a sharp knife, make 2-cm. (1-inch) slits. Place in a roasting tin, cover with a polythene bag and allow to rise until double in size, about 1 hour. Bake in a moderate oven for about 15 minutes, until light brown. Scald the 125 ml. (¼ pint) milk and add 4 tablespoons sugar. Pour over the bread, in the oven, and bake for a further 20–25 minutes to absorb the milk. (Halfway through, spoon the milk over again to give the loaf a glaze.) Sprinkle with the remaining sugar and the cinnamon. Serve with jam.

*A wedding lunch – chilled cream of cucumber soup, chicken and lobster salad, marinated mushroom salad and ice-cream bombe praline (see pages 27, 94, 95, 114, 170)*

# Wholewheat currant nut bread

Preparation time: 15 minutes
Cooking time: about 1 hour
Oven temperature: moderate (350°F., 180°C., Gas Mark 4)
Makes: one 1-kg. (2-lb.) loaf

**180 g./6 oz. white flour**
**2 teaspoons baking powder**
**½ teaspoon bicarbonate of soda**
**1 teaspoon salt**
**180 g./6 oz. wholewheat flour**
**125 g./4 oz. hazel nuts, chopped**
**125 g./4 oz. currants**
**1 large egg**
**125 g./4 oz. brown sugar**
**250 ml./½ pint milk**
**2 tablespoons/1 oz. butter**

Sift the white flour, baking powder, bicarbonate of soda and salt together in a mixing bowl. Add the wholewheat flour, chopped nuts and currants. Mix well using a wooden spoon. Combine the egg, brown sugar and milk in a bowl. Melt the butter in a small saucepan. Cool before adding to the egg and milk mixture. Pour into the flour mixture. Stir just enough to moisten the dry ingredients but do not beat the mixture. Turn into an oiled 1-kg. (2-lb.) loaf tin. Bake in a moderate oven for about 1 hour, until the top is browned and the sides have shrunk slightly from the sides of the tin. Turn out onto a wire rack to cool.

**Note** This type of tea bread improves in flavour with keeping. It will also slice better when cold. Serve plain, buttered or with a little pot of cream cheese.

# Banana bread

Preparation time: 10 minutes
Cooking time: 45 minutes
Oven temperature: moderate (350°F., 180°C., Gas Mark 4)
Makes: two ½-kg. (1-lb.) banana loaves

**6 medium-sized bananas**
**125 g./4 oz. butter**
**250 g./8 oz. castor sugar**
**2 eggs**
**3 tablespoons sour milk**
**1 teaspoon vanilla essence**
**55 g./2 oz. shelled walnuts, chopped**
**250 g./8 oz. flour**
**1 teaspoon bicarbonate of soda**
**½ teaspoon salt**

Mash the bananas. Cream the butter thoroughly until light and fluffy – use an electric hand-mixer or wooden spoon. Add the sugar gradually. Continue beating until the mixture is creamy. Beat the eggs and add to the mixture. Beat for 1 minute. Add the sour milk and vanilla essence. Fold in the mashed bananas and chopped walnuts. Sift the flour, bicarbonate of soda and salt. Fold into the mixture until well blended. Divide between two greased and floured ½-kg. (1-lb.) loaf tins. Bake in a moderate oven until golden brown and firm. Cool on a wire tray. Store in an airtight container or tin. Serve sliced thinly, buttered and with kumquat or quince preserve.

# Snacks and savouries

Rolls, sandwiches and toasts – these are indispensable snacks at any hour. Thin crustless cucumber triangles or moist asparagus fingers are delicious with morning or afternoon tea. And nothing is as good as something hot and savoury on slices of toast last thing at night with a hot drink. When the unexpected guest arrives, heat rolls from the freezer. Hollow out and stuff or sandwich together with good fillings. Keep selected cheese, ham or salami and a small stock of seasoned butters in your refrigerator, and in your store cupboard some cans of tuna, salmon, chicken pieces, anchovies and sardines. Serve your delectable fillers with right drinks for the right occasion.

Good-looking dishes and trays to have: china dish with lid for hot toasts and snacks; plain wooden shapes – one small enough to serve just two, another large enough to hold sandwiches for 12; trays in clear plain colours – dark leaf green, deep red – and an assortment of wicker baskets are indispensable.

## Sausage breads

Preparation time: 15 minutes
Serves: 2

**1 thick spiced veal-and-pork sausage**
**4 slices pumpernickel**
**2 small tomatoes**
**2 teaspoons French mustard**
**2 tablespoons chopped parsley**

Boil the sausage for 5–8 minutes. Cool and slice into thin rounds. Arrange on the pumpernickel. Slice the tomatoes thinly and arrange in rows over the sausage rounds. Add dabs of mustard and sprinkle each slice with parsley.

## Ham and cheese slices

Preparation time: few minutes
Cooking time: few minutes
Serves: 2

**4 slices white bread**
**2 teaspoons/scant $\frac{1}{2}$ oz. butter**
**2 teaspoons French mustard**
**4 slices cold ham**
**8 thin slices sharp cheese**

Toast the bread and butter it. Spread each slice with mustard then cover completely with ham and top with the cheese slices. Place under the grill until the cheese melts and turns brown. Serve with hot strong coffee.

## Anchovy butter toasts

Preparation time: few minutes
Serves: 4

**8 anchovy fillets**
**3 tablespoons/1½ oz. butter**
**1 small clove garlic, crushed**
**1 teaspoon lemon juice**
**¼ teaspoon freshly ground black pepper**
**8 slices white bread**

Place the anchovies in a mixing bowl with the butter, garlic, lemon juice and pepper. Blend together with a wooden spoon until creamy. Toast the bread on both sides and spread with anchovy butter. Serve cut into triangles.
**Note** Anchovy toasts may be garnished with finely chopped hard-boiled egg mixed with chopped parsley.

## Fluffy cheese toasts

Preparation time: few minutes
Cooking time: 5 minutes
Serves: 3

**8 tablespoons coarsely grated mature Cheddar cheese**
**1 egg, beaten**
**1 tomato, chopped**
**1 teaspoon mustard**
**¼ teaspoon salt**
**pinch freshly ground black pepper**
**2 teaspoons milk**
**1 teaspoon/scant ¼ oz. butter**
**6 slices wholewheat or French bread**

Mix the cheese in a bowl with the egg, tomato, mustard, salt and pepper. Add the milk and butter and blend well. Toast the bread on one side only. Cool for 2 minutes then spread fairly thickly with the cheese mixture. Place under the grill for 5 minutes, or until puffy and golden brown. Serve with smoked veal sausages.

## Banana cinnamon toasts

Preparation time: few minutes
Cooking time: few minutes
Serves: 2

**2 large bananas**
**juice of ½ lemon**
**pinch nutmeg**
**4 slices cinnamon bread or white bread**
**4 teaspoons/scant 1 oz. butter, melted**
**pinch cinnamon**

Thinly slice the bananas. Sprinkle with the lemon juice and nutmeg. Toast the bread slices. Cover with rows of sliced banana and brush with a teaspoon of melted butter and a little cinnamon. Place under a preheated grill for 2–3 minutes, until bananas just begin to soften and turn golden. Serve with frothy hot chocolate.

## Asparagus and egg slices

Preparation time: few minutes
Serves: 4

**4 teaspoons/scant 1 oz. butter**
**4 slices wholewheat brown bread**
**2 hard-boiled eggs**
**½ teaspoon salt**
**pinch freshly ground black pepper**
**6 thick asparagus spears**
**1 tablespoon thick mayonnaise**
**1 dessertspoon chopped parsley**

Butter the wholewheat bread. Slice the eggs and place in rows on each piece of bread. Sprinkle with salt and pepper. Top each slice with asparagus and a dab of mayonnaise and sprinkle with chopped parsley.

## Anchovy fingers

Preparation time: 15 minutes
Cooking time: about 10 minutes
Oven temperature: moderately hot (400°F., 200°C., Gas Mark 6)
Makes: about 15 anchovy fingers

**2 tablespoons/1 oz. butter**
**5 teaspoons flour**
**125 ml./¼ pint milk**
**1 teaspoon prepared mustard**
**4 tablespoons grated cheese**
**1 egg yolk**
**250 g./8 oz. frozen puff pastry, thawed**
**1 can anchovy fillets**
**½ teaspoon salt**
**¼ teaspoon freshly ground black pepper**

Melt the butter in a saucepan, add the flour and when the mixture bubbles gradually add the milk, stirring constantly. Add the mustard and grated cheese. When thickened, cool for 10 minutes and gently stir in egg yolk. Leave to cool completely. Roll out the pastry into a square, about 6 mm. (¼ inch) thick. Spread the cold cheese sauce over the square and arrange drained anchovy fillets on top, leaving small spaces. Add salt and pepper. Cut the pastry into fingers between the anchovies; place on a baking sheet and cook in a moderately hot oven for about 10 minutes, until well puffed and golden brown.

# Sandwiches

## Stuffed French bread

Preparation time: 5 minutes, plus overnight chilling
Serves: 4–6

**1 French loaf**
**10 slices liver polony**
**2 hard-boiled eggs**
**1 teaspoon chopped capers**
**1 teaspoon chopped parsley**
**2 teaspoons chopped black olives**
**1 teaspoon Worcestershire sauce**
**1 teaspoon prepared mustard**
**¼ teaspoon grated onion**

Trim the ends of the French bread and scoop out the centre to make a long hollow tube with a 6-mm. (¼-inch) crust. (Reserve the bread for use in a stuffing or a bread pudding.) Place all the ingredients in a large bowl and blend together until smooth. Fill the French bread case with the smoothly blended stuffing. Wrap in foil and chill overnight. To serve, cut in 6-mm. (¼-inch) slices.

## Miniature golden puffs

Preparation time: 10 minutes
Cooking time: few minutes
Serves: 6

**24 slices white bread**
**1½ teaspoons/about ½ oz. butter**
**1 teaspoon flour**
**3 tablespoons hot milk**
**1 teaspoon Kirsch (optional)**
**125 g./4 oz. mature Cheddar cheese, grated**
**1 egg**
**pinch freshly ground black pepper**
**4 tablespoons finely chopped bacon, crisply fried**
**2 tablespoons chopped parsley**

Cut the slices of bread into 4-cm. (1½-inch) rounds using a scone or biscuit cutter. Place on a large piece of foil and toast on one side only. Melt the butter in a saucepan. Add the flour, stirring constantly. Gradually add the milk. Cook over a low heat until thick and smooth. Add the Kirsch (if used) and the grated cheese. Cook stirring until the cheese melts. Remove from the heat. Separate the egg and beat a little of the hot sauce into the egg yolk. Add to the cheese mixture with the pepper. Cool for 5–8 minutes. Whisk the egg white stiffly. Fold into the cheese mixture with bacon and parsley. Place 1 teaspoon of the mixture on each round of toast. Place the rounds on a lightly buttered baking sheet and place under the grill until the cheese puffs up and turns golden brown. Serve in a heated earthenware dish.

# Little egg mayonnaise rolls

Preparation time: 15 minutes
Serves: 4–6

**24 little white rolls**
**6 large hard-boiled eggs**
**2 tablespoons/1 oz. soft butter**
**3 tablespoons thick mayonnaise**
**pinch salt**
**pinch freshly ground black pepper**
**1 jar caviar or lumpfish roe**
**4 lettuce leaves, shredded**

These little rolls can be bought from a confectioner or they may be made using a half quantity of milk or water bread dough (pages 142–3) and shaped into round bite-sized rolls.

Cut a slice from the top of each roll and hollow out the centre. (Reserve the bread for a stuffing or a bread pudding.) Mash the eggs together with the butter in a bowl. Add the mayonnaise, salt and pepper. Pack into the hollowed-out rolls. Place a dab of caviar on the top of each roll. Wash, dry and finely shred the lettuce leaves. Ring the top of each roll with lettuce.

# Salmon mayonnaise on black bread

Preparation time: 10 minutes
Serves: 4–6

**1 200-g./8-oz. can pink salmon**
**4 tablespoons thick mayonnaise**
**1 tablespoon thick cream**
**about 2 teaspoons capers**
**1 tablespoon lemon juice**
**$\frac{1}{2}$ teaspoon salt**
**$\frac{1}{4}$ teaspoon freshly ground black pepper**
**2 tablespoons/1 oz. soft butter**
**12 thin slices black bread**
**1 small cucumber**
**4 tablespoons chopped parsley**

Drain the salmon, reserving the juice. Remove all the silvery skin from the outside of the salmon and any bones. Place in a bowl with the mayonnaise, cream, capers, lemon juice, salt, pepper and salmon juice. Blend well. Butter the bread and spread fairly thickly with salmon mixture. Cut into triangles. Place in overlapping rows on a serving tray. Slice the cucumber finely and place a slice in the centre of each triangle. Sprinkle the parsley thickly down the centre of each cucumber section.

# Rolled sandwich platter

Preparation time: 20 minutes, plus chilling time
Serves: 4–6

*ham and mustard*
**8 thin slices chilled fresh white bread**
**3 tablespoons/1$\frac{1}{2}$ oz. soft butter**
**4 teaspoons prepared mustard**
**4 slices ham**
**pinch freshly ground black pepper**
*garnish*
**sprigs watercress, or celery leaves**

Trim off the bread crusts using a sharp knife. Cream the butter and mustard together in a small bowl. Sliver the ham and add to the bowl. Sprinkle with freshly ground black pepper. Spread each slice of bread fairly thickly with the filling and gently roll up like a Swiss roll. Wrap each one in wax or grease-proof paper and chill for 30 minutes. Remove the paper and slice each roll into 2–3 slices. Place on a dish and garnish with sprigs of watercress or celery leaves.

*avocado pear and Danish blue cheese*
**1 small avocado**
**4 tablespoons Danish blue cheese**
**1 tablespoon lemon juice**
**pinch freshly ground black pepper**
**8 slices chilled brown bread**
**2 tablespoons/1 oz. soft butter**
*garnish*
**sprigs watercress**

Skin and stone the avocado. Mash in a bowl with the Danish blue cheese, lemon juice and freshly ground black pepper. Trim the crusts off the bread and follow the above recipe for preparing the rolls. Arrange sandwiches together in groups and garnish with sprigs of watercress.

# Sauces, stuffings, preserves and other accompaniments

Some of the recipes in this chapter are those which demand a little more time and trouble, but they are well worth it for the extra fillip they add to the simplest dish – home-made mayonnaise with different flavourings, special preserves and sauces; chocolate truffles to hand around with the after-dinner coffee.

## Sauces

### Basic thick mayonnaise

*Illustrated on page 100*
Preparation time: 5 minutes
Makes: about 250 ml. (½ pint) mayonnaise

**2 egg yolks**
**1 teaspoon vinegar**
**½ teaspoon salt**
**½ teaspoon dry mustard**
**white pepper to taste**
**250 ml./½ pint salad or olive oil**
**1 teaspoon lemon juice**

Gently heat a mixing bowl for 2–3 minutes. Add the egg yolks, vinegar, salt, dry mustard and white pepper. Whisk until well blended using a large balloon whisk or an electric beater set at medium speed. Add the oil, drop by drop at first, until about 4 tablespoons have been used. Then add the remaining oil in a thin steady stream, beating continuously. From time to time stop adding oil but continue beating to combine the ingredients thoroughly. At the end add the lemon juice.

**Note** If the mayonnaise should curdle, wash the beater and add a fresh egg yolk to another bowl. Slowly add the curdled mayonnaise to the egg yolk beating constantly to form a fresh emulsion. Once you have learnt to make a basic mayonnaise, you will always want to make your own. Flavourings, see below, can be added to the basic mayonnaise; serve with cold meats, poached chilled fish or salads.

**Variations**

**Curry mayonnaise** *(Illustrated on page 100)* Fold 4 tablespoons curry powder into the mayonnaise.

**Chive mayonnaise** Fold 3 tablespoons chopped, fresh chives and 2 teaspoons lemon juice into the mayonnaise.

**Caper mayonnaise** Fold 2 tablespoons chopped capers and 2 tablespoons chopped parsley into the mayonnaise.

**Garlic mayonnaise** Peel and crush 3 cloves of garlic. Fold into the mayonnaise.

**Pink seafood mayonnaise** *(Illustrated on page 100)* Fold 2 tablespoons tomato purée, 2 dessertspoons lemon juice, 1 teaspoon grated lemon rind, ¼ teaspoon rose paprika or paprika pepper and 2 tablespoons cream into the mayonnaise.

# Herb mayonnaise (made in a blender)

Preparation time: few seconds
Makes: about 250 ml. ($\frac{1}{2}$ pint) herb mayonnaise

**1 small clove garlic**
**1 egg**
**250 ml./$\frac{1}{2}$ pint salad or olive oil**
**2 tablespoons wine vinegar**
**1 tablespoon coarsely chopped chives**
**1 tablespoon coarsely chopped leaf celery**
**1 teaspoon dry mustard**
**$\frac{1}{2}$ teaspoon salt**
**$\frac{1}{4}$ teaspoon freshly ground black pepper**

Peel the garlic and place with the egg, 4 tablespoons of the oil and remaining ingredients in the blender goblet. Cover and switch on to low speed. Immediately remove the cover. Add the remaining oil in a thin steady stream. When all the oil has been added, switch off the blender. Spoon the mayonnaise into a jar and chill well before serving. Spoon over whole hard-boiled eggs or serve with poached fish or salads.

# Green mayonnaise

Preparation time: 10 minutes
Makes: about 250 ml. ($\frac{1}{2}$ pint) green mayonnaise

**10 young spinach leaves**
**3 tablespoons chopped parsley**
**1 teaspoon crushed garlic**
**250 ml./$\frac{1}{2}$ pint thick mayonnaise**
**3 tablespoons chopped chives**
**1 teaspoon salt**
**$\frac{1}{4}$ teaspoon freshly ground black pepper**
**1 tablespoon lemon juice**

Blanch the spinach leaves for 1 minute in boiling water, drain well and chop finely; press out all moisture. Combine the spinach with the parsley and garlic, and fold the mixture into mayonnaise. Add the chives, seasoning, and blend in the lemon juice. Place in a sauceboat and serve.

# Lemon mayonnaise

Preparation time: 10 minutes
Makes: about 250 ml. ($\frac{1}{2}$ pint) lemon mayonnaise

**2 egg yolks**
**1 small lemon**
**1 teaspoon vinegar**
**1 teaspoon salt**
**$\frac{1}{2}$ teaspoon dry mustard**
**250 ml./$\frac{1}{2}$ pint olive or salad oil**
**2 tablespoons grated lemon rind**
**1 tablespoon grated onion**
**3 sprigs parsley, chopped**
**3 sprigs dill (optional)**
**1 tablespoon milk**
**1 tablespoon hot water**

Place the egg yolks in a bowl with lemon juice and vinegar. Add the salt and mustard. Slowly, drop by drop, begin adding oil. Beat constantly either with an electric beater or a large balloon whisk. After the first 2 minutes, begin adding the oil in a fine steady stream. Continue beating until the mixture thickens. Add the lemon rind and onion. Fold in the chopped parsley and dill, if used, and mix well. To thin, add the milk and water. Mix thoroughly and store in an airtight container in the refrigerator.
**Note** This is an excellent mayonnaise to serve with fish.

# Seafood sauce

Preparation time: few minutes
Makes: about 250 ml. ($\frac{1}{2}$ pint) seafood sauce

**250 ml./$\frac{1}{2}$ pint thick mayonnaise**
**2 tablespoons chopped black olives**
**2 tablespoons chopped parsley**
**2 tablespoons tomato sauce**
**1 teaspoon prepared mustard**

Blend the ingredients together thoroughly and spoon into a sauceboat.

# Light Hollandaise sauce

Preparation time: 5 minutes
Makes: 250 ml. ($\frac{1}{2}$ pint) light Hollandaise sauce

**125 g./4 oz. butter**
**4 egg yolks**
**1 tablespoon single cream**
**2 teaspoons lemon juice**
**pinch white pepper**
**pinch salt**

Divide the butter into six parts. Lightly beat the egg yolks and cream in the top of a double boiler. Set over a low heat. Whisk quickly until the yolks thicken. Add a little butter. Beat until the butter melts. Continue adding the butter a little at a time until all the butter is incorporated and the sauce is light and fluffy. Remove from the heat and beat for 1 minute. Add the lemon juice, pepper and salt. Serve with fish.

# Quick béarnaise sauce

Preparation time: 5 minutes
Makes: 250 ml. ($\frac{1}{2}$ pint) quick béarnaise sauce

**2 tablespoons white wine**
**1 tablespoon tarragon vinegar**
**2 teaspoons chopped spring onion**
**$\frac{1}{4}$ teaspoon dried tarragon or 1 teaspoon fresh**
**$\frac{1}{4}$ teaspoon white pepper**
**light Hollandaise sauce (see above)**

Combine the wine, vinegar, onion, tarragon and pepper in a saucepan. Cook over high heat until liquid has reduced to about 1 tablespoon. Add this liquid slowly to the Hollandaise sauce, whisking with a hand beater.

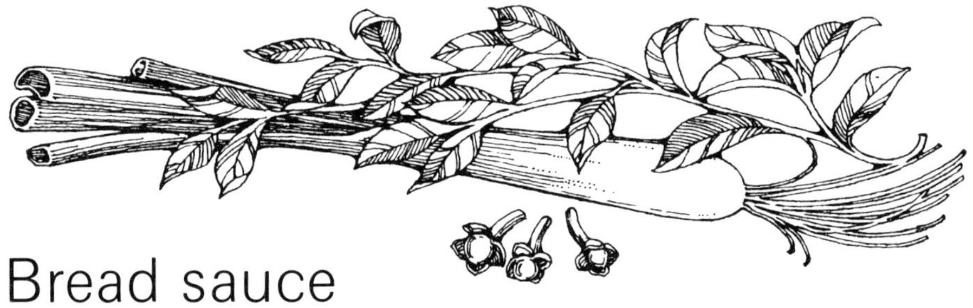

# Bread sauce

*Illustrated on page 101*
Preparation time: 5 minutes, plus standing time
Makes: about 500 ml. (1 pint) bread sauce

**500 ml./1 pint milk**
**6 tablespoons/3 oz. butter**
**1 large onion**
**3 cloves**
**1 bay leaf**
**$\frac{1}{2}$ teaspoon salt**
**$\frac{1}{4}$ teaspoon white pepper**
**125 g./4 oz. fresh white breadcrumbs**

Mix the milk and butter together in a saucepan. Peel the onion and stick cloves into it. Add to the pan with the bay leaf, salt and pepper. Bring to near boiling point. Remove from the heat and add the breadcrumbs. Cover and allow to stand for at least 30–40 minutes. Remove the onion and bay leaf. Heat before serving, stirring well with a wooden spoon. Pour into a warmed sauceboat to serve.

# Orange sauce

Preparation time: few minutes
Makes: 375 ml. (generous $\frac{1}{2}$ pint) orange sauce

**4 egg yolks**
**2 tablespoons lemon juice**
**250 g./8 oz. butter**
**1 teaspoon finely grated orange rind**
**8 tablespoons fresh orange juice**
**$\frac{1}{4}$ teaspoon salt**
**pinch freshly ground black pepper**

Place the egg yolks in a blender. Add the lemon juice. Cover and turn blender on to low. Melt the butter and add in a thin, slow stream. Turn off and add the orange rind. Strain the orange juice and add, together with salt and pepper. Serve immediately with hot poached or grilled fish.

# White butter sauce

Preparation time: 5 minutes
Makes: 250 ml. (½ pint) white butter sauce

**4 tablespoons white wine vinegar**
**1 tablespoon finely chopped spring onion**
**1 tablespoon finely chopped parsley**
**¼ teaspoon salt**
**pinch white pepper**
**125 g./4 oz. butter**

Combine the vinegar, onion, parsley, salt and pepper in a saucepan. Simmer until the mixture is reduced by half. Gradually whisk in the butter until all is incorporated. Serve hot and foamy with fish or vegetables.

# Horseradish sauce

Preparation time: 5 minutes, plus chilling time
Makes: 500 ml. (1 pint) horseradish sauce

**250 g./8 oz. horseradish root**
**90 g./3 oz. fresh white breadcrumbs**
**4 tablespoons milk**
**2 tablespoons sugar**
**1 teaspoon dry mustard**
**2 tablespoons vinegar**
**250 ml./½ pint cream**
**1 teaspoon salt**
**¼ teaspoon white pepper**

Peel and grate or mince the horseradish. Moisten the breadcrumbs in the milk. Add to the horseradish, together with the sugar, mustard, vinegar, cream, salt and pepper. Blend well. Spoon into jars and refrigerate until needed. Serve with cold poached fish or pickled meats.

# Cumberland sauce

Preparation time: few minutes
Makes: about 250 ml. (½ pint) Cumberland sauce

**3 tablespoons lemon juice**
**1 tablespoon redcurrant jelly**
**1 tablespoon double cream**
**½ teaspoon salt**
**¼ teaspoon freshly ground black pepper**
**8 tablespoons salad oil**
**¼ teaspoon finely grated lemon peel**

Pour the lemon juice into a bowl. Add the redcurrant jelly. Whisking constantly, add the cream, salt, pepper, salad oil and lemon peel. Serve with venison or pigeon.

# Piquant sauce

Preparation time: few minutes
Makes: about 250 ml. (½ pint) piquant sauce

**125 ml./¼ pint vinegar**
**125 ml./¼ pint oil**
**2 tablespoons lemon juice**
**2 hard-boiled eggs**
**1 tablespoon chopped pickled beetroot**
**1 tablespoon chopped green olives**
**1 teaspoon grated onion**
**1 teaspoon chopped parsley**
**1 teaspoon salt**
**¼ teaspoon freshly ground black pepper**

Pour the vinegar into a bowl. Add the oil and lemon juice. Chop the hard-boiled eggs and add together with the beetroot, olives, onion, parsley, salt and pepper. Blend well. Serve with cold sliced roast meats.

# Spiced cranberry sauce

*Illustrated on page 101*
Preparation time: few minutes, plus chilling time

**1 large can cranberries**
**½ teaspoon finely grated lemon rind**
**½ teaspoon finely grated orange rind**
**½ teaspoon cinnamon**
**¼ teaspoon freshly grated nutmeg**
**¼ teaspoon ground cloves**
**½ teaspoon cornflour**
**about 2 teaspoons cold water**

Pour the cranberries and juice into a saucepan. Add the lemon and orange rind, cinnamon, nutmeg and cloves. Mix the cornflour in a cup with cold water until smooth. Add to the pan, stirring constantly. Bring to the boil for 1 minute. Remove and cool before serving with roast turkey.

# Garlic and herb sauce

Preparation time: few minutes
Makes: about 125 ml. (¼ pint) garlic and herb sauce

**1 large clove garlic**
**1 teaspoon salt**
**2 tablespoons brown vinegar**
**¼ teaspoon freshly ground black pepper**
**6 tablespoons salad oil**
**2 teaspoons chopped parsley**
**2 teaspoons chives**
**1 pickled cucumber**
**1 tablespoon lemon juice**
**¼ teaspoon sugar**

Peel and crush the garlic. Blend together with the salt and vinegar. Add the pepper, oil, parsley and chives. Chop the pickled cucumber and add together with the lemon juice and sugar. Whisk well for 1 minute. Serve with cold pickled meats.

# Stuffings

## Apricot raisin stuffing for roast duck

Preparation time: 20 minutes
Makes: enough for a 2-kg. (4½-lb.) duck

**250 g./8 oz. raw long-grain rice**
**140 g./5 oz. dried apricots, chopped**
**2 tablespoons chopped leaf celery**
**2 tablespoons seedless raisins**
**3 tablespoons/1½ oz. butter, melted**
**3 tablespoons chopped parsley**
**1 teaspoon grated lemon rind**
**1 teaspoon grated orange rind**
**1 dessertspoon chopped onion**
**1 dessertspoon chopped chives**
**pinch ground nutmeg**
**pinch rosemary**
**pinch thyme**
**1 teaspoon salt**
**¼ teaspoon freshly ground black pepper**

Cook the rice, steam in a colander and cool. Mix the cold rice with the remaining ingredients. Blend thoroughly and use to stuff a duck.

## Banana bacon stuffing for roast chicken

Preparation time: 5 minutes
Makes: enough for a 1.5-kg. (3-lb.) chicken

**4 slices bacon**
**4 ripe bananas**
**1 tablespoon lemon juice**
**¼ teaspoon grated lemon rind**
**1 teaspoon sweet sherry**
**½ teaspoon salt**
**pinch freshly ground black pepper**

Fry the bacon in a pan until crisp. Crumble into a bowl. Mash the bananas and mix with the lemon juice, lemon rind, sweet sherry, salt and pepper. Combine the banana mixture with the bacon. Blend and pack into the chicken.

# Turkey stuffing

Preparation time: 20 minutes
Cooking time: about 20 minutes
Oven temperature: moderate (350°F., 180°C., Gas Mark 4)
Makes: enough for a 6-kg. (13½-lb.) turkey

**250 g./8 oz. raw long-grain rice**
**500 g./1 lb. spicy beef sausages**
**2 tablespoons oil**
**2 large onions**
**1½ litres/3 pints boiling water**
**2 chicken stock cubes**
**6 sprigs celery, chopped**
**6 mushrooms, chopped**
**3 tablespoons/1½ oz. butter**
**125 g./4 oz. pine nuts or walnuts, chopped**
**2 teaspoons salt**
**½ teaspoon freshly ground black pepper**

Cook the rice, steam in a colander and cool before using. Chop the sausages finely and fry lightly in a pan with half the oil. Peel and chop the onions. Fry lightly in a flameproof casserole with the remaining oil. Mix the boiling water with the stock cubes. Add to the onion, together with the rice. Bring to the boil and cover. Bake in a moderate oven for 18–20 minutes, until the stock has been absorbed. Lightly fry the celery and mushrooms in a pan with the butter. Add the nuts. Remove and place in a bowl. Mix in the salt, pepper, rice mixture and sausages. Allow to cool completely before stuffing the turkey.

# Lemon poultry stuffing

Preparation time: few minutes
Makes: enough for a 1.5-kg. (3-lb.) chicken

**180 g./6 oz. soft wholewheat breadcrumbs**
**grated rind of 2 lemons**
**2 tablespoons lemon juice**
**2 teaspoons poultry seasoning**
**¼ teaspoon freshly ground black pepper**
**1 teaspoon salt**
**3 tablespoons finely chopped onion**
**2 tablespoons/1 oz. butter**
**2 tablespoons chopped almonds**
**2 teaspoons chopped celery**

Mix the wholewheat breadcrumbs, lemon rind and juice together in a bowl. Add the poultry seasoning, pepper and salt. Fry the onion in a pan with the butter until soft, about 5 minutes. Add the almonds and chopped celery. Add to the bowl and mix thoroughly. Cool before using.

# Flavoured butters

# Brandy butter

*Illustrated on page 101*
Preparation time: 5 minutes

**125 g./4 oz. butter**
**4 tablespoons castor sugar**
**1 tablespoon ground almonds**
**2 dessertspoons brandy**
**½ teaspoon finely grated orange rind**
**1 whole nutmeg**

Cream the butter in a bowl until light and pale in colour using a hand mixer. Add the castor sugar. Beat in the almonds. Chill thoroughly in the bowl. Just before serving add the brandy and orange rind. Sprinkle with a little freshly grated nutmeg or grated orange rind. Spoon into a glass bowl to serve with mince pies or Christmas pudding.

# Anchovy butter

Preparation time: 5 minutes

**250 g./8 oz. butter**
**1 can anchovy fillets**

Cream the butter and add the anchovies with their oil, pounding the mixture together in a mortar or with a wooden spoon until smooth.
**Note** This is a delicious savoury base, particularly for a scrambled egg or egg mayonnaise sandwich. Or better still, fill hollowed-out baby brioche with the anchovy butter, and egg mayonnaise; dust the tops with paprika pepper.

# Danish blue butter

Preparation time: 5 minutes

**6 tablespoons Danish blue or Roquefort cheese**
**8 tablespoons/4 oz. soft butter**

Cream the cheese and butter together, pack the mixture into small pots and store in the refrigerator. Serve with Melba toast, or piped into celery stalks.

# Mustard curry butter

Preparation time: 5 minutes, plus chilling time

**3 tablespoons prepared mustard**
**1 teaspoon dry mustard**
**1 teaspoon curry powder**
**1 teaspoon lemon juice**
**250 g./8 oz. soft butter**
**seasoning to taste**

Combine the prepared and dry mustard with the curry powder and lemon juice and blend the mixture with the soft butter. Season to taste and chill thoroughly. Serve with grilled steak or rich fish such as herring or mackerel.

# Devilled butter

Preparation time: few minutes

**6 tablespoons/3 oz. butter**
**3 tablespoons lemon juice**
**3 tablespoons Worcestershire sauce**
**2 tablespoons prepared mustard**
**$\frac{1}{2}$ teaspoon salt**
**$\frac{1}{4}$ teaspoon freshly ground black pepper**

Melt the butter and add the remaining ingredients. Heat, stirring until piping hot. Serve with rare steaks.

# Preserves

**To prepare jars for preserves**
Use standard jars in perfect condition. An airtight seal is essential. Wash first in hot, soapy water. Rinse with scalding water. Drain and dry in a very cool oven (225°F., 110°C., Gas Mark $\frac{1}{4}$) for 10–15 minutes. Dry the rings, etc. with paper towels. The jars must be hot and dry when the preserve is placed in them. Stand the jars on a cloth or asbestos mat when filling them as contact with a cold surface may crack them. Glass jars are available in various sizes. Pack preserves into the small ones. It is essential to have the jars filled to within 1$\frac{1}{4}$ cm. ($\frac{3}{4}$ inch) of the top if you are going to seal them. Pack the preserve into the jar and refrigerate it if you do not intend to store it for a period of time.

# Plum and orange preserve

*Illustrated on page 81*
Preparation time: few minutes
Cooking time: about 50 minutes
Makes: 1.5 kg. (3 lb.)

**2 kg./4$\frac{1}{2}$ lb. ripe red plums**
**2 kg./4$\frac{1}{2}$ lb. sugar**
**2 tablespoons grated orange rind**
**8 tablespoons orange juice**
**4 tablespoons lemon juice**

Wash the plums, cut in half and remove the stones. Combine the plums, sugar, orange rind, orange and lemon juice in a saucepan. Bring to the boil slowly, stirring constantly with a wooden spoon. Reduce the heat to moderate. Cook, stirring occasionally, for 45–50 minutes until the preserve thickens. Remove and carefully skim off the foam from the surface with a metal spoon. Ladle into hot dry jars and fill to within 1$\frac{1}{4}$ cm. ($\frac{3}{4}$ inch) of the top of the jar. Seal and label.

# Heavenly strawberry preserve

Preparation time: few minutes, plus standing time
Cooking time: about 10 minutes
Makes: about 750 g. ($1\frac{1}{2}$ lb.)

**1 kg./2 lb. stawberries**
**1 kg./2 lb. sugar**
**8 tablespoons lemon juice**

Hull the strawberries, wash and drain. Cut away any blemishes but otherwise leave whole and place in a large saucepan. Cover with the sugar and leave to stand and draw for 3 hours. Bring to the boil slowly, stirring carefully with a wooden spoon. Cook for 8 minutes, stirring continuously. Add the lemon juice and boil for a further 2 minutes. Allow the mixture to cool, then skim the foam from the top with a metal spoon and stir. Pack into a hot dry jar. Fill to within $1\frac{1}{4}$ cm. ($\frac{3}{4}$ inch) of the top, seal and label.

# Lemon curd

Preparation time: 5 minutes
Cooking time: about 10 minutes
Makes: about 250 g. (8 oz.) lemon curd

**2 medium thick-skinned lemons**
**4 cubes loaf sugar**
**4 tablespoons granulated sugar**
**3 large eggs**
**4 tablespoons/2 oz. butter**

Holding the lemons in one hand over a bowl, firmly rub with the loaf sugar. As each lump starts to crumble, begin with another. Four lumps should be enough to absorb the oil from the peel of each lemon. Place the granulated sugar in the bowl with the flavoured sugar lumps. Squeeze the lemons and strain the juice. Whisk the eggs and juice together. Cube the butter. Place the bowl of sugar over a saucepan of boiling water and add the egg and lemon mixture. Then add the butter, piece by piece. Whisk with an electric beater for about 8 minutes, until the consistency is thick and creamy. Remove from the heat and stir until the curd has cooled. Pour into a glass jar. Cover and refrigerate. This is a delicious filling for a shortcrust tart, or for small pancakes.

# Mincemeat

Preparation time: 15 minutes, plus standing time
Makes: about 1.5 kg. (3 lb.) mincemeat

**125 g./4 oz. minced fresh beef suet**
**500 g./1 lb. seedless raisins**
**250 g./8 oz. currants**
**125 g./4 oz. blanched almonds, coarsely chopped**
**125 g./4 oz. watermelon konfyt, coarsely chopped (see note)**
**125 g./4 oz. dried figs, coarsely chopped**
**4 tablespoons coarsely chopped candied orange peel**
**4 tablespoons coarsely chopped lemon peel**
**250 g./8 oz. cooking apples, peeled and chopped**
**125 g./4 oz. soft brown sugar**
**1 teaspoon grated nutmeg**
**1 teaspoon ground allspice**
**1 teaspoon ground cinnamon**
**250 ml./$\frac{1}{2}$ pint brandy**
**8 tablespoons dry sherry**

Place the suet, raisins, currants, almonds, konfyt, figs, orange peel, lemon peel and apples in a bowl. Add the brown sugar, nutmeg, allspice, cinnamon, brandy and sherry. Mix, using a wooden spoon until all the ingredients are thoroughly moistened. Cover the bowl with foil and leave to stand in a cool place for 1 week. Pack tightly in sterilised, well dried glass jars. Cover securely with the lids. Store in a dry, cool, dark place until ready to use. Mincemeat will keep for up to 6 months without refrigeration.
**Note** If watermelon konfyt is not available, add an extra 50 g. (2 oz.) each of raisins and sultanas.

# Orange peel in chocolate

*Illustrated on page 84*
Preparation time: 20 minutes
Serves: 4–6

**4 oranges**
**8 tablespoons water**
**250 g./8 oz. sugar**
**2 tablespoons syrup**
**250 g./8 oz. bitter chocolate**

Remove the peel from the oranges in sections. (Reserve the flesh for an orange salad.) Place the peel in a saucepan with cold water to cover. Bring to boiling point, reduce the heat and simmer until the peel is soft. Drain and scrape off any of the white pith. Cut the peel into long strips with a very sharp knife. Place the 8 tablespoons water in a saucepan with the sugar and syrup. Add the orange peel. Boil the mixture until it reaches thread stage, that is, when the slightly cooled syrup spins a 5-cm. (2-inch) thread when dropped from the tip of a spoon. Pour the mixture through a sieve and cool the coated strips on wax paper. Melt the chocolate in a double boiler. Dip each strip separately into the melted chocolate and leave to set on wax paper. Serve with coffee after dinner.

# Hot salted almonds

Preparation time: few minutes

**500 g./1 lb. blanched almonds**
**250 ml./½ pint oil**
**2½ teaspoons coarse salt**

Cook the almonds in a saucepan with the oil over a low heat for 3–5 minutes, until golden brown. Drain on absorbent paper. While the nuts are still hot, sprinkle with salt. Serve in a wicker basket or in an earthenware dish.

# Sugared almonds

*Illustrated on page 84*
Preparation time: few minutes
Cooking time: about 2 hours
Oven temperature: very cool (250°F., 130°C., Gas Mark ½)

**500 g./1 lb. sugar**
**1 teaspoon nutmeg**
**1 tablespoon cinnamon**
**2 egg whites**
**1 tablespoon water**
**500 g./1 lb. blanched almonds**

Mix the sugar, nutmeg and cinnamon together. Grease a piece of foil. Sprinkle half the sugar mixture on the foil. Lightly beat the egg whites and water in a bowl for 30 seconds. Add the nuts and blend gently to coat the almonds thoroughly. Spread out onto the sugar mixture. Sprinkle thickly with remaining mixture. Place in a very cool oven for about 2 hours. Break up the crispy sugared almonds and store in an airtight glass jar.

# Hot wholewheat porridge with honey

*Illustrated on page 137*
Preparation time: few minutes
Cooking time: about 8 minutes
Serves: 6–8

**1½ litres/3 pints milk**
**500 g./1 lb. wholewheat meal or porridge oats**
**pinch salt**
**6 teaspoons honey**
**6 teaspoons brown sugar (optional)**

Heat the milk in a saucepan. Add the wholewheat meal and salt. Bring to the boil stirring continuously. Lower the heat and simmer, still stirring, for 5–8 minutes. Pour into heated bowls and swirl a teaspoon of honey on the top of each.
**Note** Brown sugar is very good with this wholesome porridge and butter could be added, although as the porridge is being cooked in milk it is usually rich enough.

# Compote of apple rings and prunes

*Illustrated on page 137*
Preparation time: few minutes, plus overnight soaking
Cooking time: about 20 minutes
Serves: 4–6

**250 g./8 oz. dried apple rings**
**250 g./8 oz. prunes**
**1 tablespoon sugar**
**2 cinnamon sticks**
**1 lemon**

Wash the fruit thoroughly. Soak the apple rings and prunes in a bowl with water to cover, overnight. The next morning, place the fruit in a saucepan together with the water in which the fruit was soaked. Add the sugar and cinnamon sticks. Peel a lemon in a continuous circle. Add the peel to the saucepan. Bring to the boil and cook covered for 15–20 minutes, until the prunes are plumped out and the apples a little softer. Spoon into a bowl and top with cinnamon sticks, if liked.

# Mocha chocolate truffles in walnuts

*Illustrated on page 84*
Preparation time: 15 minutes, plus chilling time

**125 g./4 oz. bitter cooking chocolate**
**2 tablespoons strong coffee powder**
**2 tablespoons water**
**3 egg yolks**
**125 g./4 oz. butter**
**4 tablespoons icing sugar**
**1 teaspoon vanilla essence**
**4 tablespoons cocoa powder**
**6 tablespoons very finely chopped walnuts**

Melt the cooking chocolate together with the coffee and water in a double boiler. Remove from the heat and stir in the egg yolks, one at a time, blending well. Add the butter. Sift the icing sugar and add with the vanilla essence. Mix until thoroughly blended. Pour into a bowl and chill for 5–6 hours. Form into 2-cm. (5-inch) balls. Mix the cocoa powder with the chopped walnuts and place on a sheet of greaseproof paper. Roll each truffle lightly in the mixture to coat.

**Flavoured sugars**
**Cinnamon sugar** Blend together 500 g. (1 lb.) sugar and 2 tablespoons cinnamon. Store in an airtight jar.
**Lemon sugar** Grate the rind from 6 lemons and mix with 250 g. (8 oz.) sugar. Add a drop of lemon juice if necessary to make the mixture slightly damp.
**Note** 1 tablespoon lemon sugar substitutes for 1 teaspoon grated lemon rind and 1 tablespoon ordinary sugar in a cake or pudding recipe.
**Orange sugar** Follow the recipe for lemon sugar (above), substituting oranges for lemons.
**Vanilla icing sugar** Split a piece of vanilla bean or pod and remove the seeds. Crush them together with 500 g. (1 lb.) icing sugar. Store in an airtight jar.
**Note** Vanilla sugar is used more for the aroma in a recipe and should not be substituted for vanilla essence in a recipe. Dust onto a cake just before serving.
**Vanilla granulated sugar** Add a $2\frac{1}{2}$-cm. (1-inch) piece vanilla bean or pod to 500 g. (1 lb.) granulated sugar. Store in an airtight jar for 3 days before using. If you wish to use vanilla sugar in a cake or pudding substitute 1 tablespoon vanilla sugar for 1 tablespoon ordinary sugar. Do not omit the vanilla essence.
**Vanilla powder** The beans kept in the sugar will eventually dry up. When you have six or eight absolutely dry vanilla beans, break them up and place in a blender. Use the fine powder blended with ice-cream or whipped cream for serving with fruit. The blended powder will keep indefinitely in an airtight container.

## Potted Roquefort cheese

Preparation time: few minutes
Makes: about 250 g. (8 oz.) potted Roquefort cheese

**4 tablespoons Roquefort cheese**
**250 g./8 oz. cottage cheese**
**8 tablespoons sour cream**
**125 g./4 oz. sweetmilk or Cheddar cheese, grated**
**2 tablespoons chopped chives**
**6 tablespoons dry sherry**

Place the Roquefort and cottage cheese in a bowl together with the sour cream, grated cheese, chives and sherry. Blend with a hand mixer until thick and creamy. Pour into earthenware pots. Cover tightly with the lids and refrigerate for 2–3 days before serving.

## Potted cheese

Preparation time: 10 minutes
Makes: about 250 g. (8 oz.) potted cheese

**250 g./8 oz. Cheddar cheese, grated**
**4 tablespoons cream**
**4 tablespoons sherry**
**3 tablespoons/1½ oz. butter**
**2 teaspoons freshly ground black pepper**
**pinch salt**

Place the grated cheese, cream, sherry, butter, pepper and salt in the top of a double boiler. Stir constantly using a wooden spoon until creamy, about 8 minutes. Remove from the heat and turn into two small earthenware pots. Cover with clarified butter and cover tightly with the lids. Refrigerate until needed.

## Nougat

Preparation time: 10 minutes
Oven temperature: moderate (350°F., 180°C., Gas Mark 4)

**250 g./8 oz. almonds**
**250 g./8 oz. sugar**

Blanch the almonds by adding them to boiling water. Melt the sugar in a heavy saucepan. Coarsely chop the almonds and stir into the melted sugar. Pour onto a well oiled pan, spreading thinly with an oiled spatula. Before the mixture hardens cut into shapes using an oiled biscuit cutter. (The nougat hardens quickly so do this almost at once.) If the mixture does harden before you are finished, place it in a moderate oven for a few minutes to soften.

## Sugared mint leaves

Preparation time: few minutes

**2 bunches mint leaves**
**1 egg white**
**2–3 tablespoons castor sugar**

Wash and dry large perfect mint leaves. Lightly whisk the egg white. Brush onto each leaf and dredge with sugar. Allow the leaves to dry on wax paper in a cool place. Use to decorate orange or lemon soufflés, or fruit sweets.

# Drinks

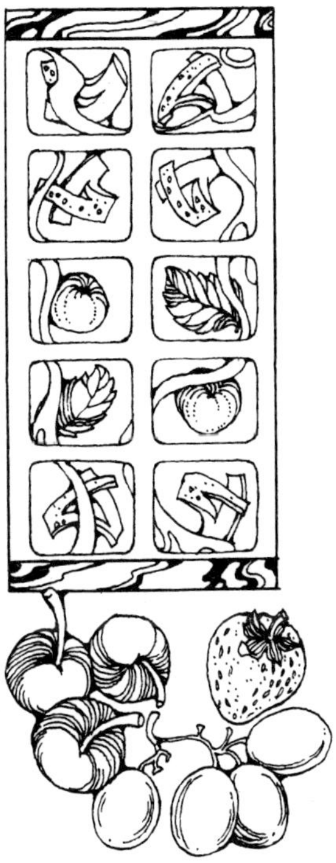

What ever thirst-quenchers you prepare do it thoughtfully. Chill the glasses for champagne and ice the jug for fruit juices in summer. Use pure chocolate for milk chocolate drinks and fresh fruit for milk shakes as a special treat.

Serve drinks with flair. It is the thin slice of lemon, the ripe cherry or plump olive with your cocktails; the iced coffee with whipped cream in summer or served the Irish way in winter, that spells entertaining with flair.

Make sure you have a large jug for iced water – glass or silver; two insulated ice boxes, one large, one small; the correct implements for removing corks from bottles; matching dishes for olives, lemons, etc.

**Ways to serve iced drinks**

Ice cubes will be crystal clear if the water is boiled before freezing. For a super-cool effect, add a few drops of green food colouring to the water before it is frozen into cubes.

Turn ice cubes into frozen islands of fruit by freezing curls of lemon or orange peel into each one. Do the same with maraschino cherries – and a mint leaf or two.

Float fruit such as fresh strawberries, grapes, a red cherry, thinly-sliced citrus, pineapple or peaches in those long, long drinks. Balls of watermelon or green melon are crunchy enough to add their own cool. Add them to a drink just before serving.

Frosted glasses make liquids look and taste more appetising. To frost glasses, dip the rims in water then dip in coarse sugar: leave in the refrigerator to firm up.

Straws to match the glass or the drink add a good final touch.

## Veranda punch

Preparation time: 5 minutes, plus standing time
Serves: 6

**1 lemon**
**1 lime**
**1 orange**
**375 ml./generous ½ pint brandy**
**4 tablespoons granulated sugar**
**1 bottle red wine**
**2 tablespoons lemon juice**
**6 ice cubes**
**1 bottle soda water**

Slice the lemon, lime and orange thinly and remove the pips. Put into a large jug. Pour over the brandy and sugar and leave to stand for 1 hour. Add the wine and lemon juice and stir well. Just before serving, add the ice cubes and soda water. Stir briskly. Pour into chilled glasses to serve.

# Nectar whip

Preparation time: 5 minutes
Serves: 4–6

**500 ml./1 pint coffee ice-cream**
**1 large can apricot nectar**
**500 ml./1 pint cold black coffee**
**3 tablespoons sugar**
**250 ml./$\frac{1}{2}$ pint cold milk**
**$\frac{1}{2}$ teaspoon almond essence**

Allow the ice-cream to soften slightly, then scoop into a blender. Add the apricot nectar, coffee and sugar. Blend at high speed for 30 seconds, until smooth. Pour into a jug. Stir in the cold milk and almond essence. Pour into well chilled glasses and serve at once.

# Grapefruit chiller

Preparation time: few minutes
Serves: 6

**375 ml./generous $\frac{1}{2}$ pint grapefruit juice**
**12 tablespoons grenadine**
**6 tablespoons lime or lemon juice**
**12 ice cubes**
**3 bottles ginger ale**
**6 wedges peeled fresh grapefruit**

Combine the grapefruit juice, grenadine and lime or lemon juice. Add the ice cubes, ginger ale and grapefruit wedges. Pour into well chilled glasses.
**Note** If grenadine is not available, use extra grapefruit juice.

# Coffee spice

Preparation time: 5 minutes, plus standing time
Serves: 6

**$1\frac{1}{2}$ litres/3 pints strong, hot coffee**
**4 tablespoons granulated sugar**
**6 cloves**
**6 small sticks cinnamon**
**6 ice cubes**
**125 ml./$\frac{1}{4}$ pint coffee-flavoured liqueur**

Combine the hot coffee, sugar, cloves and sticks cinnamon. Cover and leave to stand for 1 hour. Strain into a jug and add the ice cubes and liqueur. Stir well and pour into well chilled glasses

# Citrus and champagne

Preparation time: 15 minutes
Serves: 4–6

**750 ml./$1\frac{1}{2}$ pints freshly squeezed orange juice**
**250 ml./$\frac{1}{2}$ pint freshly squeezed lemon juice**
**500 ml./1 pint champagne**
**1 orange**
**1 lemon**
**1 sprig mint**

Pour the strained orange and lemon juices into a tall jug. Add the champagne. Peel the orange and lemon and remove the pith. Slice very thinly using a sharp knife. Add to the jug together with the mint. Chill well before serving.
**Note** Instead of the mint sprig, minted ice cubes may be added – wash a small bunch of mint and choose the nicest sprigs. Place a sprig in each ice tray compartment and top with water. Freeze.

# Creamy banana shake

Preparation time: few minutes
Serves: 2

**500 ml./1 pint cold milk**
**2 ripe bananas, chopped**
**1 teaspoon brown sugar**
**2 teaspoons honey**
**pinch cinnamon**
**1 tablespoon cream**

Place all ingredients in a blender and switch on for 15 seconds. Pour into chilled glasses. (If you do not have a blender, place the ingredients in a bowl and beat with a whisk until well blended.)

## Pineapple ginger shake

Preparation time: few minutes
Serves: 4

**500 ml./1 pint cold milk**
**250 ml./½ pint pineapple juice**
**½ fresh pineapple, chopped**
**2 teaspoons sugar**
**2 tablespoons cream or vanilla ice-cream**

Place the milk, pineapple juice, chopped pineapple, sugar and cream in a blender. Blend for 10 seconds, then pour into chilled glasses.

## Coffee chocolate shake

Preparation time: few minutes
Serves: 2

**500 ml./1 pint cold milk**
**1 teaspoon instant coffee powder**
**4 teaspoons drinking chocolate**
**pinch cinnamon**
**2 tablespoons whipped cream**
**1 tablespoon chopped walnuts**

Pour the milk into a jug together with coffee, chocolate and cinnamon. Beat thoroughly until foamy then pour into chilled glasses. Top with a spoonful of whipped cream and a few chopped walnuts.

## Cool peppermint shake

Preparation time: few minutes
Serves: 2

**500 ml./1 pint cold milk**
**2 drops green food colouring**
**1 drop peppermint essence**
**1 drop vanilla essence**
**1 tablespoon sugar**
**1 tablespoon grated peppermint chocolate**

Place the milk in a jug together with the food colouring, peppermint essence, vanilla essence, sugar and grated peppermint chocolate. Beat thoroughly until well blended, then pour into chilled glasses.

# Menus for all occasions

## Picnic fare

**Fruit**
Prepare well in advance; refrigerate and pack in airtight polythene boxes or light insulated boxes lined with wax paper. Carry in an insulated bag.
**Melon** Halve, pip and use the melon case as a container for mixed fruit salad, or a mixture of ham, cubed cheese and pecan nuts.
**Strawberries** Wash and sprinkle with sugar; marinate in orange juice for 2 hours before packing.
**Watermelon** Skin, cube, toss in rum, blend with fresh cherries and litchis.
**Pineapple** Hollow out, fill with diced fruit, chicken or turkey bound with mayonnaise.

Both pineapple and melon may be sliced or cubed, the melon sprinkled with sherry, the pineapple rolled in sugar, before packing, and served on toothpicks or cocktail sticks.
**Peaches or apricots** Refrigerate overnight; wash, dry, pack in polythene bags, then an insulated bag.

**Vegetables**
Prepare in advance, pack in light polythene boxes or insulated containers, then an insulated bag.
**Salad** Mix crisp carrot slices, radishes, onions, button mushrooms, small cauliflower heads. Pack in an airtight polythene container. Serve with a dip, anchovy-flavoured or mixed with chopped parsley, celery, chives, vinegar, oil and seasonings. Pack this separately.
**Celery** Stuff with cream cheese and seedless raisins.
**Tomatoes** Scoop out, fill with tuna, chopped capers, lemon juice, black pepper, or salmon or prawns or shrimps bound with seafood mayonnaise.

Slice thinly and pack in a shallow airtight container. Sprinkle with plenty of chopped chives or parsley.
**Cucumbers** Remove seeds, fill with chopped lettuce, cream cheese, chives and mashed hard-boiled egg.
**Avocado pears** Halve, sprinkle with lemon juice, salt and black pepper.

Combine quartered tomatoes, gherkins, olives, young courgettes, in a marinade of vinegar, oil, sugar, salt and black pepper for 1 hour. Pack in airtight containers with thinly sliced silverside or spiced sausage.

**Bread**
Brush lightly with beaten egg, sprinkle with poppy or caraway seeds. Brown and crisp in a moderately hot oven (400°F., 200°C., Gas Mark 6) for 12 minutes. Cool before packing in polythene bags. If pre-frozen, bake for 12–18 minutes.

**Rolls** Brush with beaten egg and seeds, then bake for 5–8 minutes (10–12 minutes if frozen). Hollow out rolls and stuff with a mixture of smoked salmon, cottage cheese and chives, or mashed sardines, vinegar and spiced onions or cut asparagus in salad cream. Pack in airtight polythene containers.
**French bread** Scoop out the centre, pack with one of the following: chopped ham and mustard butter, or chicken pâté or liver sausage with chopped pickled walnuts, or tongue, pickles and creamed mustard butter, or Danish blue and cottage cheese blended together.

**Eggs**
Hard-boil the night before then plunge them into cold water immediately to prevent discolouration around the yolk. For an egg salad, cover shelled hard-boiled eggs with flavoured mayonnaise – tomato, anchovy, curry or lemon. Wrap in lettuce leaves and pack in an airtight polythene container. To stuff, cut off the tops, scoop out the yolks, mash and season or combine with chopped mushrooms, capers, cream, tomato sauce and parsley. Refill, close and wrap in a slice of ham.

**Soups**
Try them cold. Make them the night before, refrigerate, then add chopped parsley, cream and chives before pouring into flasks which have been rinsed in iced water.

**Fish**
Take along crisply fried fish fingers, with seafood sauce in a separate container. Pack both in airtight polythene bowls. To make a fish salad, bake fish in oil, flake, marinate in lemon juice and season before combining with chopped pimento, avocado cubes, black olives and fresh cucumber.
**Tuna** This makes a super salad with pieces of sweetmelon, green pepper, pineapple, and a dressing of vinegar, salt and pepper.

**Meats**
Prepare no earlier than the night before and serve sliced, chilled and wrapped in foil, or in an insulated container lined with wax paper. Roll thin slices of ham or pickled brisket around gherkins, yellow peach segments, sweetmelon or pineapple.
**Meat salad** Try diced beef, gherkins and potato slices in mustard cream, or tongue slivers, rice, pine nuts, parsley, oil, lemon juice and seasonings.
**Chicken** Wrap the bird in foil, roast and unwrap; cool, cut into serving portions and reseal in foil.
**Meat loaf** Use your favourite recipe, but try wrapping the loaf in a pastry case and baking in a moderately hot oven (400°F., 200°C., Gas Mark 6) for 25–30 minutes; cool, then pack in an airtight container.
**Meat pies** Prepare them the day before and bake on the day of the picnic; cool before packing in insulated containers.

**Desserts**
A rich sponge or pound cake. Pack in an airtight container.
**Mango turnovers** Make ahead of time and freeze. Reheat, cool and pack in polythene bags.
**Biscuits** Pack in an airtight polythene container.

# Summer menus

## Picnic menus

Tomatoes with assorted fillings

Devilled chickens

Marinated vegetables

Iced watermelon wedges

Buttered milk rolls with caraway seeds

Hot coffee

Stuffed French bread

Ham and tongue salad

Fresh pineapple in vanilla syrup

Iced coffee

## Lunch menus

Stuffed cucumbers

Baked red roman with green mayonnaise
Savoury rice
Individual asparagus and leek salads

Yellow peach brûlée

Eggs in curry cream

Duck and orange salad

Strawberry fool

## Buffet menus

Chilled cream of cucumber soup

Crisp filleted fish
Lemon mayonnaise

Potato salad with lemon dressing
Marinated mushroom salad

Meringue circles

Grapefruit with preserves

Chicken tuna salad

Milk rolls with Camembert cheese

Hazel nut meringues

## Afternoon tea menu

Thin cucumber sandwiches

Rich fruitcake

Apricot cream tartlets

Tea with milk or lemon

## Dinner menus

Pawpaw with litchis

Minute steaks in French brandy sauce
New potatoes in jackets
Peas with ham

Rum chocolate puffs

Pink prawns in white wine

Veal in caper sauce
Green bean and potato salad

Banana and Curaçao crêpes

## Party menus

Avocado mousse

Chicken with spiced sausage filling
Potato slices in mustard cream
Marinated vegetables

Bowls of chilled summer fruits
Yellow peach brûlée
Strawberry fool
Plums in liqueur
Whipped vanilla cream

Pâté in a crock
Fresh peaches in white wine

Cold turkey with cherry sauce
Large salad trays

Chocolate pound gâteau with rum cream

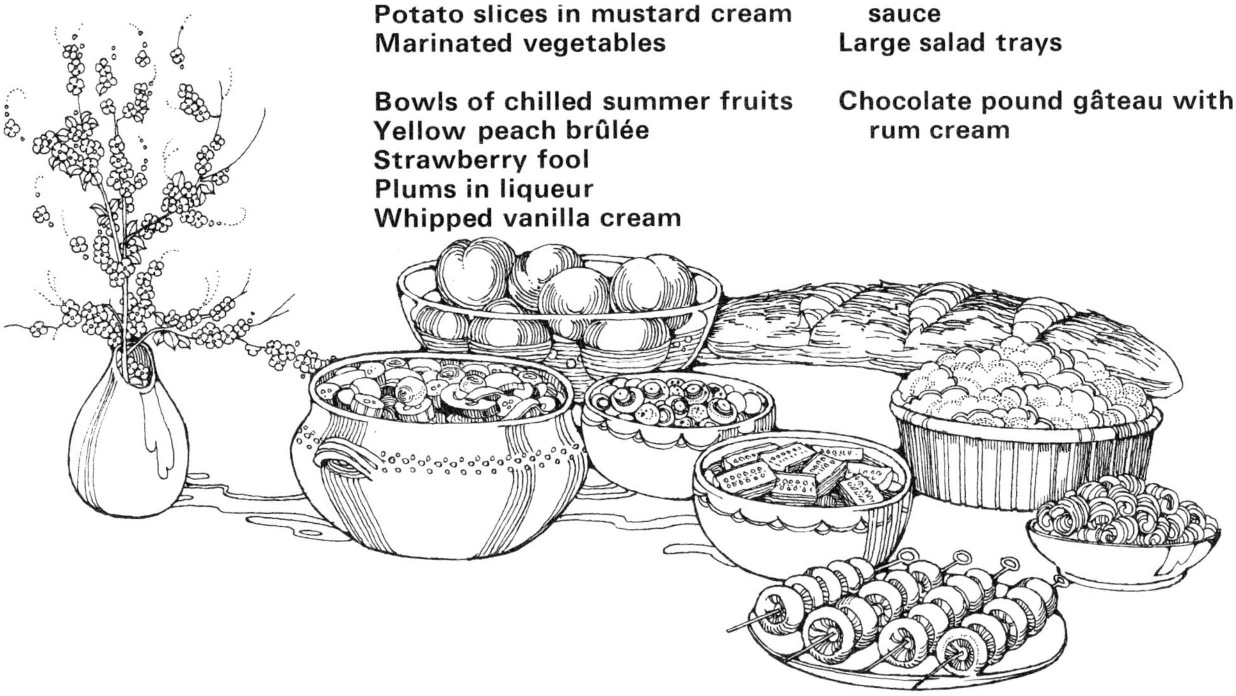

## Barbecue menus

Chilled curry soup

Barbecued chicken
Mushroom kebabs
Potatoes in lemon butter
Mixed salad bowl

Vanilla ice-cream with pineapple

Orange baskets

Marinated chops and spicy sausages
New potatoes in jackets
Chilled vegetable salad

Cherry custard flan

# Winter menus

## Morning coffee party menu

Anchovy butter toasts

Spiced oatmeal biscuits

Mango turnovers

Coffee
Hot frothed milk

## Brunch menus

Sliced fresh fruits (pawpaw crescents, dates, winter-melon, pink grapefruit, pineapple)
Baked eggs
Crisped salami with mushrooms
Grilled baby tomatoes
Fresh milk bread loaves

Strong coffee with frothy milk

Compote of apple rings and prunes
Blended orange and lemon juice
Veranda punch
Hot wholewheat porridge with honey
Buttered cheese eggs in nests
Grilled bacon and sausage twists
Walnut orange scones

Black coffee with thick cream

## Lunch menus

Creamy leek and potato soup

Rounds of lamb
Crisp potato cakes
Baby beets

Suggested salad: cucumber, orange slices and watercress

Tipsy meringue peaches

Stuffed cucumbers

Grilled snoek with lemon cream
Swirled baked potatoes
Baby tomatoes with peas

Orange sabayon

## Dinner menus

Pickled herrings with mandarin oranges

Stuffed chicken breasts
Potato puffs
Cauliflower with buttered crumbs

Suggested salad: thin cucumber slices with chives and egg topping

Individual baked lemon creams

Fluffy asparagus omelets

Stuffed fillet of beef
Thin potato rounds
Broccoli with butter

Suggested salad: lettuce and tomato wedges, sliced fennel and black olives

Orange fluff

## Drinks party menus

Little egg mayonnaise rolls

Savoury butters on a platter served with radishes, crisp celery sticks, black and green olives, ham rolls

Crisp bread, melba toast, thin black bread

Potato nuts with sour cream

Assorted nuts

Hot salted almonds

Grilled baby tomatoes

Miniature golden puffs

Hot mushroom and salami dip

Avocado mousse with toast triangles

## Buffet menus

**Crêpes with spinach and mushroom filling**

**Stuffed leg of lamb with raisins**
**Savoury baked potatoes**
**Green beans with glazed onions**
**Tomatoes with basil**

**Winter fruit medley with liqueur custard**

**Mature Cheddar cheese with wholewheat currant nut bread**

**Coffee**

**Salmon quiche**

**Savoury sliced brisket with beans**
**Herbed rice**
**Buttered spinach**
**Lettuce wedges with chopped egg and chive dressing**

**Rosy pears with vanilla cream**
**Ice-cream bombe praline**

**Brie cheese with poppyseed rolls**

**Coffee**

## Supper menus

**Avocado halves with piquant egg dressing**

**Pot roast chicken in orange gravy**
**Potato dumplings**
**Browned onions**
**Young peas**

**Pears in apple juice with thick cream**

**Fresh green pea soup**

**Baked steenbras with capers**
**Savoury rice**

**Sliced oranges in liqueur custard with almonds**

## Late supper menus

**Cream of hake soup**

**Fluffy cheese toasts**

**Compote of apple rings and prunes**

**Irish coffee**

**Velvet chicken soup**

**Milk rolls with scrambled egg**

**Grilled chipolatas with baby tomatoes on skewers**

**Rosy pears with vanilla cream**

# Wedding lunch menu for 20–30

*Illustrated on page 144*

**Chilled cream of cucumber soup**

**Chicken and lobster salad**
**Marinated mushroom salad**

**Ice-cream bombe praline**

**Wedding cake**

**Champagne**

**Soup** Make double the quantity of the recipe, but prepare it in two separate amounts. Serve from three large tureens. Replenish from the kitchen when necessary.
**Chicken and lobster salad** Make four times the quantity of the recipe, but prepare in two separate amounts. You will need three or four really large dishes for serving the chicken and lobster salad.
**Marinated mushroom salad** Make four times the quantity of the recipe, but prepare in two separate amounts.
**Ice-cream bombe praline** Make four times the quantity of the recipe, but prepare in two separate amounts. Pack in three or four large polythene containers for a really spectacular result; this looks better than serving the bombes in small containers.
**Wedding cake** Choose your favourite fruitcake recipe or order a plain large round cake covered in white or pale yellow icing. Surround the base with flowers in deeper yellow and white. Make a ribbon cluster with fresh flowers for the top of the cake as shown in the picture on page 144. This solves the problem of flowers on the buffet table and at the same time makes an attractive decoration for a very simple wedding cake. This idea can be repeated with other flowers to tie up with different colour schemes.
**Champagne** Allow about 10 bottles of champagne for a party of 30 people. Place the champagne bottles in ice buckets and surround with the glasses. Keep the remaining bottles of champagne cool, either in the refrigerator or in a white-painted wheelbarrow filled with blocks of ice. Place this near the table for quick replenishments.

**Note** When preparing food for large numbers you may find it easier to prepare it in batches, depending on how many you are catering for. If you have sufficiently large utensils and the amounts are not too large you may like to prepare the food all at once.

**Suggested layout for a buffet table and round tables**
**Table-cloths** Pale lemon cotton.
**Napkins** Sharp yellow, arranged in green goblets.
**Flowers** Lemon and white daffodils gathered into posies, each one tied with ribbon. Arrange a posy on each of the round tables.
**China** White or pale green.

# Wedding tea menu for 30

**Rolled sandwich platter**

**Lemon cheese cake in a nut crust**

**Lacy chocolate biscuits**

**Mango turnovers**

**Sugared almonds**

**Wedding cake**

**Champagne**

**Rolled sandwich platter** Prepare five to ten batches of the single recipe to allow two to four pinwheels per person. Arrange the sandwiches on leaf-covered platters.
**Lemon cheese cake** Make four in fluted flan dishes. (Borrow these if you can.)
**Lacy chocolate biscuits.** Double the single recipe. This allows four biscuits each. Serve the biscuits in a shallow, flat bowl on lacy napkins.
**Mango turnovers** Allow one per person, plus a few extra. These, like the sandwiches, can be prepared well in advance and frozen.
**Sugared almonds** Triple the single recipe and serve them piled in green goblets.
**Wedding cake** Ice a square cake with white or very pale pink icing. Surround the base with thick loops of deeper pink satin ribbon, each one wired to stay in place; intersperse with groups of pink and white daisies.
**Champagne** Allow about 10 bottles for 30 people. Fill a suitable container with ice and set in the bottles of champagne.

**Suggested layout**
Have five medium-sized tables, each covered with pale green, pink and white patterned ground-length table-cloths. These, like the lemon cotton cloths, can be inexpensive and home-made. Borrow umbrellas in soft colours. Secure them in white barrels pre-planted with trailing ground cover.
**Napkins** Deep, plain green.
**Flowers** Bunch soft pink and white daisies in white wicker baskets, together with green leaves. Loop white satin ribbon around the baskets. Have a wicker basket for each table.
**China** White, pink or green.

# Wedding cocktail reception for 50

**Black and green olives**
**Hot salted almonds**
**Miniature golden puffs**

**Salmon mayonnaise on black bread**
**Hot potato nuts with sour cream**

**Wedding cake**

**Champagne**

**Olives** Allow a 1-kg. (2-lb.) can black olives and a 1-kg. (2-lb.) can green olives.
**Hot salted almonds** Prepare three or four times the single recipe.
**Miniature golden puffs** Double the quantity of the recipe, but prepare in two separate amounts.
**Salmon mayonnaise** Double the quantity of the recipe, but prepare in two separate amounts.
**Hot potato nuts** Double the quantity of the recipe, but prepare in two separate amounts. Allow 1 litre ($1\frac{3}{4}$ pints) sour cream.
**Wedding cake** A white-iced square cake. Decorate with white satin ribbons, silver paper leaves in four layers fanning out from around the base.
**Champagne** Allow 18 bottles for 50 people. Keep in silver coolers.

**Suggested layout for the reception room**
Cocktail receptions do away with the need for seating for each guest. Have one table, covered to the ground, for the wedding cake, flowers, olives and almonds.
**Table-cloths** Hydrangea blue.
**Napkins** Flowered in blues and white.
**China** White side plates.
**Flowers** White spiky chrysanthemums interspersed with silver leaves.
**Dishes** Use white or silver platters, or foil-covered trays. Have white china dishes heated for the nuts. Pile the almonds, olives and the cream in small, very plain thick glass bowls and place them around the room.

# Index